THE EUROPEAN UNION SERIES

General Editors: Neill Nugent, William E. Paterson

The European Union series provides an authoritative library on the European Union, ranging from general introductory texts to definitive assessments of key institutions and actors, issues, policies and policy processes, and the role of member states.

Books in the series are written by leading scholars in their fields and reflect the most up-to-date research and debate. Particular attention is paid to accessibility and clear presentation for a wide audience of students, practitioners and interested general readers.

The series editors are **Neill Nugent**, Professor of Politics and Jean Monnet Professor of European Integration, Manchester Metropolitan University, and **William E. Paterson**, Honorary Professor of German and European Studies, University of Aston. Their co-editor until his death in July 1999, **Vincent Wright**, was a Fellow of Nuffield College, Oxford University.

Feedback on the series and book proposals are always welcome and should be sent to Steven Kennedy, Palgrave Macmillan, Houndmills, Basingstoke, Hampshire RG21 6XS, UK, or by e-mail to s.kennedy@palgrave.com

General textbooks

Published

Desmond Dinan **Encyclopedia of the European Union**
[Rights: Europe only]

Desmond Dinan **Europe Recast: A History of European Union**
[Rights: Europe only]

Desmond Dinan **Ever Closer Union: An Introduction to European Integration** (4th edn)
[Rights: Europe only]

Mette Eilstrup Sangiovanni (ed.) **Debates on European Integration: A Reader**

Simon Hix **The Political System of the European Union** (2nd edn)

Paul Magnette **What Is the European Union? Nature and Prospects**

John McCormick **Understanding the European Union: A Concise Introduction** (4th edn)

Brent F. Nelsen and Alexander Stubb **The European Union: Readings on the Theory and Practice of European Integration** (3rd edn)
[Rights: Europe only]

Neill Nugent **The Government and Politics of the European Union** (7th edn)

Neill Nugent (ed.) **European Union Enlargement**

John Peterson and Elizabeth Bomberg **Decision-Making in the European Union**

Ben Rosamond **Theories of European Integration**

Esther Versluis, Mendeltje van Keulen and Paul Stephenson **Analyzing the European Union Policy Process**

Forthcoming

Laurie Buonanno and Neill Nugent **Policies and Policy Processes of the European Union**

Dirk Leuffen, Berthold Rittberger and Frank Schimmelfennig **Differentiated Integration**

Sabine Saurugger **Theoretical Approaches to European Integration**

Also planned

The Political Economy of European Integration

Series Standing Order (outside North America only)
ISBN 978-0-333-71695-3 hardback
ISBN 978-0-333-69352-0 paperback
Full details from www.palgrave.com

Visit Palgrave Macmillan's
EU Resource area at
www.palgrave.com/politics/eu/

The major institutions and actors

Published

Renaud Dehousse **The European Court of Justice**

Justin Greenwood **Interest Representation in the European Union** (2nd edn)

Fiona Hayes-Renshaw and Helen Wallace **The Council of Ministers** (2nd edn)

Simon Hix and Christopher Lord **Political Parties in the European Union**

David Judge and David Earnshaw **The European Parliament** (2nd edn)

Neill Nugent **The European Commission**

Anne Stevens with Handley Stevens **Brussels Bureaucrats? The Administration of the European Union**

Forthcoming

Wolfgang Wessels **The European Council**

The main areas of policy

Published

Michelle Chang **Monetary Integration in the European Union**

Michelle Cini and Lee McGowan **Competition Policy in the European Union** (2nd edn)

Wyn Grant **The Common Agricultural Policy**

Sieglinde Gstöhl and Dirk de Bièvre **The Trade Policy of the European Union**

Martin Holland **The European Union and the Third World**

Jolyon Howorth **Security and Defence Policy in the European Union**

Johanna Kantola **Gender and the European Union**

Stephan Keukeleire and Jennifer MacNaughtan **The Foreign Policy of the European Union**

Brigid Laffan **The Finances of the European Union**

Malcolm Levitt and Christopher Lord **The Political Economy of Monetary Union**

Janne Haaland Matláry **Energy Policy in the European Union**

John McCormick **Environmental Policy in the European Union**

John Peterson and Margaret Sharp **Technology Policy in the European Union**

Handley Stevens **Transport Policy in the European Union**

Forthcoming

Karen M. Anderson **Social Policy in the European Union**

Hans Bruyninckx and Tom Delreux **Environmental Policy and Politics in the European Union**

Jörg Monar **Justice and Home Affairs in the European Union**

Also planned

Political Union

The External Policies of the European Union

The External Economic Relations of the European Union

The member states and the Union

Published

Carlos Closa and Paul Heywood **Spain and the European Union**

Alain Guyomarch, Howard Machin and Ella Ritchie **France in the European Union**

Brigid Laffan and Jane O'Mahoney **Ireland and the European Union**

Forthcoming

Simon Bulmer and William E. Paterson **Germany and the European Union**

Brigid Laffan **The European Union and Its Member States**

Baldur Thórhallsson **Small States in the European Union**

Also planned

Britain and the European Union

Issues

Published

Derek Beach **The Dynamics of European Integration: Why and When EU Institutions Matter**

Christina Boswell and Andrew Geddes **Migration and Mobility in the European Union**

Thomas Christiansen and Christine Reh **Constitutionalizing the European Union**

Robert Ladrech **Europeanization and National Politics**

Cécile Leconte **Understanding Euroscepticism**

Steven McGuire and Michael Smith **The European Union and the United States**

Forthcoming

Wyn Rees **US–EU Security Relationship**

Migration and Mobility in the European Union

Christina Boswell
and
Andrew Geddes

palgrave
macmillan

First published 2011 by
PALGRAVE MACMILLAN

Palgrave Macmillan in the UK is an imprint of Macmillan Publishers Limited,
registered in England, company number 785998, of Houndmills, Basingstoke,
Hampshire RG21 6XS.

Palgrave Macmillan in the US is a division of St Martin's Press LLC,
175 Fifth Avenue, New York, NY 10010.

Palgrave Macmillan is the global academic imprint of the above companies
and has companies and representatives throughout the world.

Palgrave® and Macmillan® are registered trademarks in the United States,
the United Kingdom, Europe and other countries

ISBN 978-0-230-00747-5 hardback

ISBN 978-0-230-00748-2   ISBN 978-1-137-28548-5 (eBook)
DOI 10.1007/978-1-137-28548-5

This book is printed on paper suitable for recycling and made from fully
managed and sustained forest sources. Logging, pulping and manufacturing
processes are expected to conform to the environmental regulations of the
country of origin.

A catalogue record for this book is available from the British Library.

A catalog record for this book is available from the Library of Congress.

10 9 8 7 6 5 4 3 2 1
20 19 18 17 16 15 14 13 12 11

Contents

List of Tables, Figures and Boxes   viii

List of Abbreviations   x

Acknowledgements   xiii

1 Studying Migration and Mobility in the European Union   1

Migration and EU population   5
Key questions   6
The EU's role   7
The complexities of European migration politics and
   policy   15
Organization of the book   18

2 Migration and Migration Policy in Europe   21

Migration and refugee flows in Europe since
   World War II   23
Making sense of migration   28
Understanding the policy process: policy failure or
   securitization?   39
A framework for analysis of European migration
   politics   45
Summary   50

3 The EU Dimension of Migration and Asylum Policy   51

The multilevel setting of EU policy   54
Relocation, relocation, relocation   67
Analysing the effects of EU migration and asylum policy   71
Summary   75

4 Labour Migration   76

Explaining labour migration policy   77
Narratives   82
Political debate   88

Administrative practice and implementation   97
Conclusions   102

5   Family Migration   **103**

The centrality of family migration   103
The right to family migration?   105
Narratives   106
Political debate   112
Administrative practice and implementation   118
Conclusion   120

6   Irregular Immigration   **122**

The dark side of admissions policies?   123
Narratives   125
Terms and their consequences   128
Political debate   135
Administrative practice and implementation   143
Conclusions   149

7   Asylum   **150**

EU cooperation on asylum: key themes   151
Narratives   157
Political debate   161
Administrative practice and implementation   167
Conclusion   174

8   Mobility, Citizenship and EU Enlargement   **176**

The EU framework   177
Narratives   178
Political debate   190
Administrative practice and implementation   195
Conclusion   199

9   Immigrant Integration   **201**

Narratives   203
Political debate   209
Administrative practice and implementation   217
Conclusion   221

10 Conclusions **225**

Multilevel migration politics? 226
Europeanization and convergence 232

Bibliography 235
Index 250

List of Tables, Figures and Boxes

Tables

1.1   Projections of population change in the EU, 2008–60   6
1.2   The EU's 'green' land borders in 2010   14
1.3   The EU's southern 'blue' maritime borders   15
2.1   Migrant population by geographic region 2010   22
2.2   Countries with the largest number of international
      migrants in 2010   22
2.3   Non-nationals in the EU-27 by continent of origin, 2008   24
2.4   Immigrants by citizenship group, 2006 or latest
      available   25
3.1   History of the Schengen system   60
6.1   Detections of illegal entry in 'frontline' EU states 2007   129
6.2   Regularizations in Greece, Spain and Italy 1982–2007   148
7.1   Asylum-seekers in EU member states, 1996–2007   153
7.2   Top 10 countries of origin of asylum applications
      lodged in Europe, 2009   160
8.1   States allowing mobility rights to A8 nationals   180
8.2   Approved WRS applications, UK, May 2004–08   185
9.1   Employment rates of nationals, TCNs and EU
      citizens, 2006   220
9.2   Unemployment rates of nationals, TCNs and
      EU citizens, 2006   222

Figures

1.1   Growth in the immigrant population in the top ten
      immigration countries in central and western Europe,
      2000–5   4
2.1   Top five countries of origin for migrants to Spain, 2006   26
2.2   Top five countries of origin for migrants to the UK, 2006   27
2.3   Main countries of origin for migrants to Italy, 2006   28

Map

3.1   The Schengen area: members, associated states,
      accession states and non-members   59

Boxes

1.1   A potted history of EU mobility, migration and
      asylum policy   8
1.2   The Lisbon Treaty   10
2.1   The 1951 Geneva Convention on the Status of Refugees   35
3.1   The Tampere, Hague and Stockholm Action
      Plans 1999–2014   52
4.1   Ageing populations and labour migration   80
4.2   Causes of labour and skills shortages   84
4.3   Mechanisms for recruiting labour migrants   86
6.1   The EU's Return Directive   140
6.2   The role of FRONTEX   146
7.1   EU cooperation on asylum: key developments   162
7.2   Safe third countries and readmission agreements   166
8.1   Free movement, the European Economic Area
      and Switzerland   183
8.2   Posted workers in North Lincolnshire   186
8.3   Sunset migration   194

List of Abbreviations

AN	Alleanza Nazionale
CARDS	Community Assistance for Reconstruction, Development and Stabilisaion
C.SIS	Central Schengen Information System
CEC	Commission of the European Communities
DG	Directorate General (European Commission)
DGEAS	Directorate General Employer and Social Affairs
DGJLS	Directorate General Justice, Liberty and Security
EC	European Community
ECHR	European Convention on Human Rights
ECJ	European Court of Justice
ECRE	European Council on Refugees and Exiles
EEA	European Economic Area
EEC	European Economic Community
EFTA	European Free Trade Area
EMN	European Migration Network
EMU	Economic and Monetary Union
EP	European Parliament
EU	European Union
EUROSUR	European Border Surveillance System
FRONTEX	Agency for the Management of Operational Cooperation at the External Borders of the Member States of the EU
GLA	Gangmasters Licensing Authority
HSMP	High Skilled Migrants Programme
ICMPD	International Centre for Migration Policy Development
ICT	Information and Communication Technologies
IND	Immigration and Nationality Department
IOM	International Organization for Migration
JHA	Justice and Home Affairs
LN	Lega Nord
MEDA	European Mediterranean Partnership
N.SIS	National Schengen Information System
NAFTA	North American Free Trade Agreement

OECD	Organisation for Economic Cooperation and Development
OMC	Open Method of Coordination
QMV	Qualified Majority Voting
REGINE	Regularizations in Europe Report
SAP	Stabilization and Association Process
SCIFA	Strategic Committee on Immigration, Frontiers and Asylum
SIS	Schengen Information System
SIS II	Schengen Information System Second Generation
SIVE	Integrated System of External Vigilance
TACIS	Technical Aid to the Commonwealth of Independent States
TCN	Third Country National
UDC	Unione dei Democratici Cristiani e di Centro
UKIP	United Kingdom Independence Party
UNHCR	United Nations High Commissioner for Refugees

Acknowledgements

This book draws from research we have both carried out over the past decade or more and our engagement with scholars working on European migration. Two people deserve particular mention. Michael Bommes has been a friend and mentor for both of us and we are deeply grateful for all the support that he has provided over the years. We would also like to thank Virginie Guiraudon, who as well as being a friend has been an important influence on many of the ideas in the book.

Our idea of developing a new approach to the analysis of European and EU migration policy was to a large extent inspired by a Seminar Series funded by the Economic and Social Research Council that we organized in 2007–9, on 'Migration Policy and Narratives of Societal Steering'. We are grateful to the ESRC for its support and the opportunities that it provided to develop our ideas. We would like to thank in particular Alex Balch, Richard Black, Simon Green, James Hampshire, Elena Lazarou, Christina Oelgemoeller and Peter Scholten, all of whom contributed very useful ideas, feedback and support at various stages in this ESRC series.

In addition a number of friends and colleagues have provided wisdom and insight over the years. These include, Erik Bleich, Grete Brochmann, Adrian Favell, Gary Freeman, Randall Hansen, James Hollifield, Gallya Lahav, Anthony Messina, Sam Scott, Paul Statham and Eiko Thielemann.

Christina would like to thank her colleagues at Edinburgh who have shared ideas on public policy, especially Caitriona Carter and Richard Freeman, as well as the Migration and Citizenship Research Group which has provided an excellent place for discussing work on these themes. Andrew would like to thank academic colleagues and (particularly) support staff in the Department of Politics at Sheffield University who have allowed him some space, while he has been serving as Head of Department, to continue with research work and writing. In particular, some of the work in this book draws from research carried out as part of an ESRC-funded project analysing 'Multi-Level Governance in South-East Europe' with three Sheffield colleagues, Andrew Taylor, Ian Bache and Charles Lees.

Just after finishing the first draft, a new arrival, Imogen Rose, meant that Christina had rather less time to work on revisions. Andrew would like to thank Jacopo and Beatrice Geddes who helped with these revisions by colouring in the map on page 59. They probably now know more about the Schengen area than most 7- and 4-year-olds.

During the writing of this book we were both saddened to hear of the death of Maria Ioannis Baganha whose work has been and will continue to be a major influence on European migration studies. This book is dedicated to her memory.

CHRISTINA BOSWELL
ANDREW GEDDES

Acknowledgement: Table 8.1 contains public sector information licensed under the Open Government Licence v1.0.

Chapter 1

Studying Migration and Mobility in the European Union

'It was filthy, we had nothing, no water, little food, but it was our only hope,' said one asylum-seeker from Afghanistan to describe his experiences in a makeshift camp close to the town of Sangatte on the coast of northern France. He spoke as the French government sent bulldozers to destroy the camps set up by people whose hope was to somehow enter the UK. *The Guardian* newspaper in the UK condemned the approach of the French and British governments by arguing that the governments acted first and only thought about the consequences of their actions later. It also condemned what it called 'buck-passing' between European Union (EU) member states seeking to offload immigration problems onto each other (*The Guardian* 2009).

What do these events and this newspaper story about them tell us about migration and mobility in the EU? First, they hint at some of the variation in the way different types of migrants are treated in politics and the media. In this case, the migrants in question were people seeking refuge. The story would have been different if the migrants concerned were high-skilled labour migrants or seeking to join family members. Second, asylum-seeking migration has an EU-wide resonance. The story recounted above suggests that this cooperation is actually quite weak as the French and British seem to prefer to offload problems rather than seek a Europe-wide framework. Third, by making a decision between what it calls 'thought' and 'action' when discussing the plight of these people, *The Guardian* alludes to different stages of the political process and to a fairly widespread consensus that migration policies fail because 'thought' and 'action' do not connect. By failure is meant that policies fail to achieve their objectives, or could actually make things worse.

These perspectives all offer fascinating ways of exploring the dynamics of migration and mobility in the EU: through thinking about different types of migration; exploring policy responses;

1

analysing the EU framework within which national policies are now located; and considering the notion of policy failure. The challenge that we set for ourselves is to integrate these various elements into a coherent analytical approach that provides a framework for understanding the EU's impact on migration and mobility (and vice versa). Before we do that, however, there are two important issues that need to be dealt with.

First, we need to specify what we mean by migration. We define an international migrant as someone living outside their country of origin either regularly or irregularly for a period of 12 months or more (IOM 2008:2). We thus exclude tourism and short-term travel, for example for business purposes. Look beneath the surface of the 12-month definition and things get more complicated because there is real uncertainty about the meaning of international migration. Temporary and seasonal migration flows are clearly important, but may not fall within the framework of this 12-month definition that is commonly used by policymakers. Immediately, it becomes apparent that international migration can come in many shapes and forms and be simultaneously represented as a solution (to an ageing population, skills shortages), a problem (because of labour market competition or as a threat to national identity) and – perhaps more realistically – as a natural component of an interdependent and globalized international system.

Of the world's 6.7 billion people around 3 per cent are international migrants. So with 97 per cent of the population remaining immobile, international migration is in fact a rather unusual condition. One reason for the relative lack of mobility is the various social and psychological costs of migrating to another country. After all, it is risky to leave one's own country, family and friends and move to another. Another reason is that the countries that receive a lot of migrants – or 'receiving states' – have established elaborate schemes to regulate and control international migration. This is partly why population movement *within* the borders of one country is far more common than international migration. In most countries, such internal movement is subject to few or no restrictions. It is usually only where mobility involves movement between states that it is the object of attempts at control and restriction. It is these efforts to regulate cross-border movement into and between EU countries that are the focus of this book.

Second, as can be seen from this book's cover, we refer to migration *and* mobility. We need to be clear from the outset about the distinction that we make between these two types of population movement.

International migration refers to movement from outside the EU by people who are not nationals of a member state. This extra-EU migration is by non-EU or third country nationals (TCNs).

EU mobility refers to nationals of EU member states – exercising their rights of free movement as EU citizens.

The prevailing image for most people when 'immigration' is mentioned may well be movement from outside the EU by TCNs. The image then conjured is of the kind of scene we sketched in this book's first paragraph describing the plight of Afghans living in a makeshift camp in northern France. This is not the whole picture; far from it, in fact. International migration is incredibly diverse, fluid and fast-changing.

The key point here is that there are important legal, social and political distinctions made at EU level between 'migration' by non-EU citizens and 'mobility' or 'free movement' by EU citizens. As we show, mobility rights for nationals of member states/EU citizens are a key feature of the Treaty of Rome (1957) and of subsequent treaties and legislation at EU level.

Extra-EU migration by TCNs is a relative newcomer on the EU policymaking scene, essentially since the Maastricht Treaty came into effect in 1993. And it is only since the Amsterdam Treaty (1999) that migration and asylum have been included in the EU's main legal and political framework. For this reason, we focus in particular on the period since the Maastricht Treaty and show that there is something new and distinct about the post-cold-war context. We see:

- greater intensity of migration flows to and within the EU;
- more countries affected by immigration;
- a growing role for the EU; and
- ostensibly new manifestations of the immigration problem, for example growing concern about irregular flows, people-smuggling and human trafficking.

By analysing mobility, migration and asylum in this post-cold-war period, this book deals with a highly topical set of issues whose political salience seems unlikely to decline. In 2005, there were 44.1 million migrants living in western and central Europe. This includes the 27 EU member states, three European Economic Area

(EEA) states of Iceland, Liechtenstein and Norway, Switzerland and two EU candidate countries, Croatia and Turkey. Of these, around 30 per cent originated from other western or central European countries. In absolute terms, Germany was Europe's largest country of immigration, with 10.1 million migrants living on its territory in 2005. Next on the list was France with 6.5 million migrants, followed by the UK with 5.4 million, Spain with 4.8 million and Italy with 2.5 million. Figure 1.1 shows the migrant population in the 10 central and west European countries with the largest migrant populations, in absolute terms.

Spain and Italy are often referred to as 'new' countries of immigration, although migration to these countries accelerated at the end of the late 1980s and early 1990s so the novelty of immigration is waning. In both, there has been a rapid increase in the numbers of immigrants. Between 2000 and 2005, Spain's migrant population rose by a staggering 194.2 per cent (3.1 million immigrants) while in Italy during the same period the numbers of migrants increased by 54.1 per cent (884,000 immigrants). Both the Spanish and Italian government have been keen to see a stronger EU role in managing migration. In August 2009, the

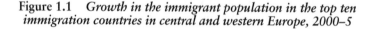

Figure 1.1   *Growth in the immigrant population in the top ten immigration countries in central and western Europe, 2000–5*

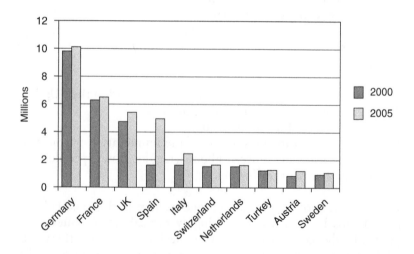

Source: Data from IOM (2008:456).

Italian foreign minister, Franco Frattini, called for solidarity among EU member states, by which he meant the proportional redistribution of migrants across the EU (*Corriere della Sera* 23 August 2009). In February 2010 rumblings of anti-immigration discontent were reported in Spain as the immigrant population had risen steeply from 2 to 12 per cent of the Spanish population (a total of 5.6 million people) in the first decade of the twenty-first century. This was at a time of economic recession and the level of unemployment approaching 4 million.

Newer member states that joined the EU in 2004 and 2007 are also showing signs of becoming immigration countries. In 2005, there was a positive net migration balance (meaning that more people were entering than leaving) in Cyprus, the Czech Republic, Hungary, Malta, Slovakia and Slovenia. That said, in Bulgaria, Estonia, Latvia, Lithuania, Poland and Romania more people left than entered. Of these, however, many were moving to other EU member states – for example Poles moving to the UK benefiting from EU free-movement provisions, but with cheap and easy travel options – a 'Ryanair effect' – making return very feasible.

Migration and EU population

Migration has been, is and will continue to be an important factor in EU population change. EU-wide demographic data consistently show declining birth-rates and raise concern about the effects of an ageing population. This has led to discussion about the role that migration can play in offsetting the effects of an ageing population. In 2008, the EU population reached 495.4 million, with 4 people of working age (aged 15–64) for each person over the age of 65. By 2060, this ratio is projected to fall to 2:1, that is 2 people in work for every person retired. These changes are not evenly distributed. Poland and Slovakia are projected to see an increase in the median age of their population by 15 years between 2008 and 2060 whereas the increase in the median age is expected to be less than 5 years in Belgium, Finland, France, Germany, Luxembourg, Sweden and the UK.

Table 1.1 shows that migration is projected to remain an important driver of population growth in the EU. Immigration could be part of the solution to population ageing because it means importing younger people, but it is not a magic bullet – not least

Table 1.1   *Projections of population change in the EU,*
2008–60 (millions)

Estimated population, 1 January 2008	495.394
Cumulative births	250.897
Cumulative deaths	298.799
Natural change	-47.902
Cumulative net migration	58.227
Total change	10.324
Projected population, 2060	505.718

Source: Data from Eurostat (2008).

because migrants get old too. This means that high levels of immigration would need to be sustained, as the previous wave of migrants themselves would age. There are other possible solutions such as an increase in the retirement age or increased female participation in the labour market that can also help to address some of these problems. It also seems reasonable to suppose that high and sustained levels of immigration to EU member states would cause some political controversy.

Key questions

Thus far we have demonstrated the political salience and complexity of immigration, but to chart a path through them we identify three sets of questions central to our analysis:

- Given that international migration is highly diverse in terms of the forms it takes, how do we make sense of this diversity and relate it to the politics of migration? How can we distinguish, for example, between the ways in which issues such as asylum, high-skilled migration, illegal/irregular migration and intra-EU mobility become social and political issues?
- Given that the politics of migration are complex, how can we make sense of the ways in which migration is articulated as a concern in public debate, in decision-making and, then, in policy implementation?

- Given that these are now issues with distinct EU competencies, how can we make sense of this EU role and understand what it means for the politics of immigration in Europe?

These three sets of questions concern themselves with different but closely related aspects of the politics of migration and mobility in Europe. They take seriously the distinctions between: different types of migration; different stages of the political process; and the multilevel context of EU politics.

The EU's role

There is a common EU migration and asylum policy, which has been further consolidated by the Lisbon Treaty after it finally limped to ratification in December 2009 (it was signed by national leaders in December 2007). EU policies do not cover all aspects of migration and asylum (admissions policy being a very notable exception), but they have had important effects on border controls, asylum and irregular migration. EU action has also played a key role in policy change and adaptation in southern European countries such as Greece, Italy and Spain and was a crucial component of adaptation by the 12 countries that joined the EU between 2004 and 2007 (10 of them in central and eastern Europe).

The EU Treaty framework established back in the 1950s for what we now know as the EU provided mobility rights for workers holding the nationality of a member state. This provision for free movement for workers has since been extended to a more general right of free movement (CEC 1997; Guild 2005; Favell 2007). Mobility rights for EU citizens are central to the framework for economic integration established back in the 1950s.

In contrast, migration from outside the EU by TCNs was not part of the founding Treaty and was not included until the Maastricht Treaty came into effect in 1993 and, even then, only in a loose, informal way that kept member states firmly in the driving seat. A key impetus for cooperation between EU governments at Maastricht was fear of large-scale migration in the aftermath of the cold war. Europe's post-1989 geopolitical shakeup played a key role in driving EU action on migration because the understanding of Europe changed, becoming wider – as too did the perception of migration potential from the south and east to the EU.

Box 1.1   A potted history of EU mobility, migration and asylum policy

Mobility rights
Free movement for workers was a key provision of the Treaty of Rome (1957). An EU-wide law introduced in 2004 replaced 10 previous pieces of legislation to create a common EU-wide framework specifying that all EU citizens have a right to move to another member state, to take family members with them and to become resident in that state, provided that they are able to support themselves.

Immigration and asylum policy
Cooperation on internal security developed in the 1970s, but there was particular acceleration in the 1980s linked to single market integration in the form of the Schengen Agreement (1985), initially between the Benelux countries, France and Germany, as well as looser forms of intergovernmental cooperation within the EC.

The Maastricht Treaty formalized cooperation by creating an intergovernmental 'pillar' dealing with Justice and Home Affairs. This pillar was intergovernmental because it was based on unanimous decision-making, largely precluding a role for supranational EU institutions such as the Commission, Parliament and Court of Justice.

➡

By 2009 and the ratification of the Lisbon Treaty both migration by TCNs and mobility by EU citizens had become central components of EU action. They must be analysed together if we are to understand how national responses have developed and, moreover, how these national responses mesh with the developing EU framework. Box 1.1 provides a potted history of key EU developments before the Lisbon Treaty and introduces themes that will be covered in more detail in the chapters that follow. What is demonstrated generally is the intensification of EU action since the end of the 1990s.

The Lisbon Treaty was agreed in 2007, but was only finally ratified at the end of 2009. It was rejected in referenda in the Netherlands and Ireland and encountered strong opposition in other member states too. As Box 1.2 shows, the Lisbon provisions

➡

The Amsterdam Treaty, which came into force in 1999, was important because it moved this intergovernmental cooperation by taking migration and asylum out of the JHA pillar and putting them alongside free movement in a new Title IV of the Treaty covering free movement, migration and asylum. This created a legal base for EU action on migration and asylum policy, as well as extended jurisdiction to the Commission, European Parliament and European Court. Articles 62-4 set out Community competencies in the area of internal and external border controls and conditions for the ability of TCNs to travel within the territory of the member states

In particular, article 63 set out Community competencies in the area of asylum and immigration policy:

- responsibility for assessing asylum claims;
- minimum standards on reception of asylum-seekers;
- minimum standards on qualification as refugees;
- procedures for granting or withdrawing refugee status; measures on temporary protection and displaced persons;
- conditions of entry and residence for TCNs
- procedures for issuing long-term visas;
- action against illegal immigration;
- defining the rights of legally resident TCNs.

The Nice Treaty (2001) made provision for use of QMV and codecision in areas of migration and asylum.

mark a further development of the EU's common migration and asylum policy. They are consistent with the direction of travel established by the Amsterdam Treaty and have a strong focus on those forms of migration defined as unwanted by member states' policies, such as asylum and irregular immigration. Box 1.2 specifies Lisbon's key provisions.

All the various issues covered by the treaties specified in Boxes 1.1 and 1.2 are analysed more fully in the chapters that follow. It is not possible to account for the contemporary politics of migration in Europe without accounting for the EU dimension; but, likewise, this EU dimension cannot be accounted for without analysis of political responses in member states. The politics of migration and mobility in the EU are thus entwined, multilevel and multidimensional.

Box 1.2   The Lisbon Treaty

The Lisbon Treaty marked the full incorporation of migration and asylum within the Treaty framework.

Migration and asylum would become 'normal' EU issues with qualified majority voting in the Council, co-decision with the European Parliament and a full role for the Court of Justice to consider annulment of legislation, to rule on failure to act on the part of EU institutions and in cases of infringement where member states have failed to fulfil their obligations.

Articles 77–80 set out provisions on borders, asylum and migration:

- Article 77 (1) provides for the absence of internal border controls, checks at external borders and an integrated approach to border management.

- Article 77 (2) provides for the following measures:
  - Common policy on visas and short-term residence permits;
  - Checks to which those crossing external borders are subject
  - Conditions under which TCNs are free to travel within the EU
  - Gradual establishment of an integrated management system for external borders
  - The absence of controls on those crossing internal borders

- Article 77 (3) provides that where it is necessary to facilitate mobility rights, the Council may adopt measures on passport, identity cards, residence permits and other such documents. The Council must act unanimously and consult the European Parliament (i.e. this is not covered by co-decision procedures, under which the Parliament has more powers).

- Article 78 deals with a common policy on asylum, subsidiary protection and temporary protection comprising:
  - A uniform status of asylum for TCNs valid throughout the EU;

➤

Multilevel politics

We need to think about what 'multilevelness' might mean, how it is made manifest and its implications for understandings of immigration policy and politics that have often been seen as closely bound by the national contexts of particular European states. EU politics are multilevel, but this doesn't get us far because all polit-

- • A uniform status of subsidiary protection for TCNs;
  - • A common system of temporary protection for displaced persons in the event of a massive inflow;
  - • Common procedures for granting and withdrawing uniform asylum or subsidiary protection status;
  - • Criteria and mechanisms for allocating responsibility for asylum claims;
  - • Standards concerning reception of applications for asylum or subsidiary protection
  - • Partnership and cooperation with third countries to manage inflows of persons applying for asylum or subsidiary or temporary protection;
- • Article 79 sets out a common immigration policy comprising:
  - • Conditions for entry and residence and standards on the issue of long-term visas and residence permits;
  - • Definition of the rights of TCNs legally residing in a member state including free movement and residence in other member states;
  - • Illegal immigration and unauthorized residence;
  - • Combating people trafficking.
- • Article 79 (3) allows for the conclusion of readmission agreements between the EU and third countries.
- • Article 79 (4) provides for the possibility of incentive measures to promote integration of legally resident TCNs.
- • Article 79 (5) states that measures on immigration 'do not affect the right of member states to determine volumes of admission of TCNs coming from third countries to their territory in order to seek work, whether employed or self-employed.'
- • Article 80 provides for 'solidarity and fair sharing of responsibility' in the areas of migration and asylum.

ical systems are multilevel to some extent. To move beyond stating the obvious, we have to decipher particular aspects of multilevelness as they impinge on EU migration politics. This means looking at the distribution of power and authority in the EU across levels of governance, thinking about the actors involved in these processes and about interactions between levels and actors.

The rise of the EU has been described as amounting to a 'rebundling' of authority (Ansell 2004) with important implications for borders, territory, territorial relationships and population control. This rebundling can help to generate some questions that specify key aspects of multilevel politics:

- How, why, when and in what form have EU governance structures emerged and developed?
- How do they impinge on policy areas that are closely associated with national sovereignty?
- Which actors have been empowered within this multilevel system?
- How does this multilevel distribution of power and authority play out across different types of migration policy, as in some areas there is a strong EU role (for example asylum) while in others the EU role (for example admissions policy) is less developed?
- How do EU member states seek to shape and influence EU policy, but, also, how has EU action affected policy in member states?

In addressing these questions, we show that the EU framework is partial, as it does not cover all aspects of migration and asylum policy, and differential, in that its effects are more pronounced on some member states than on others. We show significant variation by policy type and that this then helps us to better understand:

- relationships between member states and the EU;
- the partial nature of EU mobility, migration and asylum policy, with some areas more highly developed than others; and
- the differential effects of EU mobility, migration and asylum policy, with more impact on some member states than on others (and impact varying by policy type too).

The paradox of Europe's borders

This focus on multilevelness also points to the paradox of Europe's borders: the EU and its member states are simultaneously removing some borders, relocating others and building new ones. This paradox could actually be seen as an EU-level reflection of responses to population control and immigration that developed at state level from the nineteenth century, as internal consolidation of territory associated with state-building was accompanied by moves to regulate access to that territory (Bade 2003). Such processes were integral to the establishment of sovereign authority (Krasner 1999). This is one fairly obvious reason why member states can get so worked up about immigration and its effects, as immigration goes to the very heart of their self-definition as states. Member states do not passively observe these developments; they are key players.

It is the borders of states that make international migration visible as a distinct social process. If there were no such things as state borders then there would be no such thing as international migration (Zolberg 1989). It is the categories and meanings attached to international migration at Europe's borders that are central to the analysis that follows. We need to understand how organizations and institutions 'make sense' of international migration (Weick 1995). One way they make sense of international migration is to put migrants into categories – high-skilled migrant, low-skilled migrant, family migrant, and the like – that each determine conditions of entry, residence and associated rights and entitlements. As Bowker and Leigh Star (1999:5) put it:

> Each standard and each category valorizes some point of view and silences another. This is not inherently a bad thing – indeed it is inescapable. But it *is* an ethical choice, and as such it is dangerous – not bad, but dangerous.

Categorizations that occur at Europe's borders are central to the understanding of migration as a set of issues and concerns within the EU's multilevel system and to the constitution of a European political space. They can have a profound resonance that amounts to far more than just their representation as lines on maps. As Walker (2006:57) points out:

> Almost all the hard questions of our time . . . converge on the status of borders; of boundaries, distinctions, discriminations, inclusions, exclusions, beginnings, endings, limitations and exceptions, and on their authorization by subjects who are always susceptible to inclusion or exclusion by the borders they are persuaded to authorize.

Similarly, Balibar (1998) writes of how Europe's borders have 'multiplied and reduced . . . thinned out and doubled'.

Table 1.2   *The EU's 'green' land borders in 2010*

Border between		Length (km)
Finland	Russia	1,340
Estonia	Russia	455
Latvia	Russia	276
Lithuania	Belarus	651
Lithuania	Russia (Kaliningrad)	272
Poland	Russia (Kaliningrad)	232
Poland	Belarus	418
Poland	Ukraine	535
Slovakia	Ukraine	98
Hungary	Ukraine	136
Romania	Ukraine (east and west of Moldova)	649
Romania	Moldova	681
Bulgaria	Turkey	259
Greece	Turkey	215
Greece	Albania	282
Greece	Macedonia	246
Bulgaria	Macedonia	165
Bulgaria	Serbia	341
Romania	Serbia	546
	Total	**7,958**

Source: Data from House of Lords (2009:16).

Where are the borders at which these categorizations occur? They are most obviously territorial (land, air and sea), but they can also be 'organizational' (governing access to, for example, the labour market and welfare state) and can be 'conceptual' (concerned with questions of identity and belonging) (Geddes 20056). In 2010 there were 1636 land, sea and air border crossing-points in the EU, but we can add to these social security offices, housing authorities, healthcare providers and a wide range of other organizations and institutions that give meaning to international migration by determining who can enter the territory of a state, on what basis, for what duration and, once they have entered, the rights, entitlements and responsibilities they will have.

In 2010 the 27 EU member states had external land borders of around 8000 km and sea borders of 80,000 km. The EU does not itself have external frontiers because it is not a state. Instead the

Table 1.3   *The EU's southern 'blue' maritime borders*

Country	Length (km)
Portugal (including Azores and Madeira)	2,555
Spain (including Canaries)	4,964
France	4,720
Slovenia	48
Italy	7,600
Greece (including over 3,000 islands)	13,676
Malta (including Gozo)	253
Cyprus	293
Total	34,109

Source: House of Lords (2009:17).

external frontiers of its southern and eastern member states have become the focus of much EU activity designed to strengthen and enhance border control capacity. Tables 1.2 and 1.3 show the extent of the EU external land ('green') and southern European sea ('blue') borders.

Borders are central to the analysis of migration, but they are not some natural and immutable presence in the global order. Borders as powerful social constructions govern access to resources and signify a powerful relationship between controllers and those who are controlled (Sack 1986). They tell us something about relations between 'us and them'. Borders are intrinsically and inescapably political and are our route to the analysis of migration and mobility in the EU.

The complexities of European migration politics and policy

Having just staked out how important all these issues are, we could immediately run aground as we hit a pretty serious problem. Migration and mobility are rather diverse and complex, debates play themselves out in different ways in various EU member states and it's all very 'multilevel'. Moreover, the nature and type of these debates may have changed over time. To make things even more complicated, the EU and its institutions are now heavily involved

in this policy area, which means that we need not only to understand their role, but also to penetrate the sometimes rather peculiar
and complex ways that the EU itself has of describing its activities
(the issuance of 'Directives' and 'Regulations', the use of 'qualified
majority voting' (QMV) and so on). If this wasn't enough, we then
need to think about how the EU connects with these domestic
debates.

We think that it is important to create a framework that cuts
through this complexity without being so simplistic that we lose
analytical value. There are three possible ways to go about this:

- We could analyse how, why and when national responses to
  immigration have changed, but we choose not to do this
  because this would downplay the ability to look across these
  countries and pick out points of similarity and divergence.
- We could analyse the rapid development of EU policy and look
  at how, why and when these competencies have developed, but
  we choose not to do this because it would tend to separate the
  EU from the member state contexts that have been so central to
  the evolution and development of European integration.
- We could analyse migration types – labour, family, asylum,
  irregular, EU mobility as well as debates about immigrant integration – in order to look at how specific types of migration
  engender particular forms of political response and at how
  these play out at across the various levels of the EU's multilevel
  system connecting subnational, national and supranational/EU
  levels.

We choose this third and last approach because it actually encompasses the other two by allowing analysis of variation by policy
type, drawing from experiences in member states *and* accounting
for the EU's role.

We focus on migration types but recognize that there are powerful overlaps or linkages between migration categories. We also
recognize that categories are fluid and that people move between
them with different legal, political and social implications.
Someone arriving to study may stay on to work and then be joined
by family members. We explore these linkages because it allows us
to also analyse the ways in which categories are contingent, con-
junctural, interlinked and can change. By doing so, we go to the
core of many policy dilemmas that EU states face. We also see that

the term 'immigration' is too broad-brush and has very limited analytical usefulness.

To sum up, we focus on different forms of migration for four reasons. First, these are precisely the categories that EU states have developed and use to make sense of international migration. Second, changing understandings of migration are made evident through the redefinition of categories. Third, the forms and types of politics can differ quite substantially by migration type – with, for example, the politics of high-skilled labour migration differing greatly from those for asylum. Finally, the EU uses these categories to make sense of its role in relation to migration and mobility policy.

In the chapters that follow, we will not seek to immerse the reader in all the various complexities of migration policy in all twenty-seven EU states across all main migration types. Nor will we launch into detailed paragraph-by-paragraph analysis of various EU missives (and there are a lot of them). Rather, our objectives are to:

- create a framework for analysis that distinguishes between: types of migration; aspects of the policy process; and the extent to which these aspects of the policy process and types of migration have become part of a wider EU framework for the management of migration and mobility;
- draw from examples from across the EU to show how these debates play out;
- assess how, why, when and with what effects the EU now plays a role in migration and mobility and the extent to which this changes the ways in which debate occurs, decisions are made and policies implemented.

Thus, by providing a map (through, for instance, empirical analysis of different forms of migration and associated forms of politics) and a method (the framework for analysis of migration policy-making and the multilevel EU setting that we develop in Chapters 2 and 3) we can help the reader negotiate and understand these important issues. What should also become clear is the extent to which we have moved from a *politics of migration in Europe* to a *European politics of migration* with some common elements and the EU as a source of pressure for some convergence; but without pretending that member states have somehow been swept help-lessly along by the pressures of European integration.

Organization of the book

In Chapters 2 and 3 we set out a framework for analysing migration policy based on concepts drawn from public policy analysis. After laying the ground for our analysis of European policymaking, Chapters 4 to 9 address different areas of migration policy. Chapter 4 analyses one of the most important forms of immigration, and one that dominated European policy in the decades after World War II – labour migration, or migration for the purpose of paid employment. We show how approaches to labour migration have fluctuated over time and still vary widely between different European countries. While some governments have promoted labour migration as a means of addressing skills and labour shortages, many politicians and sections of the public remain concerned that labour migration can have adverse effects on the domestic population by displacing 'native' workers. The chapter also charts how the EU has attempted to increase its competence in this area, with somewhat limited results so far.

If labour migration can form part of a conscious recruitment drive on the part of governments or industry, Chapter 5 deals with a form of migration which tends not to be actively promoted: that of family migration. Family migration has actually often been seen by governments as an unwanted byproduct of labour migration, as immigrant workers bring their families or new spouses from abroad to settle in their country of residence. Often seen as a 'back route' for immigration, governments and the EU have had to grapple with conflicting considerations in developing policy in this area: the need to respect various international human rights and constitutional provisions on the rights of the family and their increased desire to 'select' migrants based on their perceived economic contribution. We show how attempts to introduce restrictive policies are often thwarted in practice and that we need to explore the form taken by the politics of family migration if we are to understand why this is the case, particularly the role played by courts as guarantors of rights.

European countries have found it difficult to enforce watertight control over immigration flows. Chapter 6 deals with the issue of irregular migration by those unable to enter European countries through legal channels. This can be seen as the 'other side' of legal migration flows because it is only by defining certain forms of migration as legal that others become defined as illegal. The EU is strongly committed to what it calls 'the fight against illegal immigration'(CEC 2006b). It is also a phenomenon that is difficult to observe and measure, which means that governments often have limited knowledge about these migratory dynamics. The OECD estimated that the irregular population was between 1 per cent and 4 per cent of the total population. On this basis, in 2005 the Netherlands estimated that it hosted between 125,000 and 230,000 irregular migrants, Spain estimated 690,000 while Italy calculated a figure of around 700,000 (figures cited in IOM 2008:467). Chapter 6 also analyses some of the assumptions made by policymakers about the causes and levels of irregular migration, and how they address it through various forms of border control and internal checks; sanctions on those transporting, smuggling or employing irregular migrants; and, more recently, cooperation with some of the non-EU countries from which irregular migrants originate or through which they travel.

Chapter 7 addresses another thorny area of migration: asylum and refugee policy. European countries have a long history of granting asylum to refugees, but in the 1980s and 1990s, as the number of asylum applicants in Europe increased, governments introduced a gamut of measures to try to restrict or deter such flows. Asylum came to be seen, along with family migration, as the 'weak link' in the national immigration control chain. This is an area in which EU cooperation is highly developed, so the chapter considers the complex interplay between national and EU policies, including how far the EU has influenced the nascent asylum policies of 'new' asylum recipients in southern and central Europe.

Chapter 8 analyses intra-EU mobility. EU nationals have the right to reside and work in other EU countries, an entitlement enshrined in the Treaty of Rome. Although originally a measure to ensure the more efficient operation of labour markets, mobility rights have been given a more political and civic spin, as the EU has developed since the Maastricht Treaty the concept of 'EU citizenship'. The chapter explores the impact of these provisions on migration between EU countries and how they impact on immigrants from outside the EU. It also considers how, why and when mobility rights became controversial as new member states joined the EU in 2004 and 2007.

Turning away from different types of migration, Chapter 9 explores how EU states have sought to 'integrate' the migrants who settle on their territory. The background for this is the 'crisis' or 'retreat' of multiculturalism – or, at least, multicultural policies given that many EU member states are multicultural societies – and a renewed emphasis on socio-economic integration and linguistic adaptation by migrant newcomers. We examine the various frameworks that have developed and the resonance of various 'national models' in the face of convergence pressures (Wimmer and Glick Schiller 2002). To tie in with the analysis in Chapter 8 we analyse how the EU now intervenes in these debates and how the promotion of EU mobility has also created some space for EU measures on the rights of long-term residents that are not EU citizens and to combat discrimination on grounds of race and ethnicity. We also consider the many variables that intervene in the relationship between 'integration policy' and 'integration outcomes'. By doing so, we see that migration policy is not just about migration. By this we mean that the organization of welfare states and their interactions with labour markets are crucial variables. If we think about these broader factors that influence the organization of welfare and work we can see that migration is not just about the people that move to the EU; it's also about how EU societies are organized, how they change and about self-understandings. If we don't see this, then we don't see the effects of migration (whoever 'we' are).

Chapter 10 is a concluding chapter that ties together some of the themes dealt with in earlier chapters to draw conclusions and consider the implications of our analysis both for the study of migration and for the development of the European politics of migration.

Chapter 2

Migration and Migration Policy in Europe

This chapter sets out the approach that we adopt to the analysis of European and EU migration policy and politics. It begins by providing some data on the main forms of migration and then developing a critique of existing approaches to the analysis of European and EU migration and mobility. We then specify key features of the approach to be developed in this book.

The movement of people across international borders is nothing new. Despite the recent resurgence of interest in the effects of globalization on migration, people have relocated to seek new opportunities, colonize territory, or escape persecution since ancient times. Well before the consolidation of the European state system, architects, artists, technicians, seasonal labourers, tradesmen, soldiers and sailors were moving between different parts of Europe to ply their trade (Bade 2003). In some cases, whole communities were encouraged to settle in other regions of the continent, often as part of colonization. Europe also saw flows of refugees seeking asylum from religious persecution from the late fifteenth century onwards (Marrus 1985). Flows of migrants and refugees in Europe continued throughout the nineteenth and twentieth century, including mass emigration from Europe to the New World. The postwar years produced several million refugees fleeing the Holocaust, ethnic persecution, fascism and communism. A massive 30 million people were displaced by the Second World War.

Seen in this historical context, European experiences of immigration since World War II appear less dramatic. Another important aspect of context is to think about European migration flows in relation to those in other parts of the world. The International Organization for Migration (IOM) reported on migrant populations by region and by countries hosting the largest numbers of migrants (Tables 2.1 and 2.2). In this IOM analysis Europe is far wider than the 27 member states of the EU and encompasses all 47 members of the Council of Europe. Table 2.1 informs us that both

21

Table 2.1   *Migrant population by geographic region 2010*

Geographical area	Migrants (millions)	Percentage of the area's population
Europe	69.8	9.5
Asia	61.3	1.5
North America	50.0	14.2
Africa	19.3	1.9
Latin America	7.5	1.3
Oceania	6.0	16.8

Source: Data from IOM (http://www.iom.int/jahia/Jahia/about-migration/facts-and-figures/regional-and-country-figures).

Table 2.2   **Countries with the largest number of international migrants in 2010**

Country	Migrants (millions)
USA	42.8
Russian Federation	12.3
Germany	10.8
Saudi Arabia	7.3
Canada	7.2
France	6.7
UK	6.5
Spain	6.4
India	5.4
Ukraine	5.3

Source: Data from IOM (http://www.iom.int/jahia/Jahia/about-migration/facts-and-figures/regional-and-country-figures).

North America and Oceania have larger migrant populations than Europe while, as Table 2.2 shows, the overall migrant population in the USA is massively larger than that in any EU member state.

Migration and refugee flows in Europe since World War II

Most west European countries have experienced substantial immigration since the end of World War II, and almost all European countries are now net immigration countries, meaning that the number of immigrants moving to them exceeds the number of their own nationals leaving.

In 2006, around 3.5 million people settled in a new country within the EU; of these about 3 million were not nationals of the country to which they moved (Eurostat 2008). The rest (around 500,000 people, or 14 per cent of the total) were nationals returning to their own country. Of these 3 million non-nationals moving to a new country, 1.8 million were not citizens of a member state (that is, TCNs). This means that around 1.2 million of those moving were doing so within the EU. This distinction between people moving to and within the EU is central to this book's distinction between migration and mobility. We can now divide this 2006 picture into its broad components:

- 52 per cent migration by citizens of non-EU countries;
- 34 per cent mobility by citizens of other member states;
- 14 per cent return of nationals.

If we now look at the origins of foreign immigrants (that is, excluding the return of nationals) then the areas of origin were as shown in Table 2.3 which establishes the importance of analysing migration from outside the EU *and* mobility within the EU alongside each other because both are central to the population movement between EU states and from outside the Union. It also shows that the four largest sources of third country national (TCN) migration to EU member states are non-EU Europe, Asia, America and Africa, in that order.

Table 2.4 expands on this analysis to show the total number of immigrants in EU states (and the candidate countries of Croatia and Macedonia).

Table 2.3   *Non-nationals in the EU-27 by continent of origin, 2008*

Continent	Percentage of EU-27 total foreign population, 2008
EU member states	36.7
Non-EU Europe	19.6
Africa	15.2
Asia	12.0
America	10.3
Oceania	0.7
Unknown	5.5

Source: Adapted from Eurostat (2009).

We can now drill down a little deeper into these statistics and look at how these patterns played out in particular member states.

First, we can think about the immigration hotspots, namely the three EU member states with the largest immigration inflows in 2006. In 2006, Spain was the largest country of immigration in Europe with more than 840,000 people moving to the country. Spain is often characterized as a new immigration country, but Spain has now been an immigration country for more than 20 years and is a key destination. Of those people moving to Spain in 2006, just under 500,000 were TCNs while just over 300,000 were citizens of another EU member state. Figure 2.1 looks more closely at Spain's immigration profile in 2006 to specify the top five origin countries.

Within these data, we see the centrality of intra-European migration with substantial movement from Romania (the year prior to its accession). The second-largest flow was from Morocco. Spain's sea border with Morocco – and the Spanish enclaves of Ceuta and Melilla – are key EU external frontiers. In movement from Bolivia and Colombia we see the continued resonance of colonial, historical and linguistic ties. Migration from the UK may seem more of a surprise, but comprised people retiring to Spain (many of whom were later to be stung by the collapse of the Spanish property market in the post-2008 economic crisis) and those moving to work in economic sectors, such as tourism. The Romanian and Moroccan populations are likely to be labour migrants working in sectors such as agriculture, tourism and domestic employment,

Table 2.4   *Immigrants by citizenship group, 2006 or latest available*

Country	Total number of immigrants	Of which:			
		Nationals	Non-nationals		
			Total	EU 27 citizens	Non-EU citizens
Austria	100,972	15,588	85,384	45,170	40,214
Belgium (2003)	81,913	13,113	68,800	35,143	33,657
Bulgaria	*	*	*	*	*
Cyprus	15,545	1,010	14,535	6,017	8,518
Czech Republic	68,183	2,058	66,125	10,912	55,2,13
Denmark	56,750	22,469	34,281	16,833	17,448
Estonia	*	*	*	*	*
Finland	22,451	8,583	13,868	5,368	8,500
France	*	*	182,390	5,403	176,987
Germany	661,855	103,388	558,647	320,727	237,740
Greece	*	*	86,693	18,588	68,105
Hungary	21,520	2,153	19,367	10,516	8,851
Ireland	103,260	18,895	84,365	65,002	19,363
Italy (2003)	440,301	47,530	392,771	102,045	290,726
Latvia	2,801	496	2,305	1,066	1,239
Lithuania	7,745	5,508	2,237	396	1,841
Luxembourg	14,352	621	13,731	11,512	2,219
Malta	1,829	1,171	658	*	*
Netherlands	101,150	33,493	67,657	31,921	35,736
Poland	108,02	8,978	1,824	409	1,415
Portugal	*	*	27,703	4,392	23,311
Romania	*	*	7,714	1,085	6,629
Slovenia	201,06	1,765	18,251	1,741	16,510
Slovak Republic	12,611	1,302	11,309	6,096	5,213
Spain	840,844	37,873	802,971	304,349	498,662
Sweden	95,750	15,352	80,398	25,482	54,916
UK	529,008	77,306	451,702	141,407	310,256
Candidate countries					
Croatia	14,978	13,994	1,029	284	,745
Macedonia	2,077	487	1,590	259	1,331

* No data available.

Source: Data from Eurostat (2008: 9).

Figure 2.1   *Top five countries of origin for migrants to Spain, 2006*

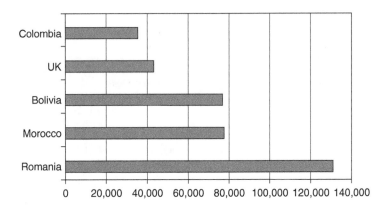

Source: Data from Eurostat (2009).

with gendered distinctions as female migrants are more likely to be employed in sectors such as domestic work while male migrants toil in sectors such as construction. Migration to Spain is spatially and sectorally particular – people move to certain places to undertake certain types of employment. This means that the effects of migration are highly specific.

The second immigration hotspot in 2006 was the UK. Figure 2.2 identifies the top five origin countries of migrants moving to the UK in 2006.

In the UK we see the continued legacy of post-colonial and commonwealth ties with migration from India, South Africa and Australia, but we also see very clearly an intra-EU dynamic in the form of large numbers of Polish migrants. These Polish people are, of course, EU citizens. They have a right to move to the UK and, of course, a right to return. These data showing large-scale migration to the UK need to be put into the context of perceptions of the UK as a 'zero immigration country' that supposedly closed the door to 'primary' labour migration by legislation introduced between 1962 and 1971. In fact, in the decade between 1998–2008 the UK experienced the largest wave of in-migration in its history. As with Spain, there is a gendered distinction in employment patterns, with male migrants more likely to be found in sectors such as construction and female migrants in care sectors. Again, migration's effects are likely to be highly specific.

Figure 2.2 *Top five countries of origin for migrants to the UK, 2006*

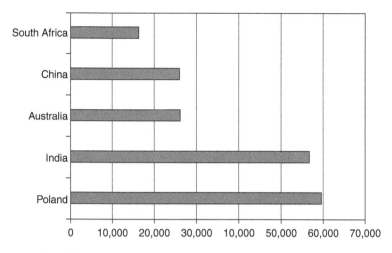

Source: Data from Eurostat (2009).

The third-largest immigration country in 2006 was Italy (Figure 2.4), which is, like Spain, a relatively new immigration country. Italy is a fascinating case because the period 2001–6 saw a centre-right government led by Silvio Berlusconi (and again since 2008) that took a tough line on immigration, enacted apparently draconian legislation but also presided over the largest increase in the foreign population in Italian history and one of the most generous regularizations ever seen in Europe (Einaudi 2007; Geddes 2008a). Here we have a good example of a government saying one thing and doing another. 'Policy failure,' one might think, but if we look more closely – as we do in Chapter 6 – we see the importance of dynamics within a coalition government and that success or failure are not simple aggregate categories but are, in fact, distributed across all stages of the political process with a more complex set of payoffs.

Key issues for Italy are its location close to neighbouring major sending and transit countries and a continued demand for migrant workers in the Italian economy in sectors such as construction, agriculture and domestic work/care. These came to a head in January 2010 in the small town of Rosarno in the southern region of Reggio-Calabria, where there were outbreaks of disorder as around 1500 people, mainly Africans, rebelled against the exploitation, abuse and racism that they were experiencing (*Corriere della*

Figure 2.3   *Main countries of origin for migrants to Italy, 2006*

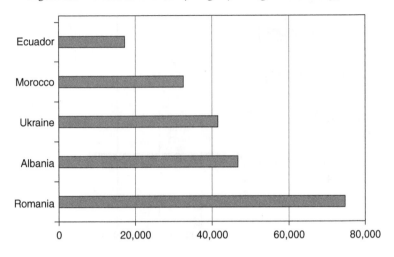

Source: Data from Eurostat (2009).

Sera 2010b). The situation was complicated by the strong presence in Rosarno of organized crime. In a TV interview on 27 January 2010, Prime Minister Berlusconi even suggested that illegal immigration fuelled organized crime. Even the interior minister, Roberto Maroni, appearing alongside Berlusconi on the same television programme, argued that these two issues needed to be separated. The leader of the centre-left Partito Democratico, Pierluigi Bersani, said that Berlusconi was instigating racism (Corriere della Sera 2010a).

Making sense of migration

This section sets the scene for the analysis in Chapters 4 to 9 by specifying in broad terms the differences between the main migration types, and then moves onto analyse the kinds of policy dilemmas that arise in relation to each of them.

Labour migration

The phenomenon of moving country for the purpose of work is not new. Nonetheless, the post-World-War-Two period saw large-scale immigration to many western European countries, mainly in the context of the major economic reconstruction taking place at that time. From the 1950s until the early 1970s, many European countries recruited large numbers of labour migrants to meet gaps in labour supply. Austria, Belgium, France, West Germany, the Netherlands and Switzerland all recruited additional labour through so-called 'guest-worker' schemes, which imported foreign labour for a temporary period. The assumption was that after a few years of work, migrants would return to their countries of origin (Castles and Miller 2008).

West Germany was one of the most important destination countries for guest-workers. The government concluded its first bilateral agreement with Italy in 1955, followed by agreements in the 1960s with Spain, Greece, Turkey, Portugal, Tunisia, Morocco and Yugoslavia. Between 1960 and 1972, the proportion of foreign nationals in the West German workforce increased from 2 per cent to 11 per cent with a net immigration of 12.6 million people between 1950 and 1993 (Joppke 1998). France signed bilateral agreements with Italy, Greece, Spain and Portugal, as well as drawing on immigrant labour from its overseas territories and former colonies in North and West Africa. Belgium similarly recruited labour migrants from Greece, Italy, Morocco, Spain and Turkey in the 1950s and 1960s. By 1970 it hosted a total of 700,000 foreign residents (Fassmann and Muenz 1994).

The UK also received large numbers of immigrants from abroad, but within a somewhat different framework. Rather than actively recruiting labour migrants from Mediterranean countries, migration to the UK came largely from the colonial or Commonwealth countries in the West Indies and Indian subcontinent, whose subjects or citizens were – according to the terms of the British Nationality Act 1948 – British subjects and entitled to move to the UK. By 1961 there were around 172,000 residents of West Indian origin, and 106,000 from India and Pakistan. A series of laws limiting access to British citizenship between 1962 and 1971 restricted immigration flows from these former colonies, particularly those in what was called the 'New Commonwealth' of the Indian subcontinent and the Caribbean (Hansen 2000).

The UK was not alone in attempting to limit immigration in the early 1970s. Other western European countries converged around similarly restrictive approaches from about 1973. By the late 1960s it became clear that many migrants who had moved to continental west Europe as guest-workers were becoming permanent residents, settling in their countries of destination and bringing their families to join them. Meanwhile, the oil price crisis of 1973 triggered recession across Europe, with many sectors that had recruited migrant workers experiencing rising unemployment. In response, European governments by and large called a halt to their recruitment policies. Policies aiming at 'zero immigration' (or 'zero labour migration', to be more precise) continued for the next two decades or so. As has been charted in much of the literature, this supposed immigration stop did not lead to a decline in immigration. Many resident migrants brought over their families and the numbers of asylum-seekers began to rise from the 1980s. Moreover, many countries introduced a number of derogations to the ban on recruitment, in order to meet labour shortages in particular sectors.

Meanwhile, in the late 1980s and 1990 a number of traditional emigration countries began to receive larger numbers of labour migrants. Ireland, Italy, Portugal and Spain all became net receiving countries during this period (Baganha 1997). A large factor in this shift was growing economic prosperity in these states; but immigration also increased because of a redirection of migration flows following the introduction of more restrictive policies in other European receiving countries. Similarly, central and east European countries have more recently become host countries. For most of the countries that recently joined the EU, economic growth and political stability have rendered them countries of destination for labour migrants. The Czech Republic, Cyprus, Hungary, Slovakia and Slovenia all now have positive net migration (Wallace 2002).

All this could give the impression that labour migration is relatively straightforward, but this is actually far from being the case. The wide variety of arrangements for the admission, work and settlement of labour migrants in different countries has led to a complex array of immigration statuses. Each country has tended to define and measure levels of labour migration based on the different entry and settlement programmes available to immigrants.

Thus labour migrants defined as 'seasonal' or 'temporary' migrants and recruited for strictly limited time periods (often 3 or 6 months) to work in specific jobs in agriculture, construction or hotels and catering often have highly circumscribed rights, with no entitlement to be joined by their families or to switch to other forms of employment or immigration status once their allotted period of stay is over.

On the other hand, migrants recruited to fill shortages in particular sectors, which often required skills that cannot be provided by the domestic workforce, are usually directly recruited by employers who cannot fill vacancies, for example in engineering, information technology or catering. They may have permission to be joined by their immediate family, but often have only limited rights to stay in the country, depending on the continuation of their employment contract.

More recently, some European countries such as the UK have introduced 'points systems' for recruiting labour migrants. Under these programmes migrants (usually high-skilled) are admitted for longer periods of time, based on fulfilling criteria such as qualifications, experience and language skills. They are then free to look for employment, and may have more generous entitlements to family reunion and even permanent settlement.

The attentive reader may have noticed that reference was made in the preceding paragraphs to national responses. There was scarcely a mention of the EU and yet this book is about migration and mobility in the EU. The point here is that policies concerning the admission of TCNs are not the subject of EU legislation. Member states may well be unlikely to accept EU regulations that constrain their capacity to recruit labour migrants given that there is an excess supply of potential migrant workers over demand plus fluctuations in economic performance that are likely to restrain or prompt increased use of migrant workers (Meyers 2002). Why would EU states constrain their ability to recruit labour migrants as they see fit? Yet EU member states have comprehensively constrained their ability to regulate labour migration with regard to the other 26 member states of the EU and are now looking at ways in which might develop a sectoral approach to labour migration for TCNs. The point here may be that greater openness within the EU plays a strong role in generating external closure.

The core dilemma

In many EU states there is a serious conflict between the economic and demographic case for expanded labour migration, and public resistance to increased migration. Some European governments, such as Germany, Spain and the UK, have responded by introducing new provisions to increase labour migration. Explicit attempts at expanding programmes have been politically controversial. One way of 'selling' them has been for liberalization to be accompanied by promises of stricter control of other, non-economically-beneficial migrants or refugees. Alternatively (or in addition), governments have placed the emphasis on temporary programmes, with the goal of avoiding permanent settlement. In other cases, governments have avoided political conflict by introducing liberalization by stealth, through acts and decrees that do not require parliamentary scrutiny and receive little media attention.

Family migration

Family migration continues to provide a major part of immigration flows to Europe. OECD data show that in 2006 around half of all permanent immigration to the EU was family migration, including 62 per cent in Portugal, 59 per cent in France, 42 per cent in Italy, 32 per cent in the UK and 23 per cent in Germany (OECD 2008:36). The EU's role in family migration has been limited because states have been reluctant to cede responsibility to supranational authority in areas related to admissions policy. In 2003, however, an EU Directive was introduced on the rights of family migrants.

When western European governments tried to halt immigration in the early 1970s they had not taken account of the fact that many labour migrants would settle in their host countries and bring their families to join them. Family migration, or 'family reunion', has accounted for a large proportion of immigration to western Europe from the 1970s onwards. Chapter 6 shows how European governments have been constrained in their capacity to restrict this type of movement, with some protection for family migrants in national legislation and constitutions, as well as international law.

Family migration has also taken the form of marriage between citizens or residents of European countries and partners from other countries. In many cases, the children of immigrants have sought husbands or wives in their parents' countries of origin, thus providing another channel of immigration. Despite attempts to restrict this type of migration, it has in practice been difficult for governments in liberal states to limit the rights of their residents to choose a spouse. Finally, higher-skilled labour migrants and resettled refugees can be entitled to bring their families with them when they migrate to European countries.

For both labour and family migration – for admissions policies affecting TCNs – the EU's role has been relatively weak. This contrasts with asylum and irregular migration, which have seen a strong presence of EU action. This reinforces the point that it is important to distinguish between types of migrants because the attendant forms/types of politics and policymaking can differ.

Core dilemma

Family migration is a key migration flow and has been represented as less economically productive and/or connected to concerns about the 'integration capacity' of immigrants. Both of these perceptions can be questioned. It is also the case that migration to join family members can be a right protected by law and could make an important contribution to integration.

Irregular migration

The 'fight against illegal immigration' (CEC 2006b) is a central component of EU migration policy, but with a particular resonance in relatively new countries of immigration in southern Europe and in those countries that joined the EU in 2004 and 2007. Irregular migration is a byproduct of national policies to restrict the legal entry of certain types of immigrants. Those migrants who enter European countries without relevant authorization are then defined as illegal or irregular.

Illegal migration first emerged as a political problem in a number of western European countries in the early 1980s. But by the end of the decade all EC states were more or less affected. This was in large part a consequence of new legislation on migration and asylum. Restrictive provisions made it increasingly difficult for migrants to find legal routes into European states. Meanwhile, the removal of emigration restrictions in former communist countries after 1989 increased the possibilities for illegal entry via land borders to the east and south of Europe. But probably the most significant contributor to irregular migration has been the extensive possibilities for living and working in European countries on an irregular basis. The persistence of irregular migration reflects the fact that many parts of the labour market in Europe welcome cheap migrant labour, and are happy to employ workers on an irregular basis. At the same time, many social services are quite accessible to migrants, whether their stay is authorized or not. The facility with which immigrants can and do participate in the labour market, find accommodation and access health and education services, helps explain the scale and persistence of irregular migration, despite state attempts to restrict it.

It is notoriously difficult to measure the level of irregular migration in Europe. In Chapter 7 we look far more closely at policy responses to irregular migration and the ways they have become embedded in an EU framework. This also serves to reinforce the point made throughout this book that a focus on particular types of migration allows us to take the diverse forms and types of policy responses to migration and mobility into account while also looking at the EU's differential impact. The EU has become more closely involved in irregular migration and asylum than it has in policies governing the admissions of labour or family migrants.

Core dilemma

Irregular migration raises some pressing policy dilemmas in relation to both the regulation of external borders and the regulation of labour markets and welfare states. The risk is that a 'myth of invasion' creates the mistaken belief that irregular migration is some overwhelming external pressure on the EU when, in fact, there are powerful internal drivers (de Haas 2007).

Asylum and refugee flows

In post-cold-war Europe, asylum-seeking migration rose in both scale and intensity. The Amsterdam Treaty (1997) created far more substantial EU competencies in the area of asylum, and, by the end of the first decade of the twenty-first century there was a standardization of rules across the EU. The member states then expressed their intention to create a common asylum system for the whole Union. Asylum is thus extensively Europeanized.

The concept of 'refugee', and the practice of granting 'asylum' to those suffering political or religious persecution, have existed in Europe at least since the seventeenth century. However, it was not until after World War II that international provisions on these practices were codified, in the form of the 1951 Geneva Convention. Box 2.1 specifies the Geneva Convention's main features. Most west European countries integrated the provisions of the Convention into their national laws or constitutions, recognising a duty to protect those suffering persecution on grounds of race, religion, political opinion or social group. The general practice has been to offer such people refugee status, which confers a

---

Box 2.1   The 1951 Geneva Convention on the Status of Refugees

The Convention was originally negotiated by 26 states, including countries from Europe, the Americas, the Middle East and Australia. It was initially limited to European refugees who had been displaced due to events occurring before 1951, but was subsequently expanded in terms of its temporal and geographic scope. The 1967 New York Protocol confirmed its applicability to refugees from all countries. Currently, there are 147 states signatory to the Convention.

The key provisions of the Convention are:

- Article 1A, which defines a refugee as a person outside his or her country 'owing to a well-founded fear of being persecuted for reasons of race, religion, nationality, membership of a particular social group or political opinion'.
- Article 33, which obliges states not to expel or send back (*refouler*) refugees to countries where their 'life or liberty would be at risk'. This is known as the principle of *non-refoulement*.

The Convention also sets out the type of legal protection and social and other rights that asylum-seekers and recognized refugees should receive from signatory states. It allows for the exclusion of certain refugees because they are guilty of 'crimes against humanity', or pose a threat to internal security.

---

generous range of rights akin to citizenship, including a right to permanent residence. The practice of granting refugee status is referred to as 'asylum', and those seeking such protection as 'asylum-seekers'.

Prior to the late 1970s, the number of asylum applications was low (rarely over a few hundred per year in most countries), and most applicants were lauded as victims of communist persecution in the Eastern bloc. Western European countries were by and large happy to grant refugee status to communist dissidents, whose flight provided a powerful symbol of the superiority of the capitalist West. This began to change from late 1970s and 1980s, as some countries experienced a rise in asylum applications. Moreover, the countries of origin of asylum-seekers were changing, with many emanating from non-communist countries in Africa, Asia, Latin

America or the Middle East. Although most refugees from these areas remained in their regions of origin, there was a strong perception in many European countries that Europe was being flooded with asylum applicants; and, moreover, that many or most of these applicants were not *bona fide* in the sense of the Geneva Convention. Table 2.4 breaks down asylum flows for the period between 1980 and 2006 and shows the distribution between EU member states. It is clear that numbers fell back after the peaks of the early 1990s that were strongly linked to the civil war in ex-Yugoslavia. The conflict in Kosovo contributed to a spike in numbers in 2000. It is also clear that some EU states, particularly Germany, were more exposed to asylum flows.

Core dilemma

What will the EU's focus on tougher and tighter external border controls and its 'fight against illegal immigration' mean for the rights of asylum-seekers to seek protection? Does the EU run the risk of creating the *de facto* category of the 'illegal asylum-seeker' (Morrison and Crosland 2000).

Intra-EU mobility

We have already demonstrated the salience of intra-EU mobility by EU citizens exercising mobility rights and the distinction that is made within the EU between 'migration' by TCNs and 'mobility' of EU citizens. To develop this point, Chapter 8 looks at provision for free movement by EU citizens coupled with the consolidation of this space in the form of cooperation and integration on internal security measures.

Core dilemma

At least in official discourse, mobility by EU citizens is seen as more virtuous because it is linked to the attainment of the EU's core economic objectives (CEC 1997; Favell and Hansen 2002; Guild 2005). The dilemma that arises is between openness and closure, with some EU states either – advertently or inadvertently – seeing or experiencing large increases in EU migration that form part of the solution to labour market shortages. In Germany, Italy, Spain and the UK, we saw that movement from within the EU is a key component of recent migration. This intra-EU movement brings challenges because of variation in labour laws and welfare rules, but a mobility framework that allows people to come and go may well be preferable to immigration laws that often encourage people to stay precisely because of the difficulty that immigration laws and visas systems create for TCNs to come and go.

Integration

This is traditionally an area in which approaches have shown significant levels of divergence. National approaches tend to reflect longstanding traditions of thinking on identity, citizenship and the role of the state.

Core dilemma

The perception of policy failure is endemic and has helped to instigate a backlash against multicultural policies. A particular focus has been on the integration of Europe's Muslim population, which has intensified since the Al Qaeda terror attacks of the first decade of the twenty-first century. Islamic beliefs have been singled out by some as incompatible with liberal democratic and human rights standards in European countries (Caldwell 2009). The risk is of painting with a broad brush for Muslim populations across Europe and creating a caricature. It is also the case that the Muslim population has a younger age profile and higher fertility rates, which has led to some predictions of rapid growth. More measured research does point to a growth in Europe's Muslim population, but also highlights how age and fertility patterns are likely to converge around European levels to reduce the rate of growth while non-Muslim immigration is also growing as a proportion of inflows to European countries (Kaufman 2010). The 'demography as destiny' argument is also weakened by its tendency to ignore the effects of social and political institutions. Historical research has shown the capacity of institutions to promote integration and adaptation by immigrant newcomers. That said, it is Caldwell's (2009) argument that it is precisely the diminished power and resonance of these institutions – that in turn are indicative of a collective loss of self-confidence in European countries – that leaves these societies and their values vulnerable to the effects of groups or communities that are more confident of their values and keen to assert them, by which Caldwell means Muslims.

In a not dissimilar vein, Joppke explores the 'limits of integration' in the UK for group-based claims by Muslims as Muslims

(Joppke 2009). His argument is that the institutional pathologies of UK race relations stimulate the production of group-based demands by Muslims that cannot actually be accommodated. Joppke draws from survey research done as part of the Pew world values survey of 2004 to note that this research suggests that 81 per cent of British Muslim survey considered themselves Muslims first and only 7 per cent considered themselves to be British citizens first. This compared with 42 per cent of French Muslims who saw themselves as French first and 46 per cent who saw themselves as Muslims first. Joppke looks admiringly at the capacity of the French state – or 'the dreaded Jacobin state across the Channel', as he puts it (p. 467) – where Muslims and non-Muslims according to Pew hold equally benign views of one another. This can be seen as a 'failure of British multiculturalism and a success of French Republicanism' (p. 467; see also Hansen 2007). Joppke argues that a pathology of the UK race relations model is that it leads people to expect the wrong things of the state – respect and recognition – when it is 'multiple adjustments' in areas such as markets and culture that are the essence of integration.

Other survey research can usefully contextualize the Pew data and allow us to explore the attitudes of British Muslims. The UK government's 'citizenship survey' analysed Muslim attitudes in 2008. More than 9 in 10 Muslims agreed that they felt part of British society. They expressed high levels of trust in institutions, indeed they seemed to have far more trust in elected politicians than the general population. There were widespread perceptions of discrimination targeted at Muslims and a sense that this was increasing. The citizenship survey suggests that British Muslims do tend to see their place in British society in terms of the kinds of multiple adjustments of everyday life mediated by local communities, by social and political institutions and by the labour market and welfare state. In turn this points to the importance of analysing these intervening factors and not rushing to assume that immigrant/ethnic minority groups are defined by such characteristics when, in fact, interactions with the places where they live are affected by more day-to-day factors such as employment, schooling, health and housing. These experiences may be shaped or influenced by the ethnic identities of migrants and their descendants, but it is equally plausible to imagine that these institutions can also play a role in shaping identities. This goes back to the point made earlier about the power and resonance of key social and political institutions in affecting the integration of immigrant and immigrant-origin populations.

Understanding the policy process: policy failure or securitization?

Broadly speaking there are two main approaches to the analysis of migration to the EU. One focuses on the inability of states to achieve their stated migration policy objectives. This can be called the 'policy failure' approach. The other argues that states are actually quite good at realizing their migration policy objectives and that states seek to justify draconian control measures through high-lighting the security threats associated with migration. This can be called the 'securitization' approach. Both 'policy failure' and 'securitization' contain powerful and important insights, but we argue that both tend to focus on the rhetorical construction of migration in public and policy debate and on the visible outcomes of policy. We argue that it is also important to factor the decision-making process into the analysis and explain later in this chapter what we mean by this and how we plan to do it.

Policy failure

The first approach to explaining migration policy holds that policy interventions are almost inevitably destined to fail and that the evidence for this is that migration levels seem persistently to exceed the stated intentions of governments to limit and control migration (Cornelius *et al.* 1994; Brettell and Hollifield 2000; Castles 2004a; 2004b). The perception of failure is quite broadly grounded across the political spectrum from right to left, and has worked its way into a good deal of the academic literature on migration. For example, postwar guest-worker policies in European countries such as Austria, West Germany and Switzerland were designed to provide temporary labour migration, but actually led to permanent immigration (Castles and Miller 1998; Herbert 2001). Similarly, post-imperial attempts by countries such as Britain and the Netherlands to maintain power and influence inadvertently formed the backdrop for large-scale migration (Hansen 2000). More recent examples of apparent failure include policies at state and EU level designed to counter trafficking and smuggling, which have unintentionally led to increases in irregular migration (Castles 2004c; 2004a). Similarly, policies to recruit migrants through temporary programmes frequently result in overstay or even permanent settlement (Ruhs 2002; Martin 2003). As one prominent exponent of the 'policy failure' thesis puts it, 'Paradoxically, the ability to control migration has shrunk as the desire to do so has increased. Borders are largely beyond control and little can be done to really cut down on immigration' (Bhagwati 1998).

These kinds of observations of policy failure have worked their way into analyses of developing EU migration policy competencies, particularly in analyses of the aspiration to achieve a 'fortress Europe', which is considered to have produced numerous negative and unanticipated consequences (Joly 1996; Noll 1997; Morrison and Crosland 2000).

A number of reasons are typically given for this apparent failure:

- Policies are based on misconceived assumptions about the migration process.
- Policy interventions are seen as inadequate in grappling with the complexity of the dynamics they are seeking to steer because they are based on insufficient knowledge of migration dynamics and the motivations of immigrants. In other words, they misunderstand the phenomena they are trying to control.
- Policymakers prefer to base policies on more simplistic or symbolic ideas about migration processes. So even if more complex and reliable accounts of migration dynamics are available, they prefer to stick to simpler notions. This is likely to be because they are under political pressure from the media or party politics to adopt clear-cut and populist responses to complex problems.
- Policy failure may derive from the inherent problems of securing compliance in a complex policy area such as migration. Thus the dynamics that policymakers seek to control – such as irregular movement, illegal labour, or permanent settlement – may be, to a considerable extent, beyond the influence of state controls. For instance, migrant networks or smuggling operators are able continually to bypass government measures, while employers or irregular migrants are adept at evading state regulations.
- Liberal institutions exert constraining power as governments are impeded from introducing the types of restrictions neces-

sary for effective migration control because of a 'liberal constraint' (Hollifield 1999). Such constraints kick in at two levels. First, liberal-democratic institutions such as international treaties, constitutions, the judiciary, and norms of human rights and equality constrain the implementation of more draconian approaches (Soysal 1994; Joppke 1998; Hollifield 1999). Second, liberal economic interests militate in favour of more open policies on labour migration, thus making states reluctant to be too restrictive in their entry policies (Hollifield 1992; Freeman 1995; Favell and Hansen 2002).

These assumptions about policy failure are not casual observations of little importance. Policy failings in the area of migration and mobility strike at the heart of our understanding of state authority and capacity. If the thesis of failure is correct, it could imply a serious malfunctioning of states, suggesting they are handicapped in carrying out a range of core functions: controlling their borders; keeping track of their population; and preventing infringements to labour, welfare, social policy and residency laws. If we take this perspective of failure at face value, then we might be tempted to agree with diagnoses about migration as a threat to sovereignty, or certainly as a challenge to the nation-state at the least (for a discussion, see Joppke 1998)

We will return to this possibility later and suggest why we consider the 'failure' thesis to neglect some dynamics of policy processes that contextualize sweeping notions of failure. In the meantime, it is worth reviewing a second, rather different, account of migration policy, which starts from almost the opposite premise about state capacity.

Securitization

On this account, migration is being 'securitized' by states and other political actors. There is a great deal of power behind this account as it is clearly the case that there is a strong security logic that underpins debates about immigration in Europe. Unlike the policy failure account, this approach does not see states as incompetent entities constantly failing to deliver on policy objectives. On the contrary, they are viewed as essentially expansionist, power-maximizing agents, permanently on the lookout for new ways of enhancing control over migration (and population generally).

Governments are willing and able to mobilize public support through pursuing highly restrictionist or 'securitarian' approaches to immigration. Indeed, adopting securitarian rhetoric serves a number of important political functions, by: consolidating a sense of a shared collective identity; mobilizing loyalty for the relevant political community; and legitimizing the state in its function of protecting citizens from external threats (Bigo 2001; Huysmans 2006). Crucially, such securitarian rhetoric can justify restrictive approaches to controlling migration, which may derogate from human rights or constitutional provisions (Wæver *et al.* 1993). In this way, otherwise illegitimate policies become 'normalized' as part of the repertoire of justifiable practice. This strategy of securitizing migration is not limited to politicians. In a similar way, so the argument runs, the officials responsible for elaborating and implementing policies are constantly seeking new opportunities to expand practices and technologies of control, to enhance their power, or, borrowing a term from Michel Foucault, their 'governmentality' (Foucault 1994; Huysmans 2006).

These accounts have inspired a considerable body of literature on the apparent 'securitization' of migration, at both national and EU level. The popularity of the approach was boosted in the aftermath of the 11 September 2001 attacks, with a number of critics charting European responses in the area of migration policy, and pointing out incidences of securitarian approaches (Bigo 2001; Tirman 2004; Huysmans 2006; Hampshire 2008). The terrorist threat was seen as providing a justification for introducing more draconian migration control measures, stricter asylum procedures, and extended surveillance of (potential) migrants through EU-wide databases (Mitsilegas 2007).

Again, though, we should pause for thought and consider the implications of adopting this sort of explanation of European migration policy. It implies that states have a fundamental interest in maximizing restriction and control, considerations that apparently outweigh business and economic arguments for migration, questions of social cohesion, or relations with countries of emigration. In fact, there is considerable evidence that European governments are acutely aware of these social, economic and political factors in forging immigration policy. By pursuing a securitarian approach, they would be implementing highly restrictive and punitive policies that would jeopardise many of these considerations. By adopting rhetoric that linked migration to security threats, they would be undermining public support for beneficial forms of labour migration and undermining interethnic relations. Thus while it is clearly the case that some politicians adopt securitarian discourses, it is also the case that politicians and governments have been cautious about pursuing outright 'securitization' of migration policies (Boswell 2007).

Understanding migration policymaking

Beyond the various queries we have raised, we believe there is a deeper flaw in both of these approaches. Despite their very different assumptions about the state, both the policy failure and the securitization theses could be argued to offer a somewhat simplistic account of the political system. In their different ways, they seem to both attribute too much rationality and uniformity to the policy process.

A more general observation about the policy failure thesis is that if we look across public policies more generally then the failure to attain stated objectives is actually a rather standard feature. If we analyse the attainment of stated objectives and take these as the basis for assessing whether policy succeeds or fails then most policies in most areas probably fail to some extent (Pressman and Wildavsky 1982). In the immigration literature, the 'policy failure' thesis seems to accept at face value the stated policy objectives of governments, and then goes on to assess the success of policy by comparing outcomes with stated intentions. This seems to imply acceptance of a classic policy-cycle model with policymaking understood as a linear process starting with the definition of objectives, followed by the elaboration of measures designed to meet these objectives and ending with the implementation of these measures. Policy is then evaluated based on whether implementation achieves the original specified goals. If we assess the record of European states or the EU on this basis, then we can hardly avoid the conclusion that migration policies are subject to systematic failure.

Yet on further inspection, this policy-cycle model seems too simplified. The politicians and officials that are engaged in formulating policy are guided by a range of often conflicting considerations, and policies that are often a reflection of compromises or delaying tactics, rather than of clear-cut and unified goals. Apparently successful outcomes are frequently attributed to government policies, whereas in fact these outcomes can be largely brought about by exogenous factors that had little to do with such interventions. Moreover, electoral considerations, special interests and expert or practitioner advice often pull governments in different directions, encouraging a gap between restrictive rhetoric and more permissive practice. These are all common features of European migration policy responses, but none of these features is adequately captured by the instrumentalist perspective of the 'policy failure' approach. Its emphasis on formally accepted policy goals and on policy outputs could provide a misleading snapshot of the policy process, obscuring the more complex dynamics of how policy problems and solutions are defined, the messy and often incoherent compromises involved, and the frequently ambiguous interests and goals of policymakers. This is not to mention the very real practical difficulties associated with policy implementation.

The securitization literature has a less benign understanding of the rationality of states, conceived in terms of an impulse to expand control through enhanced intelligence, surveillance, steering and sanctions (Huysmans 2006). However, as with the policy failure account, these theories may well attribute too much unity and rationality to the actions of states and the EU. They can exaggerate the extent to which different parts of the political system and administration develop proactive strategies for controlling migration while underestimating how far politicians and agencies are involved in more reactive 'firefighting' and struggles to retain legitimacy in the face of often unrealistic public and media demands about state interventions. They also gloss over the distinctive logics guiding organizational behaviour in different sectors: economics, labour, welfare, interior, justice and foreign ministries all can have quite different objectives in relation to migration policy, making it problematic to conceive of the state as a unified actor or of migration as a unified policy field.

In the analysis that follows we draw from a number of seminal contributions in public policy and political sociology that have questioned the more rationalist accounts of the policy process (Meyer and Rowan 1977; March and Olsen 1983; Majone 1989; March and Olsen 1989; Scott and Meyer 1991; Kingdon 1984; Brunsson 2003). We draw from this body of literature to suggest a rather different understanding of the policy process, which we believe provides a better basis for making sense of European migration policy and its dynamics. We now specify the main elements of this approach.

A framework for analysis of European migration politics

The analytical framework that we develop throughout this book does not commence from the aspects of policy that are most easily visible, namely government rhetoric or outcomes of policy. In fact, it is not possible to work back from the outcomes of policy to make assumptions about the policy process. It is necessary to study the process itself. Similarly, while government rhetoric can tell us much about the signals that states want to send about their policy aspirations and can have important effects on the 'framing' of migration issues, a focus on this sort of discourse often obscures the complexity of state interests and goals. This rhetoric is also often highly symbolic, designed to appease different constituents or signal commitment to a particular course of action. In reality, policy practice may end up being effectively 'decoupled' from such rhetoric. By decoupling we mean that policymakers are often quite happy to tolerate a discrepancy between discourse and practice, or what Nils Brunsson (2003) calls their 'talk', 'decision' and 'action'. In all the chapters that follow, we identify how this decoupling can take place and show that it makes little sense to compare stated policy goals with outcomes, since these latter may well be successful in meeting a variety of interests about which states prefer to remain reticent and which don't figure too much in public rhetoric. So instead of focusing solely on stated goals and outcomes, our approach also explores the often opaque process of policymaking, conceiving of states in rather less rationalistic and uniform terms. To do this we draw from three fundamental insights from mainstream and widely used approaches to analysis of policymaking, albeit ones that have not always figured too prominently in analyses of migration (for exceptions see, for example, Guiraudon 2003, Geddes 2008a and Boswell 2009).

'Talk', 'decision' and 'action'

The first of our core concepts is captured in Brunsson's (2003) three-way distinction between 'talk', 'decision' and 'action'. The key idea here is that different parts of the political system and administration have different ways of deriving legitimacy. In many areas of policy, politicians and bureaucrats sustain their legitimacy not so much through how they actually affect the dynamics they are seeking to control (Brunsson's notion of 'action'). Indeed, these impacts are often diffuse and difficult to observe. Instead, policy-makers rely on more symbolic means of gaining support for their policies: talk (or rhetoric), and being seen to take decisions.

Scott and Meyer (1991) make a similar distinction between modes of legitimation in 'institutional' and 'technical' sectors. Institutional sectors are those in which decision-makers derive legitimacy from conforming to certain expectations about appropriate action – that is, through rhetoric and symbolic decisions. In these areas, it is difficult to judge the impact of policies, so the government relies on talk and decisions to bolster support for its programme. By contrast, technical sectors are those in which decision-makers are rewarded for their substantive output, or the change they effect on their environment (action). In other words, the impacts of their actions are visible and may be punished or rewarded by the electorate. In later chapters we show that irregular migration possesses characteristics of an institutional sector because the causes and dynamics are unclear and there is uncertainty about numbers. We would thus expect – and do indeed find – a strong focus on rhetoric. This contrasts with asylum, where data on flows have been systematically available and have led to a strong focus on measures to reduce the numbers of applicants (measured on a 6-monthly basis as new data are released), although in Chapter 7 we identify ambiguities in the politics of asylum too.

Once we start distinguishing between talk, decisions and action as ways of securing support for policies, then it becomes clear that these different elements may not always converge. Put another way, talk, decisions and action may be 'decoupled' from one another. In other words, policies may claim to pursue certain objectives, but end up doing the opposite (Castles 2004c). It may be that:

- Statements and pledges are made, but cannot be implemented – for example, 'controlling immigration', in the literal sense of preventing all forms of irregular movement.
- Decisions are taken which seek to appease key interests within, for example, a coalition government.
- Actions are taken without any explicit declaration by policy-makers, for example facilitating some forms of higher-skilled labour migration that are beneficial to the economy, while continuing to claim to be restricting new immigration.

This 'decoupling' may occur because political organizations in complex environments concentrate their efforts on reaching some kind of 'symbolical accord' with their environment that reflects rather than resolves inconsistencies (Brunsson 2003). An example of a symbolical accord would be tough talk on immigration, particularly focused on efforts to secure external frontiers, but with less focus on regulation of the domestic labour market where many regularly and irregularly employed migrants may work (and are valued for the contribution that they make). There may be a sound political logic for this, as enforcement of external frontiers affects non-citizens seeking to enter the country who cannot vote, while tough measures of internal enforcement affect citizens who can vote (Sciortino 1999). Tough talk may well not translate into tough action if this symbolical accord is threatened.

This is not to say that 'talk', 'decision' and 'action' do not link and that there is always a radical disconnect in the political system that means that objectives can never be attained. What it can help us to comprehend is some of the underlying dynamics of a policy area such as migration and mobility where there is a lot of 'tough talk' but some major difficulties actually turning that talk into action. Conversely, when action is achieved it may be because the issue is extracted from 'politics' – or at least the more public and visible manifestations of it – and dealt with in more secreted administrative or judicial venues, again decoupled from talk (Guiraudon 2003).

Deliberate malintegration

The second key concept we would like to introduce is what Hall (1984) has termed 'deliberate malintegration'. As we have seen, migration policies are often the object of a range of competing interests, whether between different government agencies, interest groups, sections of the electorate and media, or even different European countries at the level of EU policymaking. In order to satisfy competing demands, policies will often reflect an intentional jumble, or 'fudging', of different goals and priorities. Legislation or programmes may be designed to keep different interests happy, with the result that policies appear to be quite inconsistent or contradictory.

Typical examples of this in migration policy would be policies on labour migration and the problem of 'brain drain'. Many European countries, and (more recently) the EU, have been keen to find ways to attract skilled labour from third countries, including from developing countries that may be detrimentally affected by losing qualified staff. Development and foreign ministries have attempted to promote responsible practice in recruitment in order to avoid this problem of brain drain – indeed, they would rather governments desisted entirely from this sort of 'cherry picking' of skilled workers. The outcome is often a rather incoherent combination of selective recruitment policies, and the introduction of ethical practices for certain sectors such as health professionals (Martineau *et al.* 2004). This is a good example of 'deliberate malintegration'. So unlike in the case of decoupling talk and action, conflicts are resolved through combining quite inconsistent types of policies in the same package of measures.

Rather than representing policy failure, we argue that this type of incoherence can be a quite rational response to unrealistic demands. For example, it can be a means of reconciling liberal economic goals with internal security considerations or of satisfying unfeasible public demands for action while ensuring that governments will not be held to account for failing to deliver. Yet if we were to assume that successful policy should be consistent and follow clear goals, then deliberate malintegration would almost certainly be categorized as yet another policy failure.

The policy stream

A substantial body of work has developed that demonstrates how the relationship between participants in a decision process, the problems they address, the solutions that might attach themselves to such problems and the points in time at which decisions are made may not be smooth-flowing (Cohen *et al.* 1972). In his seminal book, Kingdon (1984) suggested that there is no clear causal and temporal sequencing of policy problems and solutions: there may actually be different rates of flow in the streams of ideas, solutions and problems. It is not self-evident, for example, that problems initiate policy responses, because there may well already be a stream of solutions waiting to attach themselves to a particular problem. Equally, calls for 'better' or 'more coordinated' policies are staple components of reform agendas, but these agendas come and go (Pressman and Wildavsky 1982). Even the most casual observer of politics would have noticed that reforms are easy to initiate but hard to achieve. Instead, the solutions favoured by politicians for dealing with particular policy problems may have been on the agenda for years, but were never taken up because they did not garner support. Such discarded solutions may be revived, or rescued from the 'garbage can' (Cohen *et al.* 1972), as convenient ways of dealing with new problems that have emerged. One good example of this would be proposals to protect refugees in their 'regions of origin', promoting better support for refugee camps, reception centres or safe areas in areas neighbouring civil conflict or violence. The idea was to encourage people to stay closer to their place of origin, rather than travel to Europe to apply for asylum. This scheme was mooted by various commentators and organizations in the mid 1990s, but received insufficient political backing at the time. The notion was subsequently 'rediscovered' by the UK government in the late 1990s, as a good way of justifying more restrictive asylum policies. In fact, this idea keeps resurfacing periodically in EU discussions of asylum, each time presented by its proponent as a new solution.

Finally, favourable outcomes which were never planned or intended may be retrospectively attributed to policy interventions. In other words, policymakers may try to get credit by passing off certain outcomes as attributable to their past actions (Weick 1995). Thus policymakers have taken credit for reducing asylum numbers, even though there is some evidence that other factors such as conditions in countries of origin played a more significant role than did national legislation (Sasse and Thielemann 2005). Again, this challenges the idea that it makes sense to evaluate policy by comparing outcomes to stated policy goals: certain outcomes may have little to do with the actions of policymakers.

In short, the policy stream literature provides us with three alternatives to the linear sequencing of policy posited by the 'policy cycle' literature:

- Responses can precede problems and be fished out from a range of discarded solutions when required.
- Preferred responses can influence which problems get selected for attention, and how these are constructed.
- Exogenously caused events or outcomes can trigger a shift in how policymakers explain their previous actions, whereby they seek credit for achieving outcomes they had little or no influence over.

To sum up, these three concepts – talk, decision and action; deliberate malintegration; and the policy stream – can help to provide an important corrective to prevalent ways of conceiving migration policymaking, drawing attention to the often piecemeal, reactive, inconsistent and ambiguous nature of policy in this area.

Summary

This chapter has introduced key elements of the approach to be developed in the remainder of this book. It began by seeking to clarify the distinction between different types of migration. It did so by looking at some empirical data that show the relevance and salience of immigration issues and also by identifying some of the policy dilemmas that arise. Our empirical analysis also illustrates how migration issues play out in different ways in different parts of the EU. For example, asylum was more of an issue in 'older' immigration countries such as Germany, the Netherlands and the UK than it was in 'newer' immigration countries in southern Europe. Similarly, irregular migration has been a more prominent concern in southern Europe than in 'older' immigration countries. We then moved on to specify the approach that we take in this book, setting out a framework for understanding policymaking and implementation on immigration. Our next task is to analyse in more detail the EU institutional setting. This is the task of Chapter 3.

Chapter 3

The EU Dimension of Migration and Asylum Policy

This chapter specifies the EU context of immigration and asylum policy in Europe. It identifies key features of the EU's legal, political and institutional framework in order to show how this system has evolved, how institutional roles have developed, and how these relate to the growing salience of migration and mobility as EU concerns. It also considers how these EU policies and institutions can then impact on member states as a result of 'Europeanization'.

One important aspect of the developing EU role is that interior ministers from all EU member states now meet on a regular basis to discuss a range of migration and asylum issues. This work is supported by officials who meet in a Strategic Committee on Immigration, Frontiers and Asylum (SCIFA) and various working groups within the SCIFA framework. Much EU cooperation thus occurs beneath the tip of the iceberg (ministerial meetings) at official level where much of the preparatory work is done. Cooperation has certainly increased and intensified since the 1990s and has, since 1999, been underpinned by EU laws (Regulations and Directives) on migration and asylum. It is national interior ministries that have been central to this cooperation, but foreign, justice, development, employment and social ministries have also been quite regularly involved in mobility, migration and asylum issues.

The Lisbon Treaty, ratified in November 2009, represented a recent and significant development in EU migration, asylum and borders policy (see Box 1.2 on p. 10–11 for details). To put it in straightforward terms, the Lisbon Treaty meant that migration and asylum measures would be adopted by QMV in the Council of Ministers and with use of the co-decision procedure for the European Parliament (EP), which gave the EP real legislative teeth. The Lisbon Treaty was, however, a further development of already-existing provisions aimed at creating a common migration and asylum policies, which had been in place since the Amsterdam

51

Treaty came into effect in 1999. Since Amsterdam, the framework for EU migration and asylum policy has been organized into consecutive five-year work plans that build on the Treaty's provisions. Between 1999 and 2004 the Tampere agreement set the agenda, to be succeeded by the Hague Programme between 2005 and 2009 (European Council 1999; Council of the European Union 2004). Between 2010 and 2014 a programme agreed while the Swedish government held the Council presidency and thus known as the Stockholm Programme will set the agenda. Key aspects of these three action plans are laid out in Box 3.1. They build on the formal competencies outlined in the various treaties that we specified in Boxes 1.1 and 1.2 (pp. 8–11) and thus provide a more specific take on migration and asylum competencies.

Box 3.1   The Tampere, Hague and Stockholm Action Plans 1999-2014

The Tampere programme covered the period 1999–2004 and identified four main aspects of a Common EU migration and asylum policy:

- Partnership with countries of origin, which flags the growing importance of an 'external' dimension of EU migration and asylum policy
- A Common European Asylum System leading to a common asylum procedure and a uniform status throughout the EU for those granted asylum.
- Fair treatment of TCNs through measures to combat discrimination and that extends rights to TCNs that approximate those of EU citizens.
- Management of migration flows with measures to stem irregular migration and combat trafficking and smuggling.

The Hague Programme covered the period 2005–9 and sought to build on the measures proposed by Tampere:

- A balanced approach to migration management, with measures to tackle illegal immigration, smuggling and trafficking.
- Development of an integrated approach to the management of external borders and visa policy consistent with free movement provisions.
- Work towards the creation of a common asylum area.   ➡

It is important to emphasize that these three action plans do not mean that all objectives have been attained and that there is now a single, EU-wide approach, or some kind of 'one size fits all' policy. Indeed, the development of 'mutual recognition' as a core principle of EU governance, and the use of Directives that specify EU legal objectives but that do not specify the means by which they must be achieved, does create scope for adaptation with 'national colours' (Green-Cowles *et al.* 2001).

What these action plans do imply is that the EU now plays a key role in setting the migration and asylum agenda. And, as a consequence, the context within which member states operate has changed significantly. In this chapter we show the challenges that have underpinned the development of this EU framework, analyse

---

- Work with member states to deliver better immigrant integration policies.

The Stockholm programme covers the period 2010–14 (House of Lords 2009). The document states that the 'EU needs to promote a dynamic and fair immigration policy'. This will include:

- A global approach based on partnership with third countries.
- Promotion of the positive effects of migration on the development of sending countries.
- A common framework for admissions adapted to the requirements of increased mobility and labour market demands.
- An EU immigration code and common rules to manage family reunification and support immigrant integration policies.
- Better controls on illegal immigration, including measures to combat illegal employment as well as measures on return and removal.
- A single asylum procedure and a uniform international protection status by 2012.
- A 'true sharing' of responsibility for hosting and integrating refugees, including a voluntary system for redistribution between member states and common processing of asylum applications. The aim should be mutual recognition of asylum decisions – that is, that a decision made in one member state is recognized in all other member states.
- Extension of regional protection programmes to assist non-member states.

the specific forms that cooperation has taken and specify the roles of key EU institutions. Our account will demonstrate the rapid development of EU migration and asylum policy; its centrality to core aspects of the EU project, such as economic integration and enlargement; the differentiation in EU policy between types of migration; and the differential impacts of EU action on member states. By doing so, we also provide further justification for the approach taken in this book – that is, the importance of distinguishing between migration and mobility and exploring different forms of migration as a way of better understanding the complex migration relationships that have developed within and between member states in the EU's multilevel system.

The multilevel setting of EU policy

European states are central to the process of European integration, but now share power with each other and with EU institutions. One way to think about this is to think in terms of states striking 'sovereignty bargains' where EU level decision-making could increase the likelihood of attaining policy objectives (Mattli 2000). These 'bargains' may also bring with them increased capacity as a result of the pooling of authority and resources, which is a major concern for those states, for example in southern Europe, most exposed to migration flows. A 'sovereignty bargain' can thus also be a 'capacity bargain', enhancing a government's ability to cope with migration problems. These bargains also bring with them the possibility of unexpected or unintended consequences as new decision-making arenas are established, competencies are shared and new institutional actors – such as the European Commission – become more extensively involved (Pierson 1996).

One way of understanding this multilevel system would be to see it as a series of interactions between national governments and the EU, but it is actually more complex than this. In her analysis of policy types in the EU, Wallace sees migration and asylum as being a form of 'intensive transgovernmentalism', which is distinct from intergovernmental (state cooperation) or supranational (EU-driven) policy types (Wallace 2004).

To develop this point a little further, we can ask the basic question here of 'Who's in charge?' Is it the member states that hold the upper hand and set the pace (intergovernmentalism) or is it EU institutions such as the Commission and the EP (supranationalism)? Wallace's point is that neither of these perspectives captures the rather more complex dynamics in an area such as migration and asylum where there is intensive cooperation on a regular basis between a specific group of ministers and officials with responsibility for migration and asylum. This intensive interaction is quite sectoral – that is, focused on a particular area of policy with associated specialisms and expertise. Interactions are intensive, transgovernmental and centred on networks that connect formal law-based action to more informal, socially constituted resources.

EU institutions

The EU is a treaty-based organization. These treaties agreed in public international law between member states can then be turned into laws that bind participating states (Sandholtz and Stone Sweet 1997). These can be understood as the sovereignty bargains to which Mattli (2000) refers. This ability to turn treaties between states into laws that bind those states is a unique and defining feature of the EU as no other international organization possesses this power. The treaties provide the legal framework while the Tampere, Hague and Stockholm programmes specified action plans for the period 1999–2014. These action plans have then provided a basis for common decision-making procedures involving all member states within the EU's political system. As is well known, this system contains five main institutions:

- The *Council (of Ministers)*, on which sit representatives of national governments. In addition, since 1974, the *European Council* has convened heads of state/government to set the EU's overall political direction.
- The *Commission,* which is responsible for initiating policy and for the management and implementation of EU decisions.
- The *European Parliament* (EP), which is the only directly elected body at EU level and which has become increasingly involved in decision-making through use of the co-decision procedure. The EP is based in Brussels, Luxembourg and Strasbourg with 736 members who, since 1979, have been directly elected in elections held every five years.
- The *European Court of Justice* (ECJ) based in Luxembourg with 27 judges (one from each member states) that normally

operates in configurations of 13 judges. The ECJ interprets EU law and rules in cases of dispute. Its remit in the areas of non-EU migration and asylum has tended to be circumscribed, although the Lisbon Treaty extends the ECJ's powers in migration and asylum policy.

The EU political system has supranational elements (through the EP, the Commission and the ECJ), but is best understood as hybrid in the sense that that there are also clear intergovernmental components, particularly in the Council and European Council. This hybridity also means that power-sharing and interinstitutional bargaining are everyday components of EU politics while particular dynamics become evident in different policy sectors as cooperation and integration evolve over time.

If we now focus more specifically on migration and asylum, we see that primary responsibility has lain with the Justice and Home Affairs (JHA) Council composed of interior and justice ministers from all 27 member states, which tends to meet every two months or so. This is supported by the Council's secretariat and by the work of each member state's permanent representatives, usually Brussels-based civil servants from each of the member states who do much of the groundwork for the ministers in various official working groups. More specifically, the groundwork for the JHA ministers is laid by national and EU officials meeting in SCIFA on a monthly basis, and by the plethora of subgroups belonging to SCIFA, which meet more frequently.

The Commission, meanwhile, also has responsibility for the management and implementation of policy. This responsibility for implementation is shared with the member states because the Commission possesses neither staff nor resources to monitor implementation across all 27 member states. In all this discussion of the EU, its role and its powers, it is helpful to bear in mind that the Commission employs fewer people (some 23,000) than the employees of most medium-sized European cities, and that the EU's budget amounts to little more than one per cent of the combined GNP of its members.

As we have seen, since 1999 migration and asylum issues have fallen within the legal framework of the Treaty of Amsterdam. The main legal outputs are Regulations, Directives, Decisions, Recommendations and Opinions. Regulations and Directives are particularly important because they are binding and have 'direct effect', which means they take precedence over national laws and must be implemented. Both specify the objectives that are to be achieved, but Directives leave more discretion in the method of implementation while regulations are more tightly prescriptive. For example, the EU has issued two Directives on anti-discrimination which allow more scope for differences in the implementation methods so long as stated objectives are secured. By contrast, the EU has issued a regulation specifying very clearly the 101 countries whose nationals must be in possession of a visa when entering the territory of a member state.

When analysing structures of government it is necessary to differentiate between legislative, executive and judicial authority. The argument has been made, for example, that the executive branch of government has been a key player in the development of restrictive immigration policies, with interventions made by the judiciary that have sometimes restrained restrictive impulses when they contradict national or international legal standards (Hollifield 1992; Guiraudon 2000b). Within the EU system, we can discern the following relationships between institutions:

- The Council and EP share legislative power.
- The Commission and the member states share executive power and responsibility for the management and implementation of policy.
- The ECJ is the highest court with regard to the content of the EU treaties and thus exercises judicial power, but has had only a limited immigration and asylum role. This contrasts with the extensive role it has played in the interpretation of the free movement framework.

Again, we see the importance of the legal and political distinction between the intra-EU and extra-EU migration frameworks. The Amsterdam Treaty constrained the involvement of the ECJ by only allowing reference to be made to it from the highest court of appeal in a member state. The Lisbon Treaty has changed this and allows preliminary references to be made from any court or tribunal in a member state. This does raise the clear possibility – if not likelihood – that the ECJ will become intensively involved in migration and asylum issues.

If we were to tell the story of EU competencies on migration and asylum then it would contain the following components:

- a gradual movement towards increased EU involvement as marked, particularly, by Commission involvement in decision-making;
- a growing EP role through use of co-decision procedures with a particular landmark in 2008 when the 'Return' Directive (covering expulsion for irregular migrants; see Chapter 6) was the first measure to be agreed by co-decision between the Council and Parliament;
- a continued strong role for member states in setting policy direction, but since Amsterdam, Nice and Lisbon far more emphasis on interinstitutional negotiation;
- immigration and asylum as central to the EU enlargements that occurred in 2004 and 2007;
- incorporation of migration and asylum as 'normal' issues by the Lisbon Treaty, meaning co-decision between the Council and EP, QMV in the Council and full jurisdiction for the ECJ.

Schengen

What this story lacks, however, is an additional and very important element: the importance of innovation outside the Treaty framework. The best example of this is the Schengen Convention, named after the town in Luxembourg. Schengen was an agreement in 1985, outside the Treaty framework between five EC member states (the Benelux countries, France and Germany) to liberalize free movement between themselves with compensating security measures. Map 3.1 shows the Schengen members, states that are adapting to Schengen, associated states and those EU states that are outside Schengen.

Schengen has been a 'laboratory' within which have been developed mechanisms and measures – such as the development of databases and information-sharing – to develop security measures that accompany free movement provisions (Monar 2001). The Amsterdam Treaty (1997) incorporated the Schengen provisions into the main body of the EU Treaty. This meant that the Schengen framework became a key component of EU migration and asylum and, importantly, central to the requirements that had to be met by the 12 countries that joined the EU in 2004 and 2007.

In terms of its introduction, the Schengen Convention came into effect with 9 participating states in 1995 that abolished checks at internal borders and created a single external border where entry

Map 3.1 *The Schengen area: members, associated states, accession*
states and non-members

Members
Associated states
Accession states
Non-members

checks for access to the Schengen area are carried out. These
checks are based on a common set of rules, such as a common visa
policy, police and judicial cooperation and a Schengen Information
System (SIS) to pool and share data. Table 3.1 charts Schengen's
development with an overview of its key stages.

Table 3.1   *History of the Schengen system*

1990	Schengen Convention signed to implement the Schengen Agreement. Italy signs the Convention.
1991	Spain and Portugal sign the Convention.
1995	The Convention comes into effect. Austria signs the Convention.
1996	Denmark, Finland and Sweden sign the Convention. Because of their links in the Nordic free movement area, Iceland and Norway also signed the Convention despite not being EU member states.
1999	The Amsterdam Treaty comes into force which integrates the Schengen Convention into the EU Treaty framework.
2000	The UK secures partial participation in Schengen, mainly in the areas of police and judicial cooperation.
2002	Ireland secures partial participation, mainly in police and judicial cooperation but also the SIS.
2004	All 10 new member states partially apply Schengen provisions, mainly those on external border control and police and judicial cooperation. Switzerland signs an agreement which associates it with Schengen.
2007	Bulgaria and Romania join the EU and partly apply Schengen provisions, mainly those on external border control and on police and judicial cooperation. On 1 September, Czech Republic, Estonia, Hungary, Latvia, Lithuania, Malta, Poland, Slovakia and Slovenia all start to use the SIS. On 21 December, internal land border controls are lifted with Czech Republic, Estonia, Hungary, Latvia, Lithuania, Malta, Poland, Slovakia and Slovenia.
2008	On 30 March, internal air border controls are lifted with Czech Republic, Estonia, Hungary, Latvia, Lithuania, Malta, Poland, Slovakia and Slovenia. In August, Switzerland is connected to the SIS.

The SIS is particularly important as it is a huge database aiming to gather and share information in pursuit of public security. The SIS clearly raises questions about civil liberties because of the huge amount of information about private citizens contained within it. Participating states enter 'alerts' onto the database on wanted and missing persons, lost and stolen property and entry bans. The database is immediately accessible to police and security officials across the EU. The SIS is designed to compensate for the absence of land and air border controls and contains about 30 million 'alerts'. In each of the 25 participating states there is a national system (N.SIS) connected to a central system (C.SIS). The European Commission is currently developing a second-generation SIS – the SIS II.

Schengen is an example *par excellence* of innovation outside the Treaty framework that eventually was absorbed within the main Treaty framework.

Another example of cooperation outside the Treaty within which templates for future Treaty-based cooperation may develop is the Prüm Treaty signed in May 2005 between Austria, Belgium, France, Germany, Luxembourg, the Netherlands and Spain. Prüm's objective is to step up cross-border cooperation on combating terrorism, cross-border crime and illegal immigration. The Treaty gives reciprocal access to participating states to DNA profiles, fingerprints and vehicle registration data. Like Schengen, Prüm too may serve as a laboratory for the development of ideas and practices related to the gathering and sharing of data (Monar 2001). This then raises issues about the sheer quantity of data gathered and shared, the use these data will be put to, and principles of accountability. It also raises an issue similar to the one raised when the Schengen Agreement was incorporated into the EU by the Amsterdam Treaty in 1999: how can appropriate standards of scrutiny and accountability be applied to secretive intergovernmental mechanisms such as Prüm that may well, at some point, be imported into the EU.

The Commission's role

Although often seen as a neutral broker between the interests of different member states, the Commission does in fact have quite clear views and preferences in the area of migration and asylum policy. In particular, three of its departments, or directorates-general (DGs) – those dealing with Justice, Home Affairs and with

Employment and Social Affairs (DG EMP) – have quite strong interests in the direction of policy. There is also an increased role for other DGs, such as Foreign Affairs (DG RELEX) and the DG dealing with Enlargement. In August 2010 DG JLS was split into two: DG Home Affairs and DG Justice.

Because of its organization into functionally distinct DGs, the Commission is best understood as a multi-organization comprising 27 policy-focused DGs (Cini 1996). These DGs differ from administrative agencies in national governments. They are headed by commissioners appointed by national governments, rather than ministers who are part of an elected government. In this sense they are less accountable to electorates. Moreover, it is difficult to pinpoint any coherent 'public opinion' that the Commission needs to respond to in order to justify its policies. In fact, most Commission pronouncements and legislation tend to be viewed as rather technical and rarely make it into the headlines in European countries. As such, it is difficult to talk about 'public debate' on EU policies, except in so far as these debates are taken up by national media. Debates are often quite specialized and involve a community of actors, including relevant ministries and agencies from member states, NGOs and think-tanks. Even then, most media seem more interested in the pronouncements of national politicians than in those of EU commissioners.

That said, the Commission is keen to enlist support for its policies, not just from the governments whose agreement is necessary to adopt legislation, but also from the network of interest groups and practitioners with a stake in policy. The Commission may also seek to appeal directly to electorates in EU member states. So, just like any government, the Commission is engaged in setting out political programmes in a way that can garner support, but tends to do so in specific ways that are linked to its rather technical responsibilities.

Partly because of its unusual institutional status, the Commission tends to have a style of justification rather different from those of national governments. It derives much of its credibility from its technical expertise, and its ability to rise above what may often be populist national positions, to seek a longer-term perspective. Like other international organizations dealing with economic questions (such as the OECD or World Bank), it also tends to adopt a relatively modernizing, liberal position. This generally coincides with its interest in pushing for closer economic and political integration between member states.

The Commission began to carve out a role for itself in immigration and asylum after the Maastricht Treaty was ratified in November 1993. Until then the member states in the Council had made it very clear that EC competencies did not stretch to migration and asylum. The member states were more than happy to cooperate with each other and, indeed, this cooperation intensified both after the Schengen Agreement (1985) and through informal cooperation after the Single European Act (1986) (Geddes 2008b). The Commission did accept a seat at the negotiating table when these developments were discussed, but had no formal competence and was mainly seeking to steer the member states in the direction of a common approach – with some member states also happy to see policy steered in this direction because it reflected their pro-integration stance.

The Commission's influence was particularly expanded after the Amsterdam Treaty (1997), which came into force in 1999, and gave the Commission a greater role in initiating common policies on asylum. The Commission unit dealing with JHA was upgraded into a DG in October 1999, and subsequently renamed the DG Justice, Liberty and Security (JLS). Since then, the Commission's role has been further expanded through the procedural switch of immigration and asylum to an area governed by QMV and with sole right of initiative for the European Commission.

Far from being a depoliticized bureaucracy, or 'impartial broker' between member states, DG JLS developed a clear set of preferences. In the area of asylum policy, we show in Chapter 7 that there has been a professed attachment to norms of human rights and international refugee law – at least in comparison with the position of most national interior ministries. This commitment to international law is formally codified in the Commission's role as 'guardian' of the treaties. Even more importantly, DG JLS was strongly supportive of the increased harmonization of national policies. It was a keen advocate of a common European asylum system, implying uniform standards of assistance and protection, uniform procedures for assessing claims and a single asylum status. Such a common system would, of course, imply a much greater regulatory role for the Commission and enhanced jurisdiction for the ECJ. This ECJ role is important given that asylum issues have been prominent in the national legal systems of many member states. It seems likely that they could be an important part of the day-to-day business of the ECJ, with the effect that the interpretation by the ECJ of EU asylum measures may tell us whether the EU conforms with the rights-based politics model advanced by Hollifield (1992). Will judicial authority at EU level help to create social and political spaces for migrants and asylum-seekers that confound some of the more restrictive intentions of national governments? This remains an open question.

From the perspective of DG Home Affairs, the two goals of refugee protection and harmonization are not inconsistent. Support for refugee and human rights law implies the need to ground policies in more liberal and universalistic principles, and thus the development of common standards applicable to all EU countries. The Commission's perspective also sets it apart from the more restrictionist and state-centric approaches of member states, thus marking out and legitimizing its distinctive role in the policy process. So the Commission's aspiration is to harmonize EU approaches, but where possible at a level that codifies commitment to norms of international law. These aspirations are reflected in Commission proposals, Communications and Green Papers, as well as in the 'scoreboard' recording progress in implementation of JLS goals.

The JHA Council

The second major EU actor in play is the JHA Council, the forum in which home affairs ministers and their officials meet to debate and agree upon legislation. The JHA Council has a reputation for being somewhat conservative and restrictive in its approach, taking its cue from the typically control-oriented officials it is composed of. Its state-centric control focus was very much shaped by the initial institutional setup of JHA cooperation under the Maastricht Treaty, in which the Commission had only a limited right of initiative. Thus in the early days, national officials and especially the Council's presidency had considerable influence in crafting (and vetoing!) legislation. This often resulted in individual states putting forward proposals based on their own specific legal and administrative arrangements, which did not provide the most coherent framework for collective regulation. In its early days, the 'K-4 Committee' (named after an article in the Maastricht Treaty) responsible for preparing legislation for ministerial approval met behind closed doors, with only minimal Commission presence, helping to engender perceptions of EU immigration and asylum policy being determined in the absence of public scrutiny or accountability.

With the coming into force of the Treaty of Amsterdam in 1999, the JHA Council began to open up. The Commission was granted joint right of initiative for all areas of cooperation, and the Treaty foresaw it being given exclusive right once member states had agreed to switch to QMV. In the Nice Treaty (2001), member states committed themselves to switching to these new institutional arrangements once common rules and basic principles on asylum and immigration had been agreed. The planned switch to QMV was also accompanied by a greater EP role in shaping legislation (the 'co-decision procedure'), introducing a more robust form of scrutiny. Nonetheless, the new arrangements did not immediately transform the Council's approach. Indeed, by the early 2000s there was widespread frustration on the part of the Commission and many international organizations and NGOs at the continued tendency of governments to try to impose their national approaches on EU legislation, to block legislation that implied any raising of standards of national asylum systems, or to continue to reform domestic legislation regardless of ongoing EU deliberations. The Lisbon Treaty now makes provision for use of QMV on all migration and asylum issues as well as co-decision for the EP.

The European Council

The European Council summits represent an additional institutional layer, providing the venue for higher-profile and often sweeping political declarations on various issues, including immigration and asylum. The European Council was set up in 1974 precisely to supply overall political direction that could not be delivered by the Council, the latter being sectorally organized and thus more specifically focused.

These Councils are chaired by the presidency of the day, and much of the content of decisions has been decided in advance through relevant Council committees, including the JHA Council. However, because of their high political profile, and the desire of presidencies to secure a legacy, European Council conclusions often contain quite far-reaching and ambitious political goals. Such statements are probably the most important channel for declaratory politics by member states, securing wide press coverage and also used as a proxy for measuring the success of the outgoing presidency.

Of course, European Council Conclusions are not just symbolic statements, but are intended to set out the broad parameters for subsequent EU legislation. They are generally followed up by action plans and initiatives from the Commission. However, follow-ups to European Councils can be disappointing. Often, their conclusions contain bold but rather vague aspirations, which the Commission is keen to pin down and translate into concrete measures through action plans, legislative proposals or scoreboards. The Commission follow-up, however, frequently sets the targets too high. The result is that member states block initiatives in the Council of Ministers, and there is frustration about the perceived lack of progress in relation to the European Council objectives. This has been referred to as the 'pendulum-like oscillation' of EU policy (Sciortino 1999).

The European Parliament

The EP's role has expanded considerably in recent years, particularly since the application of the co-decision procedure to some aspects of migration and asylum policy by the Amsterdam Treaty and subsequent developments within the Nice and Lisbon Treaties. The 'Return' Directive of 2008 was the first instance of co-decision being applied in the area of migration and asylum. It was indicative of a complex power-sharing relationship between the Council representing national governments and the directly elected EP. If we are to consider democratic politics in the EU then we need to factor in the EP's role. At the same time, national governments can legitimately claim to exercise powerful mandates. These tensions have been evident in discussions of migration and asylum; not least because the EP has often exhibited a pro-integration, relatively progressive bias that has led to strong criticism of 'fortress Europe' style approaches in EU policymaking.

While it is not uncommon to hear claims that MEPs are essentially powerless, it may actually be the case that they wield more power and influence than humble backbench parliamentarians in many member states. The EP is hampered by its 'multi-site' problem as it meets for plenaries in Strasbourg and for committees in Brussels while its administration is based in Luxembourg. That said, the committee with most direct oversight of migration and asylum, the Civil Liberties Committee, has become a far more prominent player.

There have also been significant shifts in the composition of the EP, with a vociferous Eurosceptic fringe, consolidated by the decision of the British Conservative Party to leave in 2009 the EP's biggest grouping (the European People's Party) and form the European Conservatives and Reformists Group in alliance with central and east European Eurosceptics. The June 2009 elections also saw the return to the EP of extreme-right parliamentarians who combine hostility to the EU and immigration, including those from the British National Party and the French *Front National*.

Relocation, relocation, relocation

How can we understand this developing EU role? We identify three types of 'relocation' that help to identify important aspects of the relationships between the EU and its member states in the areas of mobility and migration.

Spatial relocations of competence and capacity to act

The EU has acquired powers and responsibility in the areas of mobility and migration policy, constituting a spatial relocation in the sense that some aspects of decision-making now have an EU focus. National governments – and other non-governmental or international actors involved in immigration and asylum policy – now need to pay attention to the constitution of the legal and political framework at EU level.

We have already sought to make it clear that spatial relocations cannot be understood in terms of some simple state-versus-supranational dichotomy as though our main issue is one of determining whether it is states or supranational actors that are in the driving-seat when shaping EU migration and mobility policies. This is because the policy area of migration and mobility in Europe is now characterized by networks of transgovernmental action that cross state and supranational levels and mean that although states remain key actors they are no longer the only actors. Some actors and organizations are likely to have greater access to and influence within these networks. At the most basic level we can say that the operation of such networks demonstrates how states now share decision-making power with a range of other actors, including those located within EU institutions.

Temporal shifts in the making and operation of European migration policy

This refers to the effects *over time* of the spatial relocation of policy competencies and the impact of distinct *European* processes. Why at particular points in time do we see the development of EU competencies, but not at other times? How do we understand the effects over time of the development of EU competencies? We know that EU history has been characterized by rapid bursts of development (in the mid 1980s at the time of the Single European Act, for example) with other periods of stagnation or Eurosclerosis (at the end of the 1970s, for example). It is very clear that the member states still play a key role in the areas of migration, asylum and border policy. However, we also see the effects *over time* of the development of EU competencies and legislation, plus the effects *over time* of EU enlargement to take in as member states new migration countries in central, eastern and southern Europe.

We can add to this the effects at particular *points in time* of key ideas about migration and their effects on policy processes. For example, the end of the Cold War led to a strong focus on the 'threat' posed by potential large-scale migration from eastern Europe. By the end of the 1990s some member states, such as the UK and Germany, saw a more active debate about 'managed migration' and the recruitment of higher-skilled migrant workers. By 2009, there was a debate across the EU about continued migration needs in the face of severe economic recession. Thus we can see the effects of EU action over time and also explore particular temporal conjunctures.

A social relocation and its effects on migration and mobility in the EU

This third relocation concerns the question of whether or not European integration changes the preferences and identities of the actors involved in this process. As they now meet frequently with their European colleagues, do interior ministry officials set aside narrow national interests and 'become European'? Distinctions can be made when assessing the impact that European influences may have on their action. There are clear institutional linkages, but they may only be a 'thin' constraint on national actors working on migration and asylum policy. If the career structures of these officials remain national then their orientation to national politics may well remain strong (Zürn and Checkel 2005). Alternatively, European integration may have a 'thicker' effect, operating through means of influencing the interests and identities of the actors. The issue here is the scope for and effects of socialization, or 'a process of inducting actors into the norms and rules of a given community' (Checkel 2005:804; see also Dawson and Prewitt 1969). These effects could also be more noticeable among politicians and officials in newer countries of immigration and newer member states where the EU has been a decisive influence on the development of national policy.

Europeanization

So far, our focus has been on what could be called the 'ontological' dimension of European integration looking at how, why and when states have chosen to develop a framework for the development of a common migration and asylum policy. We have also considered some of the ways in which this cooperation engenders spatial, temporal and social relocations in policymaking. At this point, however, it is important to consider more broadly the ways in which this EU setting affects policy in member states. It is here that we encounter one of the biggest growth areas in EU studies, namely the analysis of Europeanization. Broadly speaking, the analysis of Europeanization addresses the extent to which 'ways of doing things' in EU member states have changed as a result of European integration, that is the extent to which the EU has been a driver of domestic change. This can be seen as implying four dimensions of the institutionalization of an EU legal and political framework (Sandholtz and Stone Sweet 1997):

- inter-state negotiation and the reaching of agreement.
- the transfer of competencies in some areas to EU level.
- the development of EU legal outputs and other forms of action.
- impacts on domestic politics in the member states – that is, 'Europeanization'.

The picture is slightly more complicated than this because of the complexities at each stage and also the feedback and loops present within this characterization. That said, it provides a useful way of thinking about the broader EU context and raising the issue of Europeanization. Five key questions can then be addressed.

First, where might we see these EU effects? The general consensus in Europeanization studies is that there are a number of places or locations within the political process at which these effects might become evident. The broad range of possibilities is made most evident in the widely used definition provided by Radaelli (2000:4) who refers to processes of (a) construction (b) diffusion and (c) institutionalization of formal and informal rules, procedures, policy paradigms, styles, 'ways of doing things' and shared beliefs and norms, which are first defined and consolidated in the making of EU decisions and then incorporated in the logic of domestic discourse, identities, political structures and public policies.

Europeanization is thus a broad and amorphous concept that encompasses almost all aspects of the political process. Being so broad, it's not actually clear whether Europeanization is a cause, an effect or both.

The second question concerns the effects that European integration might have. The point here is that there are different kinds of EU output and these might have different effects. One important characteristic of EU migration and asylum policy is that there are 'hard' legal outputs in the form of Directives and Regulations. There can also be 'softer' outputs such as EU-funded research projects, reports, consultations, conferences and seminars that provide venues for the diffusion of ideas and practices related to the developing EU policy framework. We do leave open the possibility that the EU creates new venues for socialization, but we also hypothesize that these effects are likely to be partial and differential in the effects they have, and might only amount to relatively weak forms of socialization and not necessarily mean that national officials, for example, cast off their national identities and 'become European'.

A third question concerns the need to distinguish between Europeanization as a driver of domestic change and other potential drivers of change. For example, in his seminal contribution to the analysis of immigration politics, Freeman (1995) has argued that there is evidence of convergence but that this is related to the forms of politics found in liberal states. The point is that if such changes occur outside the EU then it is hard to argue that the EU caused them. It may not be plausible to assume that because developments happen in Europe they are necessarily linked to the EU framework. Put another way, the EU can drive change, but it is likely to be one among a range of potential drivers (Faist and Ette 2007). European-ization may drive convergence, but may not be the only driver. Convergence may occur, but may not be driven by Europeanization.

A fourth question centres on the kinds of adaptation that might be seen. Here we can see a veritable growth industry of studies that look at Europeanization in country X or of policy Y, or some combination thereof. The broad consensus that seems to be emerging from this research is that the EU can have important effects on domestic politics; that greater pressure can emerge when there is 'misfit' between the EU and domestic frameworks; and that, where adaptation does occur, it tends to be with 'national colours' (Green-Cowles *et al.* 2001).

Finally, what does Europeanization mean for our framework? We do not assume that the EU is a simple and straightforward driver of change. We think that its effects are likely to be differential and partial. We also expect to see these effects to made manifest in different ways at different stages of the policy process, that is at stages of talk, decision and action. We would also expect to see contestation of the meaning of European integration within domestic politics. For example, 'Europe' might be presented as a solution to domestic political problems or as the cause of them, depending on the point of view of various actors within the political process. We should not assume that the debate about the impact of Europe is merely a technical debate about adaptation to agreed standards. Rather, Europe provides a new dimension of political contestation and mobilization that can impact across the political process and be seen in the way that narrative constructions of the immigration problem develop, in how debates and decisions about immigration are conducted, and in the ways that states and the EU seek to act on these decisions and implement agreed measures.

Analysing the effects of EU migration and asylum policy

How does this conceptual focus on multilevel and multidimensional policymaking in the EU fit with the ideas about the policy process set out earlier? In Chapter 2 we drew from scholarship on public policy and the policy process to outline three concepts that we think can help us to make sense of the dynamics of policymaking in EU and national settings. These were 'talk', 'decision' and 'action'; deliberate malintegration; and the policy stream. By exploring these dynamics we disentangle different components of the policymaking process. We do not think that it is helpful to assume that policymaking follows a clear-cut temporal sequence (from planning to elaboration, implementation, evaluation, and back to planning). So what sort of framework are we proposing to replace it? In order to observe these different elements of the policymaking, we need to disaggregate the process into three component parts.

First, we will distinguish between discourse and practice in migration policymaking. This will help shed light on how far talk, decisions and actions converge or are decoupled in the politics of migration. We therefore disentangle analysis of discourses on European migration and asylum policy from decision-making, bureaucratic practice and implementation of policies. Rather than infer practice from what is said or decided, we will examine practices and implementation as an area of policymaking that may be decoupled from rhetoric.

Second, our analysis will disentangle the various competing interests that go into shaping migration policy. This can help us to understand better the components that get welded together in often 'malintegrated' programmes. In this case, it makes sense to look both at the discourse on migration policy, and especially the ways the different protagonists frame problems and solutions. And it is also useful to look at the dynamics of party politics, whereby governments and opposition, or political actors in the EU, take up, defend or criticize different ways of framing these problems.

Third, we will analyse how more declaratory types of party politics influence bureaucratic decision-making in states and at the EU level. This will help elucidate the relationship between policy problems and solutions: how they are constructed both in public debates and in bureaucratic venues.

This approach implies teasing out four different dimensions of politics and policymaking on migration: ideas, political mobilization, bureaucratic practice, and implementation.

Narratives and ideas

The first of these, ideas, refers to the theories and beliefs that inform how policymakers frame policy problems, and how they conceive of the impact of their interventions on these. We refer to these as different 'narratives' of migration and migration policy. These narratives are shaped by a range of sources, including organizational memory, the experiences of practitioners, expert knowledge from the policy community, scientific research, the media, and party-political debates. Moreover, these are organized across various levels so there might be local reports on particular situations in certain places or the effects of migration on types of employment. There might be reports that examine national policies or national citizenship/integration models. There are also interventions by a wide range of international organizations that deploy knowledge and ideas about international migration. There will then be interaction across these levels that can promote the sharing of ideas and the diffusion of good practice. There can often be a tension between narratives emanating from more specialist communities (practitioners and researchers) that we could term 'technocratic' narratives; and those produced in more populist fora, such as mass media and populist politics.

Politics and political mobilization

Second are the dynamics of political mobilization and party-political competition to attract electoral support for their programmes. Governments and opposition debating migration policy are engaged in a constant struggle to secure backing for their policies. Similarly, more political components of the EU – Commissioners, MEPs or European Council presidencies – seek to gain national and popular support for measures at EU level. Their strategies are heavily influenced by mass media coverage, which can strongly influence the resonance of different political claims, and provide a sounding-board for politicians to gauge support for their programmes. Such political programmes are frequently more about rhetoric and symbolic decisions (talk) than practice (actions). Nonetheless, they are crucial in shaping the parameters of debate on feasible and desirable policies, and setting out the general orientations for more detailed implementation (by organizations).

Public-administrative decision-making

Third are the ministries and agencies responsible for elaborating and implementing policy – what we may term the public administration. This comprises the various organizations and officials responsible for translating political programmes into practice, at national and EU level. Unlike party politics, these organizations are not preoccupied primarily with mobilizing electoral support, but are guided by a range of internal organizational goals: securing the support and mobilizing the loyalty of members, resolving intra- and interdepartmental conflicts, and so on. Bureaucracies are often rather conservative, preferring not to deviate from established routines and procedures that have been proven to enlist support and resolve internal conflicts. However, others have more expansionist ideologies, seeing their survival as contingent on gaining more competences or exporting their practices. Organizations may also be more or less responsive to external pressures from politics: some may see their survival as contingent on being able to adjust to new political programmes, while others prefer to 'decouple' reformist rhetoric from maintaining existing practices. And they may be influenced by interaction with officials from other countries or the EU, through the kind of socialization mentioned earlier.

Implementation

Fourth, and finally, we need to consider the dimension of implementation, or the ways in which policies manage or fail to 'steer' the objects of interventions. Implementation may not be understood as merely the follow-up of decision-making. It needs to be seen as part of the process itself as policy objectives are communicated to those on the ground with responsibility for implementation and the organizational contexts within which they operate. It is also useful to distinguish between policy outputs and the outcomes of those policies. We can identify a large number of outputs, but it is not always clear that these are translated into the desired outcomes. This should not come as a surprise because it has been shown that it is not unusual for policy outputs not to secure their objectives (to become the desired outcomes). We should not necessarily be surprised if the great expectations of decision-makers founder as they are translated down the decision-making chain (Pressman and Wildavsky 1984). Outcomes may be only loosely linked to policy objectives. Stated objectives may not be implemented in practice ('decoupling'); or attempted implementation may generate unintended impacts (distortions, counter-productive outcomes). Alternatively, apparent impacts of policies may be caused by quite independent dynamics (for example labour market trends or changes in conflict dynamics may have more of an impact on asylum numbers than national legislation). There may also be more mundane reasons, as policy objectives may literally be lost in translation in an EU of 27 member states, or there are not the organizational resources (staff, funding) to secure objectives.

If policy objectives are clearly defined and there is little contestation then the possibility for implementation could be strong, but if there is ambiguity about policy and there is a high level of contestation then it may be more difficult to secure objectives (Matland 1995). It is also likely to be the case that levels of ambiguity and conflict differ across migration policy type so that it might be more straightforward to implement tightly prescribed high-skilled worker admission programmes while it could be far more difficult to implement ambiguous and highly contested policies on irregular migration.

Summary

This chapter outlined some defining characteristics of the EU's political and institutional setting and specified our analytical approach. It started by highlighting the complexities of the multi-level setting within which the EU and its member states share power. We sought to make sense of various aspects of this multi-level policymaking process ranging from the negotiation of treaty provisions through to the impact on domestic immigration politics in member states.

The chapter also set out our approach to analysing policy at these different levels. We proposed a four-way focus on ideas, political mobilization, bureaucratic decision-making and implementation. This will be applied to explore different areas of migration policy – asylum, labour migration, family migration, mobility and enlargement, irregular migration, and integration. For each of these areas, we will analyse how discourse, strategies, policies and practices flow between the levels, shaping or constraining politics and policy. The next chapter develops our focus on policy types by exploring the dynamics of labour migration.

Chapter 4

Labour Migration

This chapter analyses a form of migration that is integral to Europe's migration history, but for which EU competencies are limited. Article 79(5) of the Lisbon Treaty states that measures on migration 'do not affect the right of member states to determine volumes of admission of third-country nationals coming from third countries to their territory in order to seek work, whether employed or self-employed'. Despite this limitation, policies on the admission of labour migrants have been a central topic for debate across the EU over the past decade and there have been important EU developments. This is also an area in which the EU has ambitions. The Stockholm programme sets the EU's migration and asylum agenda until 2014 and talks about a 'common framework for a flexible admission system ... to adapt to increased mobility and the needs of national labour markets' (House of Lords 2009:7).

Around a third of the world's 86 million migrant workers reside in Europe. These could be nationals of other EU countries benefiting from mobility opportunities, or TCNs from outside the EU. The majority of these men and women work in lower-skilled forms of employment, although there has been an increased emphasis in some EU states on attracting higher-skilled migrants. (IOM 2008:32). Since around 2000, a number of European governments and the European Commission have been highlighting the potential benefits of increased labour migration into higher-skilled employment. This agenda has been hit by the severe economic recession at the end of the decade, but did mark an important break with previous policy.

This chapter charts political debates, decisions and practical implications of recent labour migration policies in Europe. We argue that part of the reason for the frequent gap between rhetoric and practice in this area is the endemic problem of conflicting interests between those with a stake in policy. As we discussed in Chapter 2, this can encourage governments to pursue various strategies to 'decouple' rhetoric from practice or to sustain a 'deliberate malintegration' of policy goals. Understanding these different types of strategy is crucial to making sense of variations and change in national policies, as well as evaluating their success. Before exploring these dimensions we begin by clarifying past and current debates about labour migration policy in Europe.

Explaining labour migration policy

Labour migration is highly diverse. It may involve lower- and higher-skilled employment for shorter- and longer-term durations. Higher-skilled and lower-skilled are definitions of the type of employment (skills level required for a job) or of the migrant him or herself (level of qualifications). Higher-skilled migrants are generally defined as those with tertiary (usually university) education or with equivalent professional or vocational skills. Migrants may, of course, move into types of paid employment below the levels of skill that they possess.

There is significant variation in the proportion of high- or low-skilled migrants received by different European states over the past two decades. Figures produced by Chaloff and Lemaitre (2009) show that some countries, such as Belgium, Denmark, Ireland, Luxembourg, Poland and Sweden, have a relatively high share of skilled migrants – in each of these countries, in 2006 more than 40 per cent of employed immigrants who had arrived in the previous 10 years were defined as high-skilled. By contrast, only 27 per cent of employed immigrants were so defined in Austria, the figure being 29 per cent in Germany, 24 per cent in Spain, and just 12.5 per cent in Greece. Analogous data from the UK were not available, but those migrants falling into the category 'managers, professionals or associate professionals' comprised 46.2 per cent of migrants in 1996 and 38.6 per cent in 2006.

These specificities reinforce the point made earlier that the politics of immigration are often quite general, but the policy dilemmas posed by international migration in its various types are much more specific. Two aspects of this specificity are particularly relevant when discussing labour migration as it is, namely:

- Sectorally specific – labour migrants are often heavily concentrated in certain types of employment at the higher- and lower-skilled ends of the labour market. There is also a gendered distinction between the kinds of work done by male and female migrants.

- Spatially specific – there tend to be certain parts of EU member states with relatively large concentrations of labour migrants because of the availability of work. These tend to be urban areas, but there can also be rural areas with relatively large concentrations of labour migrants linked to agricultural employment.

These specificities have important implications for politics and policy. While we typically see migrants as moving into countries and think about national policy frameworks, it is the case that labour migrants move into certain places and types of employment with the result that policy issues can be highly specific. For instance, the delivery of key services such as education, health and housing tends to be the concern of local authorities. High numbers of newcomers can put a strain on service provision, for example of language training for migrants' children in schools.

Before examining in more detail some of the variations and similarities between European policies on labour migration, it is worth offering a very broad picture of some of the key differences. Chaloff and Lemaitre (2009:30–1) identify migration policy strategies in four key EU member states:

- *In the UK*, there is a reliance on EU free movement with a point-based system for the highly skilled and limits on non-EU lower-skilled migration. In the UK, there is also a growing reliance in the higher-education system on international students.
- *In France*, policy seeks to protect native workers while meeting employer demands. There has been a conscious attempt to expand economic migration at the expense of supposedly less productive types (particularly family migration; see Chapter 5). Admissions policy is governed by strict labour market tests.
- *In the Netherlands*, there have been attempts to reduce immigration by the lower-skilled and those without Dutch language skills. There are exemptions from language and labour market tests for the highly skilled.
- *In Germany*, the government has sought to limit immigration generally, while allowing routes for higher-skilled migrants. Germany sees itself as competing with other economically

developed nations for high-skilled migrants. Permanent residence permits are on offer to the highest-skilled and highest-paid, but there are strict residence conditions for other immigrants. Germany has, however, experienced only limited non-EU immigration and much of this has been changes in status by students. Flows of the highly skilled have fallen short of expectations.

New policies that emerged in some EU member states after 2000 seemed to represent a move away from the type of restrictive approaches that had been favoured since the early 1970s. Many governments – and the European Commission – argued that selective labour migration could help boost productivity and growth, by filling labour and skills shortages. Some commentators also saw labour migration as a means of offsetting the impact of ageing populations, ensuring a supply of workers to fund pensions and boost the proportion of the population active in the labour market. Box 4.1 looks at the debate about population change and labour migration. Countries such as the UK also saw intra-EU migration as a way of addressing labour market shortages, particularly in lower-skilled employment.

However, we should be careful not to overemphasize the break in policy and give the misleading impression that there was 'zero immigration' prior to 2000. For a start, the shift was to some extent rhetorical. Although European countries had pursued so-called 'zero immigration' policies since the early 1970s, most governments had continued to admit certain types of labour migrants into lower- and higher-skilled work. In fact, perhaps the most significant feature of the shift in approach is not so much in terms of substantive policy, but in the discourse on labour migration: notably, a willingness on the part of some governments and also international organizations to make an explicit case in favour of labour migration. What this suggests is that it is important in our analysis to go beyond declaratory politics, and explore the relationship between the rhetoric and practice of labour migration policy. In some cases, rhetoric has remained restrictive while practice has been more lenient; in others, rhetoric embraces more liberal approaches, but practice remains largely unchanged. Clearly, the possibility of this sort of gap between stated goals and substantive policy raises questions about how best to chart and explain policy.

Box 4.1   Ageing populations and labour migration

Fertility rates in west European countries have been declining since the 1960s, while average life expectancy rose from 66 in 1960 to 77 in the late 1990s. Meanwhile, average retirement ages are getting lower, with less than half the population aged between 55 and 65 in OECD countries in employment. Taken together, these factors are likely to generate a rise in the average age of the population and a decline in the proportion of the population in employment, and thus a rise in the ratio of those dependent on state support to those economically active.

The decline in the employed population will create a major shortage of labour in all sectors, and a decrease in revenue for taxation. It will also necessitate far greater public expenditure on pensions, health and long-term care.

Some research has suggested that immigration could offset these effects, filling labour gaps and helping to meet public spending costs. A widely cited UN study argued that the EU could need an intake of almost 674 million immigrants between 2000 and 2050 to retain current dependency rations, including 1 million per year in the UK, 1.8 million in France and 3.6 million in Germany.

Other researchers are more sceptical about these findings, suggesting that immigration is not a panacea for the problem of ageing populations. Although recruiting young migrant workers may temporarily meet the demand for labour, once they are integrated migrants tend to adopt similar fertility patterns to those of nationals. Thus an increase in immigration will at best delay the process of ageing populations by a few generations.

A second important point is about how best to explain divergence between EU states and policy change. There is a fairly long-standing debate on the determinants of migration policy. One camp emphasizes the relevance of (usually national) institutions and traditions of thought in shaping policy. It posits that these factors create important variations in national policy, even where states are faced with seemingly similar types of problems (Hansen 2002). We agree that national governments are frequently hampered by a range of political and judicial constraints; and that national debates are deeply embedded in historically conditioned patterns of thought and collectively shaped memories. However, there are a number of striking similarities in the challenges confronting European states: demand for skills in a knowledge-based economy, ageing populations, strains on welfare provisions, and public anxieties about the impacts of immigration. Moreover, the frequent exchange of information and ideas between countries, not least through EU integration on mobility, migration and asylum, can create a significant degree of convergence in ideas about how best to respond to these challenges. So it is certainly possible to trace cross-national trends in policy, whether because countries face similar challenges or because they are exchanging experiences about 'good practice' in tackling them.

The other camp argues that migration policies are essentially shaped by the impact of immigration – specifically, the distribution of the costs and benefits of migration between different parts of society (Freeman 1995, 2006). In the case of labour migration, businesses stand to gain most, while costs borne by the population tend to be diffuse. Thus governments tend to be more responsive to business interests, and the policies they adopt tend towards the expansive. As a result, EU states will tend to converge because of similar policy dynamics. But again, the case of European policy suggests this account needs to be nuanced. Clearly, some governments have been more responsive to business concerns than others. The tendency of governments to 'decouple' their rhetoric from practice enables them to juggle these interests in very different ways, with important implications for policy. In some cases very restrictive legislation is combined with toleration of irregular migrants; in others, governments adopt liberal programmes as part of their official policy. Both variants represent different ways of trying to mollify business interests while addressing public concerns. Moreover, it is clear that governments are not simply reacting to a pre-given constellation of societal interests, but have in some cases been active in shaping debates and ideas about the social or economic impact of migration. The upshot is that politicians and civil servants can be quite resourceful in coming up with configurations of rhetoric and practice that address public concerns while simultaneously eliciting support from key societal interests.

This leads us to the third main point: the question of policy failure. As we saw in Chapter 2, much of the literature on migration policy argues that European migration policies, including those aimed at recruiting labour migrants, have by and large failed. They have resulted in a variety of unintended consequences, such as the permanent settlement of 'temporary' migrants, or triggered an increase in irregular movement, or created problems with attempts to integrate large numbers of immigrants and ethnic minorities.

Narratives

There is a substantial body of research in economics that suggests that labour migration brings net benefits to the economies of host countries (European Migration Network 2006). The argument tends to be that migration brings a small positive impact, but also that the costs and benefits are unevenly distributed as there are some members of the population that benefit more directly from migrant labour (by employing it or by having easier access to cheaper goods and services as a result of migrant labour) and those who may lose out because they face tougher competition in the labour market. Experts, practitioners and politicians are by no means in agreement that labour migration is a good thing. There are a range of different beliefs about the economic, social and cultural impacts of labour migration. We identify these as competing or contesting narratives and argue that it is important to explore their content in order to understand better the debates about labour migration in the EU's multilevel system. We would also note that these debates about costs and benefits tend to be circumscribed by national communities – that is, they relate to how immigration affects those within a European country. This is probably quite a narrow way to think about these issues, as immigration will have an effect on migrants, their families and the countries they move from. By opening the debate in this direction we also begin to draw in the role that international migration plays in debates about global economic development. In this regard it still seems unclear whether migration causes development or development causes migration. The relationship is famously 'unsettled' (Martin and Papademetriou 1991).

Narratives about labour migration tend to be informed by a range of different sources. Economic arguments often draw on academic studies, or the views of the business community. Claims about the effects of migration on welfare and social services often emanate from practitioners or local authorities supporting or hosting immigrants. In contrast, arguments about the socio-cultural or security impacts of immigration are often anecdotal, based on media reporting or populist political claims (Caldwell 2009). This means that debates on the impacts of labour migration often mix rather different sorts of arguments, ranging from academic studies to practical experience and more speculative or anecdotal claims. In such debates, distinctions between different categories of migrants – such as labour migrants, those entering for family reasons, asylum-seekers or irregular migrants – become blurred.

Economic arguments

There is a fairly strong body of research about the positive economic impact of immigration. According to this scholarship, foreign labour can boost productivity and growth, and high-skilled immigrants can create jobs. In fact, economists have by and large eschewed the notion that there will be a 'displacement effect' caused by immigration (Winter-Ebner and Zweimuller 1999) or a significant downward pressure on wages (Card 1990). As a UK-government-commissioned study reported in 2001: 'There is little evidence that native workers are harmed by migration. There is considerable support for the view that migrants create new businesses and jobs and fill labour market gaps, improving productivity and reducing inflationary pressures' (Glover *et al.* 2001:viii). In so far as economists have observed a downward pressure on wages or a displacement effect, these tend to be limited to very specific sectors or occupations (namely those in which migrants have been recruited), and are relatively small. In sum, then, there can be general economic gains from migration, while costs may be smaller and limited to specific sectors.

This positive account of the economic benefits of immigration, or variants of it, dominated the thinking of many governments in north-west Europe in the decades after the World War II during the era of large-scale labour migration that accompanied postwar economic reconstruction in the 1950s and 1960s (Castles 1986). More recently, beliefs about the positive impact of labour migration have been boosted by supply-side economic theory. The key insight here is that skilled and creative people can help generate new jobs (Straubhaar 2000). Indeed, in a 'knowledge-based economy', human capital has become the most important factor of productivity. Another fashionable theory holds that cultural diversity in itself can be a source of innovation. Ensuring a mix of people with different forms of 'cultural capital' not only ensures that a greater ranges of products and services are available in cities; it can also enhance productivity within firms, by generating a more creative and edgy environment in which new ideas flourish (Florida 2002).

Not surprisingly, these various narratives about the positive impact of migration are often strongly supported by business, as well as by political parties embracing liberal economic policies. Removing barriers to free movement means that people can be more flexible in responding to job opportunities, implying more efficient markets. Liberal labour migration policies can ease labour shortages, and – more controversially – can help business employ labour at lower costs. Box 4.2 details causes of the various kinds of labour and skill shortages. Box 4.3 outlines the mechanisms for recruiting labour migrants.

Similar ideas about the benefits of free movement have increasingly gained currency in organizations such as the World Trade

---

Box 4.2   Causes of labour and skills shortages

Labour and skills shortages occur where there is a demand for labour in a particular occupation, but a lack of workers who are available and qualified to do the job. Shortages can take a number of different forms.

Aggregate shortages occur in situations of full employment, where there are simply not enough workers to meet demand for labour. For example, many European economies recruited workers across a range of sectors in the 1950s and 1960s, as their economies expanded. Far more frequent, though, is the problem of shortages due to *mismatch* of labour demand and supply. This refers to a situation where the number of workers is sufficient to fill jobs, but workers are unable or unwilling to fill vacancies for one of the following reasons:

• Qualifications mismatch: workers do not have the necessary education, training or experience to fill vacancies. For example, there may be a shortage of workers skilled in new information technologies.

➡

Organization (WTO), the World Bank, the International Labour Organization (ILO) and the OECD. Such ideas dovetail neatly with the internationalist and liberalizing agendas of many international organizations, which are keen to remove barriers to exchange between countries.

A number of economists have challenged this characteristically neo-liberal account. One line of critique emphasizes some of the costs generated by mobility and free movement. Some contributions have focused on the negative consequences of migration for immigrants and ethnic minority groups. One of the most prominent theories in this respect is that of the 'segmented labour market'. Migrant workers tend to be employed in insecure, low-skilled jobs in the 'secondary' economy, and effectively get trapped within this 'underclass' (Piore 1979).

A rather different type of critique revolves around the negative impact of large-scale labour migration on the indigenous population. Here much of the evidence comes from the US, where George Borjas has famously argued that excessive or unselected immigration can lead to the displacement of indigenous workers, or a downward pressure on salaries (Borjas 1995, 2001); for a critique,

➡
- Preferences mismatch: they may have adequate qualifications, but do not want to do a particular job because of inadequate pay, status or working conditions – examples of this might include seasonal agricultural labour, or unskilled work in catering.
- Regional mismatch: they are able and in principle willing to do the job, but are located in the wrong geographical area and are not ready to move. For example, there may be a demand for workers in fish-processing factories in the Northeast of Scotland, but not enough local residents to meet demand.
- Mismatch due to information deficits: workers are not matched to jobs because of a lack of information on existing vacancies, or inadequate recruitment procedures on the part of employers. Thus there may be a high demand for hairdressers in Hamburg, but insufficient information on vacancies in other parts of Germany, so that qualified workers are not aware of these possibilities.
- Shortages due to mismatch can coexist with high levels of unemployment, as is the case in many European countries.

Box 4.3   Mechanisms for recruiting labour migrants

There are three main mechanisms for recruiting migrants to fill labour or skills shortages:

Sector-based programmes involve identifying sectors or professions with labour shortages:

- Sector-based programmes are often based on a *list of sectors or professions facing acute shortages*, such as IT or engineering. For these sectors, the normal restrictions on recruiting foreign workers may be lifted, facilitating recruitment.
- They may also take the form of *special programmes*, such as the German Green Card, introduced in 2001 to attract ICT workers to Germany.
- Sector-based programmes may take the form of *bilateral agreements* to recruit seasonal or temporary workers with low skills levels, for example in agriculture, construction, domestic work, or hotels and catering.

Employment-based schemes allow employers to recruit foreign workers to fill vacancies.

- Recruitment is usually conditional on demonstrating that there is no EEA national available for the job, or a so-called '*labour market test*'.

see Card (2005). Even where immigration brings net benefits, these may be unequally distributed between different parts of the labour market. Any costs of labour migration may be borne disproportionately by low-skilled workers, especially those in sectors such as construction or domestic work, where they are competing directly with immigrants. These effects will depend to a large extent on how flexible the labour market is. Where there exist a high minimum wage and generous employment benefits, there is less scope for immigrants to push down wages or displace indigenous workers. However, employers may have incentives to bypass these employment costs by employing immigrants on an irregular basis (see Chapter 6); if the immigrants are in the country illegally their redress against unlawful employment practices will be considerably

- Alternatively, larger firms with overseas branches may recruit workers through *intracompany transfers*, which allow foreign workers to perform contract work in another country, as long as it is temporary and within the same firm.
- Regularizations offer an opportunity for irregular migrants to legalize their status for a certain period (or in some cases permanently). This is often on the condition that they already have a job with an employer – indeed, in some cases employers apply for regularization on behalf of their employees. Belgium, France, Greece, Italy, Portugal and Spain have all introduced such programmes.

Skills-based programmes seek to select migrants according to particular skills or characteristics, such as qualifications, language skills, age or family status.

- The most common form is the *points-based system*, under which immigrants qualify for entry through meeting certain skills criteria, regardless of whether they already have a job in place. In some cases, though, points favour particular professions or sectors, implying that points systems can combine skills and sector considerations.
- Many countries permit *foreign students* to apply for jobs once they have graduated, allowing them several months to look for work. This reflects an interest in retaining highly qualified migrants who already have good language skills and knowledge of the country in which they have studied.

reduced or may indeed be effectively non-existent. By contrast, in more flexible labour markets immigrants may accept lower salaries, thus undercutting indigenous workers. They may also be ready to work on a casual or temporary basis, or with less comprehensive health and safety standards, again giving them an advantage over domestic workers.

These less-positive accounts of the economic impacts of migration tend to be in the minority. Very few economists reject the economic arguments in favour of migration, but this does not mean such ideas are not marshalled in public debates. Concerns about competition between foreign and indigenous workers continue to be flagged by both left-wing and right-wing political parties keen to be seen to protect the rights of native workers.

Political debate

How are these narratives deployed in political debate and policy-making? As we suggested in Chapter 2, it makes sense to draw a distinction between the dynamics of party-political debate, which will be discussed in this section, and that of more detailed policy-making and implementation within the administration, which we turn to later.

Unlike in the case of asylum policy (see Chapter 7), there is no obvious division of party-political views along the left–right ideological axis. A more pertinent divide is often between business-friendly parties and more protectionist, welfare-oriented ones. For this reason, most political parties with a broad membership base defined in traditional ideological terms find it difficult to adopt a clear and consistent position on labour migration. There are simply too many conflicting interests and preferences on the part of their own parties, the electorate, and organized interests. As we will see, there are various strategies that incumbents and opposition parties have adopted to deal with these different pressures.

The contours of political debate on labour migration are not solely dependent on party-political positions and societal interests. They are also shaped by various institutional factors, such as electoral systems, constitutional provisions and historically entrenched patterns of political debate. For this reason, while we do not want to overstate national differences, it does make sense to explore how debates on labour migration have evolved in different national contexts. We will also consider the rather different dynamics of political discourse around EU policies in this area.

Germany and the UK: making the case for labour migration?

In this section we delve a little more closely into developments in two EU states that were very much to the fore in debates about active recruitment of labour migrants from the late 1990s onwards. In March 2000 the German Social Democrat/Green coalition government launched a new so-called 'Green Card' (although its provisions were not as generous as the US 'Green Card') to attract up to 20,000 ICT specialists from outside the European Economic Area (EEA). This was followed by the launch of a high-profile immigration commission to set out ideas for an overhaul of Germany's immigration rules, and new legislation put before the Bundestag in autumn 2001. Similar developments were underway in the UK from around 2000, with the Labour government launching a series of reforms to labour migration rules, including an expansion of the list of industries facing acute labour shortages and thus exempt from the normal restrictions on recruitment, as well as the establishment of a new Highly Skilled Migrants Programme (HSMP). In both cases, centre-left governments with a modernising agenda were attempting to loosen rules as part of a broader economic strategy of meeting skills shortages and attracting highly qualified migrants.

Despite the similar timing and justification of provisions, public reactions to these initiatives in both countries differed profoundly. In the UK, the Labour government was largely able to convince opposition parties and the media about the economic benefits of selective migration, at least to begin with. It introduced wide-ranging reforms to immigration rules, and also was one of only three member states (Ireland and Sweden being the others) to grant immediate labour market access to nationals of the eight central and east European countries that joined the EU in May 2004. The effect of these changes was to lead to the largest inflow of migrants to the UK in its history and a renewed politicization of labour migration from 2005 onwards.

In Germany, by contrast, the government's plans were immediately opposed by the opposition Christian Democrat parties, and received a lukewarm reaction in the media. Faced with the prospect of having its legislation blocked in the upper chamber, the government effectively retreated from its plans to liberalize labour migration policy, and from its bold new rhetoric on the economic case for immigration.

One factor explaining the rather different fate of reform in the two countries is the dynamics of party-political opposition. In the UK, the main opposition party was the business-friendly Conservative Party, which was also weak because it was heavily defeated in the 1997 and 2001 general elections. In the early part of the decade, the Conservatives largely accepted the economic case for selected labour migration. The pro-immigration argument advanced by the government was bolstered by drawing on a series of research reports about the positive economic impact of migration. The mass media picked up on a number of these findings, so that the debate on labour migration became highly technocratic. Discussion on the merits of immigration were very much informed by economic arguments based on research from academic institutions or think-tanks (Boswell 2009).

By contrast, the tone of debate in Germany was striking for its absence of discussion of research. Instead, most of the criticism of government attempts to liberalize policy were based on rather more populist concerns: anxiety about potential displacement effects from admitting large numbers of foreign workers during a period of high unemployment; and worries about the impact of cultural diversity on identity and social cohesion. The government was highly sensitive to these critiques, largely abandoning a more technocratic debate about the economic impact of migration. Instead, it attempted to elicit support from the main political parties, as well as the most significant social groups: business as well as the trade unions, churches, and migrant groups. Part of the reason for its caution was its fragile majority in the upper house – a majority which was subsequently eliminated after local elections in February 2003. This meant that any legislation would require the support of the Christian Democrat opposition parties, who strongly rejected the arguments being put forward by Chancellor Schroeder. Just as important was the government's concern about how its new agenda might be picked up in mass media and public debates. As in most European countries, immigration is often a fraught political issue in Germany. Both centre-right and right-wing parties have been able to tap into public concerns about the impact of migration on German society (Green 2004; Boswell 2008). The government clearly felt it would be taking an electoral risk in coming out in favour of a more liberal approach, especially given the Christian Democrat Party's clear readiness to mobilize support against the reforms.

Similar sorts of concerns led the German government to introduce restrictions on the free movement of the citizens of what were called the A8 countries – the eight countries that joined the EU in May 2004, namely the Czech Republic, Estonia, Hungary, Latvia, Lithuania, Poland, Slovakia and Slovenia – while the UK offered them immediate access to its labour markets. Again, there was very little debate in Germany about the economic arguments for or against granting labour market access, and limited reference to relevant research. Instead, the German government appeared to largely accept arguments about the potential displacement effects of admitting labour migrants from these countries. By contrast, the UK government was keen to argue for the potential advantages to the economy of allowing access. In fact, the number of migrants from A8 countries who subsequently arrived in the UK to work was much larger than expected. Initial estimates of between 5,000 and 13,000 a year – albeit based on the assumption that all EU member states would open their labour markets, when only three actually did – were confounded by more than 600,000 people registering their presence in the UK. This has triggered broader public debate about some of the negative social impacts of labour migration.

In sum, the German and UK cases present an intriguing comparison. Both governments made similar arguments for increased labour migration at around the same time. But while the UK government was successful – at least to begin with – at shifting the argument onto more technocratic terms, the German government was not. The tide has, however, shifted in the UK, as concerns rise about the impact of migration from the A8 countries. This debate has been fuelled by recession from 2008 onwards, with controversy in the UK becoming more focused on scarce jobs and social problems arising from immigration, as was the case in Germany.

Spain and Italy: new immigration countries with fluctuating approaches

It is interesting to compare debates on migration reform in Germany and the UK – two 'old' immigration countries – with those in relatively new immigration countries. In many ways, Spain and Italy present parallel cases. Both were traditionally countries of emigration, which became net immigration countries from around the mid 1980s onwards. Italy saw a rise in foreign residents from around 300,000 in the mid 1980s (Zincone 1999) to 1.447 million by 2001, equivalent to 3.5 per cent of the population (OECD 2007). In Spain, the number of foreign residents in 2001 stood at around 2.172 million, or 5.3 per cent of the population (OECD 2007) – a fourfold rise compared with 1994 (Balch 2010). Italy and Spain also face common challenges in managing porous sea borders. In addition, irregular migrants can be drawn by the relatively large informal economy and the possibility of employment within it (Reyneri 1998; Arango 2000).

Both countries are quite heavily dependent on low- and semi-skilled labour from abroad. In the case of Italy, demand is especially high in the north-eastern regions of the country, where there is large-scale recruitment in sectors such as manual trades, tourism, construction, domestic services and homecare (Zincone 1999; Einaudi 2007; Geddes 2008a). There is also considerable demand for seasonal labour in agriculture. In Spain, a large share of recent non-EU immigration has been directed to Madrid and Catalonia, where many are employed in agriculture, construction, manufacturing and the service sector, especially the hotel trade and domestic service (Balch 2010).

Spanish and Italian immigration policies both show quite a high degree of fluctuation, mainly depending on which party is in power. In both countries, centre-right governments have tended to pursue policies aimed primarily at restricting legal channels for labour migration. Thus the Popular Party in Spain introduced an Immigration Act in 2000 that sought to strengthen border control and restrict admissions of new migrants. A supplementary memorandum was issued to all offices issuing work permits, instructing them to reject all applications that fell outside of the rather limited quota system in operation. The provision was subsequently overturned, as employers invoked their right to recruit foreign workers in cases where there was no Spanish or EEA national available for the job (Balch 2010). The point to note, though, is the very tough rhetoric advanced by the government, which sought to convince the electorate that it was willing and able to pursue a highly restrictive approach. However, as Balch points out, this restrictive approach was accompanied by a surprising degree of leniency for irregular migration, and periodic regularization programmes for illegally resident workers: a classic case of 'decoupling'.

Italian centre-right coalition governments have pursued a very similar approach, combining restrictive legislation on labour migration with a toleration of widespread regular and irregular migration in practice. In the five years between 2001 and 2006, under the administration led by Silvio Berlusconi, the legally resident foreign people in Italy rose from 1.3 million to 2.7 million, including 646,000 regularizations – the largest growth in immigration in Italy's history. Similarly, tough talk by the incoming *Popolo delle Libertà* coalition led by Berlusconi elected in 2008 was accompanied by a regularization for domestic workers and care-providers. As in the case of the Spanish government, this approach can be characterized as a classic case of tough talk and lenient practices.

Interestingly, though, both countries have also seen centre-left administrations that have been more willing to push for a more liberal approach to legislation and policies on labour migration. In

Spain, a new Socialist Workers' Party (PSOE) government was elected in 2004 under José Luis Rodríguez Zapatero. This centre-left government has ushered in a more labour market-oriented approach to labour migration, introducing a new Immigration Act in 2005 that established a new system for identifying skills shortages, and provided for a further regularization. Zapatero's rhetoric on labour migration was progressive and liberal, evocative of that of the UK Labour administration in the early part of the decade.

Both Italy and Spain have seen a similar type of fluctuation in policy, depending on which party is in power. The basic pattern is one of a fluctuation between centre-left governments, which try to align official policy with labour market needs; and centre-right administrations, which prefer to pursue (at least symbolically) tough policies, while tolerating large-scale irregular migration and periodic amnesties in practice. Nonetheless, behind the restrictive rhetoric of centre-right parties, in practice immigration levels have remained high in both countries regardless of who is in power. So the fluctuation between different governments is more a change of rhetoric than in practice, at least as concerns the level of labour migrants tolerated by the state.

The EU's limited role in labour migration policy

Any discussion of European labour migration policy needs to take into account the EU's role in shaping debates. We know that there is significant legislation to provide for an EU migration and asylum framework. At the same time, admissions policies for non-EU nationals have remained in the hands of national governments. The Commission has pushed for greater harmonization of national approaches, based on common indicators for assessing labour market needs (CEC 2005). Nonetheless, the Commission's involvement in labour migration remains somewhat paradoxical. On the one hand, it has had a huge impact on migration through its competence in the area of the free movement of workers (see Chapter 8). This has been an important, and relatively uncontroversial, component of the integration of Europe's economic systems. Barring certain temporary restrictions for newly acceding countries, EU citizens have full access to the labour market and even most welfare provisions in other EU countries.

On the other hand, the EU has very limited competence to introduce legislation in the area of labour immigration from outside the

EEA. Despite a formal mandate provided by the Amsterdam Treaty (1997) and various initiatives to develop a common approach, EU states have been reluctant to cede sovereignty or even significantly reduce differences in approach to the admission of foreign workers. A one-size-fits-all approach is unlikely to be appropriate. Instead, most EU states have their own complicated set of legislation and programmes in place to regulate the entry and employment of non-nationals, and can see little added value in granting a greater role to the EU.

Commission forays

For this reason, the Commission's various attempts to promote harmonization of national policies have not been warmly received by member states. The Commission's first real foray into the area was its November 2000 *Communication on a Community Immigration Policy*. The document emphasized the need for a controlled immigration policy to address labour and skills shortages, based on 'a common assessment of the economic and demographic development of the Union' taking into account its 'capacity of reception' (CEC 2000). It suggested that each member state compile annual reports of their labour needs, which would then contribute to an overarching EU approach to recruitment. Given the sensitivity of labour migration policy in most states, this Communication did not receive endorsement.

Not to be put off, in July 2001 the Commission produced a further Communication, recommending an 'open method of coordination' (OMC) for a Community Immigration Policy (Caviedes 2004). The idea was for each member state to gradually approximate their national approaches, based on a number of common guidelines and targets. However, when the Commission presented its proposal for a Directive on the admission of TCNs for economic purposes, it was rejected by member states after just one reading.

The Commission's hopes for developing a common policy were bolstered by European Council meetings in 2003 and 2004, which made positive (if vague) noises about the need for more coordinated policies. Trying to exploit this apparent window of opportunity, a Commission Green Paper of January 2005 on an EU approach to managing economic migration set out ideas for a common admission procedure for economic migrants. It argued that a common approach would help 'meet the needs of the EU labour market and ensure Europe's prosperity' (CEC 2005). The document set out characteristically liberal, business-friendly arguments, which very much dovetail with the EU's Lisbon objectives (a programme of reforms to enhance the competitiveness of European economies). Indeed, the Commission has partly justified its rather controversial foray into immigration admissions policy on the grounds that it is necessary for fulfilling the Lisbon objectives and economic reform more broadly. The bold suggestions of the Green Paper proved however to be a bridge too far for most member states. Indeed, the only legislation that was accepted by member states over this period covered far less controversial categories:

- A Council Direction of December 2004 dealt with the 'conditions of admission of third-country nationals for the purposes of *studies, pupil exchange, unremunerated training or voluntary service*' (emphasis added).
- In October 2005, the Council adopted a Directive on 'a specific procedure for admitting TCNs for the purposes of *scientific research*'.

It was perhaps surprising, then, that the Commission managed to push through a programme for an EU 'Blue Card', which finally gained agreement in the Council in May 2009. Provisions are set out in a Directive that covers the conditions for entry and residence of TCNs for the purpose of high-skilled employment. Holders of the card will be granted permits of between one and four years. They and their family members will benefit from a number of rights, including equal working conditions, access to education and training, recognition of qualifications, and various national provisions on social security and pensions. Significantly, after a stay of eighteen months in one EU country, under certain conditions a Blue Card holder may travel to another country to seek employment without going through the usual national procedures for admission.

There are a number of important caveats and restrictions in the Blue Card provisions. The scheme is only open to those with the relevant skills and experience, and who have a concrete job offer. Member states retain the right to determine the number of migrants entering under such a scheme, and can declare themselves, or certain regions or sectors, exempt from the provisions. Moreover, the UK, Ireland and Denmark have all decided to exercise their opt-out from the scheme.

Nonetheless, the Blue Card scheme does include a number of elements that go beyond current provisions. For example, a Blue Card holder can apply for permanent residence after a period of five years, including where some of this time has been spent in another EU country. Perhaps more importantly, the Blue Card carries a high degree of symbolic importance, arguably representing a tentative first step towards a common EU admissions policy.

The Commission has sought to further develop these proposals on what can be called a 'sectoral' basis by proposing schemes for seasonal workers, remunerated trainees and people transferred within multinational companies. The aim is to try to convince member states that there is distinct 'added value' in a common EU approach that can help member states address their labour market objectives.

How then was the Commission able to secure support for this proposal? It did so by adopting a sector-based approach that was able to marshal support for limited and prescribed measures in the area of higher-skilled migration that strengthen the EU's role and provide a measure of coordination. The proposals do not, at this stage, foreshadow extensive involvement in member states' admissions policies, but competence has been established and the Commission has managed to get its foot in the door. This does not mean that some inevitable process of 'competence creep' will be initiated, but does show how the development of EU-level cooperation and integration in the area of migration and asylum has shifted the preferences of states and understandings of the context in which they operate.

New EU thinking on migration and mobility?

In its global approach to migration, the Commission has sought to stimulate debate about new policy directions. It has done so by mooting the possibilities and potential advantages of circular migration and mobility partnerships. Both, it has been argued, provide a potentially better way of managing migration. In this area, the Commission has tried to be entrepreneurial and to stimulate new thinking. To refer to the terms used earlier, the spatial relocation of some (albeit limited) aspects of admissions policy to EU level has given the Commission some scope to think creatively about future policy development and the EU's role within it.

Both circular migration and mobility partnerships address a weakness in traditional immigration policies, namely that they

have an inbuilt tendency to encourage migration to become permanent. This is because they do not tend to create the possibility for
return – that is, once someone has moved from country A to
country B then their possibilities to return and re-enter can be very
limited. This reduces the flexibility of immigration and migrant
workers and could also diminish the attainment of potential economic development gains were people able to circulate – that is, to
move more freely from countries outside the EU to those within it.
Under the terms of its global approach to migration and funding
allocated to budget line B7-667 the Commission funded a number
of programmes that sought to develop better ways of managing
migration (CEC 2006a). These included: the development of information and advice centres for potential migrants from the western
Balkans; Spanish and Moroccan cooperation on seasonal labour
migration; national capacity-building in south Caucasus countries;
and cooperation between Italy and Tunisia.

The Commission has also sought to build mobility partnerships
both as another route to better management of migration and also
to reflect the global approach. Indeed, this global approach is a significant label because as the Commission itself noted, it provides a
potential route to a 'shift from a primarily security-centred
approach focused on reducing migratory pressures to a more trans-
parent and balanced approach' (CEC 2008:3). Partnership agreements have been reached with Moldova, Cape Verde and Georgia,
while negotiations were underway (at time of writing) with
Senegal. The agreements with Moldova and Cape Verde signed in
the summer of 2008 offer some enhanced protection for nationals
of these two countries working in EU member states, but focus
quite strongly on the development of migration policy capacity. As
Parkes (2009:2) points out, this could also be seen as consistent
with the logic of the external dimension of EU migration policy, as
'EU member states have long realised that they must offer something in return if they are to encourage third countries to fall in
with the Union's migration priorities' (see also Lavenex 2006).

Administrative practice and implementation

Political debate and rhetoric may set the general lines for policy
programmes, but, as we have argued, it is not self-evident how
directly they translate into legislation and programmes, let alone

how systematically these policies are implemented. One reason for this is the frequent discrepancy between media and political demands for (usually restrictive) policies, and the various business, legal and international considerations pushing for more liberal approaches. Another reason is the diversity of interests within government or EU departments with regard to labour migration. A third reason for the gap concerns problems with implementation: governments are not always able to steer complex social and economic dynamics in the way they would like. We will explore each of these factors in turn.

Bureaucracies and labour migration

The ministries or agencies responsible for labour migration policy in European countries clearly need to ensure their policies are at least seen to correspond to the government or minister's stated political goals. However, these organizations have multiple means at their disposal to resist change that runs counter to their interest, or that implies introducing difficult reforms. The most obvious tactic is to 'decouple' formal structures and rhetoric from informal procedures and practices (Meyer and Rowan 1977). This can help an organization to reconcile conflicting demands from its environment.

One example of this in the area of labour migration policy is the decoupling of anti-immigration rhetoric from more liberal practice. For example, the West German government introduced a so-called 'recruitment ban' in 1973, effectively calling a halt to the guest-worker programmes it had been running since 1955. However, even after the recruitment stop a number of government decrees ensured that firms would have access to labour where shortages could hamper business. For example, multinational companies were able to bring in foreign employees through little-known provisions for intracompany transfers (Kolb 2005). A government decree on 'exceptions from the general recruitment ban' allowed for a host of exemptions for different groups of persons, occupations and areas, meaning that the ban was only really symbolic (Leibig 2004), while bilateral agreements on seasonal labour with a number of central and east European countries allowed for the recruitment of temporary workers for up to 9 months in agriculture, hotels and catering. However, none of these measures became the object of intensive public political debate. The relevant ministries were able to effectively smuggle them through as low-profile decrees, meeting labour demand while pursuing an ostensibly restrictive approach.

A second strategy for resisting change, as we have seen, is the 'deliberate malintegration' of policies. Italian policy under Berlusconi between 2001 and 2006 and since 2008 provides a good example of this characterized by a combination of restrictive rhetoric and toleration of widespread irregular labour in practice, implying that strategies on entry and border control, labour market and regularization are far from 'joined up'. Yet rather than seeing this as a failure of policy, it can also be seen as a quite rational way of meeting the conflicting goals and pressures faced by centre-right administrations, and especially those working with fragile or fractious coalitions.

Attempts to meet conflicting pressures can be further complicated by divergent interests in different parts of the administration. Competence over policymaking is frequently the object of inter-agency wrangles. While interior ministries have traditionally wielded most clout in UK policy, in other European countries economics and labour ministries have played a key role in defining labour market needs and designing labour migration recruitment programmes (Hammar 1985). Departments dealing with science and technology have also been at the forefront of promoting skill-based criteria for selecting migrants, including in the UK. Welfare agencies have played a key role in developing programmes to promote the social integration of long-term residents. And foreign ministries in many countries have influenced programmes on refugee resettlement and policies to control irregular migration, and have even negotiated bilateral provisions on the recruitment of labour migrants. Not surprisingly, there have been significant tensions between different agencies in a number of European countries, as well as at the EU level.

The balance of influence between these respective ministries can shift over time. This can reflect formal decisions about the division of competence between departments. In Germany, for example, the 2004 Immigration Law granted new powers to the Federal Agency for Migration and Refugees in the area of integration policy. In the UK, the Home Office division dealing with immigration and asylum was recently given the status of a government agency. And the European Commission created a new Directorate General in 1999 to deal with Justice and Home Affairs matters. Frequently, though, shifts in power reflect changes in political priorities.

Reformist or business-friendly administrations will tend to look more to their economics and labour ministries to shape policy, rather than to traditionally more restrictive interior ministries.

There have been good examples of this tendency in Spain and the UK, under centre-left administrations keen to pursue a more business-friendly labour migration policy. In the UK, much of the impetus for reform from around 1999 came from the Performance and Innovation Unit based in the Prime Minister's Office, as well as the Department for Trade and Industry and the Department for Work and Pensions. In Spain, since the amendment to the 2005 Immigration Act, recruitment quotas for different sectors have been based on input from the network of local employment institutes in the autonomous communities (the National Institute of Employment) (Balch 2010).

Another tension in bureaucratic policymaking comes from differences in centre–periphery interests. National administrations typically have competence over admissions policy, and can therefore determine the level of labour immigration for the whole country. However, many countries experience quite pronounced variation in labour demand across different regions. Moreover, it is often local government and services that take on the main task of supporting new immigrants through providing welfare and social houses, and dealing with any local tensions that may arise. For this reason, subnational governments in countries such as Belgium, Germany, Spain and the UK have called for increased autonomy in shaping labour migration policies.

Finally, we should consider problems in implementing labour migration policies once they have been adopted. Even though governments in principle control whom they admit and for what duration, in practice it is often difficult to maintain control over processes of entry, residence and employment. Problems of implementation can occur in many different areas. For a start, governments cannot always predict exactly what demand there will be for different types of labour in different sectors. Labour shortages are caused by a complex set of economic, social and demographic factors that are difficult to track and project. Neither can they accurately forecast how many people will take up opportunities for labour migration presented by a new or expanded recruitment programme. In some cases, takeup may be less extensive than intended, as was the case with initial applications for the German 'Green Card' introduced in 2000. In other cases, the immigration resulting from a newly opened channel may be far higher than expected, as in the case of migration from Poland to the United Kingdom and Ireland after May 2004.

Even where governments are in a position to continually tweak their recruitment programmes to ensure optimal levels of immigration, they cannot always control migration flows that occur outside legal programmes. An initial influx of labour migrants can create a self-perpetuating form of 'chain migration', as friends, family or people from the same region of origin become aware of opportunities for work abroad (Faist 2000). Often such chain migration involves irregular entry or employment, as has been charted in the case of Romanian migration to Spain (Elrick and Ciobanu 2009). Migrant networks can also facilitate overstay of regular labour permits, through helping immigrants to access jobs outside of the temporary or bilateral schemes on which they originally entered. Just as importantly, once labour migrants have been resident in European countries for a number of years, a number of socio-economic and civil rights often kick in. The German government, for example, was obliged to acknowledge the rights of long-term residents through a series of constitutional court rulings in the 1970s and 1980s, implying that governments can be seriously restricted in how far they can control who stays (Joppke 1998). This re-emphasizes the point that it is necessary to study forms and types of politics and see how the actions of the executive branch of government can be constrained by the decisions of courts.

These constraints on governmental capacities to control labour migration might imply that immigration policies are indeed failing. States are simply unable to control who enters, stays and works in their territories. However, we would stress that in many ways these apparent limitations of state capacity are often less unwelcome than might be supposed. For a start, high levels of labour migration, even if irregular, are a strong indicator of a demand for foreign labour in domestic markets. Even if governments are keen to signal that they want to restrict immigration, higher levels may be beneficial to productivity and growth in certain sectors. As long as governments can get away with this kind of decoupling, then it may be a far from detrimental outcome. Moreover, this type of dualist approach may enable governments to mollify the conflicting interests of those favouring restriction, and those pressing for openness. In this sense, governments may well prefer to remain in blissful ignorance about these forms of non-compliance with labour migration rules. Only when evasion or irregularity is picked up by the media or party politics are bureaucracies forced to confront these issues. Where they do not become the object of public scrutiny, then some degree of malintegration may be the best way of meeting opposing interests.

Conclusions

The EU's role in the admission of TCN labour migrants remains limited. This is certainly not for want of trying on the part of the European Commission. However, efforts to coordinate admissions policies have met with resistance from member states. Whereas cooperation on asylum essentially implies harmonizing systems based on a logic of *restriction*, harmonization in TCN labour migration would imply adopting common approaches for the *admission* of non-EU nationals. As such, it would involve some delegation of power in a highly sensitive area of migration control. As in other areas of migration policy, the Commission has managed to slowly expand provisions, most notably through the adoption of an EU Blue Card in 2009. While still extremely limited, this step may represent the thin edge of a harmonization wedge, with further measures gradually rolled out over the coming decade. These developments could be taken to show how the dynamics of EU cooperation can, over time, slowly reshape national perceptions and objectives and create fertile terrain for EU action. At the same time, however, a note of caution is necessary. Member states have been reluctant to cede capacity to EU level to manage non-EU migration. This is true for labour migration and, as we see in Chapter 5, it's also true for family migration.

Family Migration

While much public debate in Europe about immigration focuses on labour migration, asylum-seeking and irregular migration, it is family migration that has been, is and will continue to be a key migration flow. A better understanding of 'the family' as a migration unit and of gendered processes linked to understandings of the family can enhance our understanding both of migration and of political and social processes associated with it.

The fact that family migration continued after the so-called 'immigration stop' of the early 1970s does suggest that policy-makers have not been able to attain their objectives. By looking at political debate and decision-making, we see tensions at all stages of the policy process between the role of the executive, 'rights-based politics' and the operation of judicial institutions. This tension is not easily reconciled because respect for human rights, on the one hand, and the right to determine who can access their territory, on the other, are both important components of EU state identities. The chapter also analyses the growing EU role, and, further, the ways in which EU integration in the form of a 2003 Directive on the Right to Family Reunion may not weaken the capacity of member states to regulate admission by family members, but could actually facilitate attainment of member state policy objectives.

Initially, however, it is important to explore the meaning of family migration. By this is meant the development of a better understanding of 'the family' as a relevant unit of analysis and also to see how this draws clearly into view gendered approaches to the analysis of international migration.

The centrality of family migration

In its annual survey of international migration in 2008, the OECD (2008:22) reported that 'Family migration continues to dominate among the inflows of permanent-type immigrants.' Indeed, as

OECD figures showed, in 2006, as much as 62 per cent of permanent-type migration into Portugal was family migration. In France this figure was 59 per cent, it was 47 per cent in the Netherlands and 42 per cent in Italy. At the lower end of the scale, 23 per cent of permanent-type immigration to Germany was family migration while 26 per cent and 32 per cent were the figures in Denmark and the UK respectively (OECD 2008:36).

It has been argued that the right to family life enshrined in national constitutions and laws, as well as in international legal standards, left a route open for family migrants. This helps us to see:

- a disjunction between the rhetoric of control employed by the executive branch of governments and the reality of continued immigration;
- the importance of broadening our understanding of migration beyond the migrant as an individual and thinking instead of the family units that play a key role in shaping migration decisions;
- the need to specify the venues within which decisions about immigration are made – in this case the key role played by the judicial branch of national governments, but also the roles played by EU and other international frameworks.

To give a hint of where we are heading, two other key components of the debate about family migration become apparent:

- How family migration jars with the contemporary EU-wide quest to 'manage migration', which can lead to a focus on the 'useful' or 'productive' migrant understood in economic terms rather than supposedly unproductive family migration.
- How family migration is linked to debates about integration through national and EU legislation that focus on the 'integration capacities' of family member migrants. Does family migration facilitate integration by reconstituting the family or does it inhibit integration. In its Plan Greco in 2000, Spain sought to liberalize procedures for family migration because it was seen as a route to better integration for settled migrants. In Denmark, France, the Netherlands and the UK, there has been concern that family migration inhibits integration by 'maintaining different family norms' (Kofman and Meetoo 2008: 159).

Family migration can thus enable us to develop the themes that are central to this book, namely the disjunction between talk, decision and action and the utility of exploring the political and institutional contexts within which policymaking occurs.

The right to family migration?

Family migration is a key migration route, and legal venues have played an important role in protecting the rights of migrants to be joined by their family members. It is, however, important to note that there is no positive right to family migration. The right to family life is enshrined in international law, but does not constitute a positive right to family reunification (Lahav 1997). Articles 12 and 16 of the 1948 Universal Declaration of Human Rights (UDHR) declare the right to found a family and the importance of respect for family life, respectively. Article 8 of the 1953 European Convention on Human Rights (ECHR) declares the right to respect for private and family life such that:

> Everyone has the right to respect for his private and family life, his home and his correspondence.

This does apply to all within a territory whether they be citizens or not, but, again, is not a right to family reunification. There is no positive obligation on states to accept family migrants. States can and do impose conditions by defining the family members eligible, age conditions, waiting periods and integration measures. An exception to this is the EU free movement framework, which does guarantee rights of family reunification for all mobile EU citizens. We also see that EU member states have been keen to regulate admission by non-EU family migrants, mindful of their legal obligations, but with a tendency to adopt restrictive interpretations of the family and to focus on a definition of the immediate, nuclear family (that is, spouses and children who are minors).

The EU's family reunification Directive – somewhat misleadingly entitled the 'Right to Family Reunification' Directive – does not provide a right to family migration. Each EU member state can and does make provision in its national laws for family migration, but these states can and do have the right to impose conditions. These include waiting periods for family migrants and/or income level requirements and housing conditions for the sponsor. The EU approach is closely linked to these national approaches, as the Directive on family reunification allows states to impose conditions and also to specify 'integration measures' such as language skills (Adam and Devillard 2008).

By factoring the EU into this analysis we can see how EU institutions can change the context within which decisions are made. The family reunification Directive can be understood as a sovereignty bargain that pools authority but still allows states significant leeway. The spatial relocation of some authority can however change the dynamics of policy, involve new EU-level actors in the process and raise the possibility of future developments that were not anticipated at the time that the family reunion Directive was agreed.

Narratives

In this section we unpick conceptualizations and rhetorical framings of family migration in order to develop a better understanding of how policymakers conceive of the challenges and the impacts of their interventions.

Family migration can be broken down into three main types (Kofman 2004):

- *Family reunion* refers to children, spouses and parents as and when permitted by states. Geneva Convention refugees can bring their families with them. Asylum applicants granted a secondary status normally have to wait.
- *Marriage migration/family formation* refers to children that return to their parents' country of origin for marriage partners or people wanting to marry someone they met while abroad. Only the Netherlands makes a legal distinction between family reunification and family formation (Adam and Devillard 2008:55).
- *Entire family migration* is in EU states usually reserved for highly skilled workers and their family members.

We know that 'most geographic mobility implicitly and explicitly involves families' (Bailey and Boyle 2004:229), but this is a broad category. We may have an idea of the family as the nuclear family of parents and children, but this is hardly a reflection of the contemporary reality of family life where people may choose to cohabit, divorce, separate or enter into a same-sex partnership (Bailey and Boyle 2004:232). In legal and policy terms, however: '[w]hen we speak of family migration ... we mean the nuclear family as defined by the state' (Kofman 2004: 245). It can be difficult to extend this discussion to the extended family and even more difficult to extend it to same-sex couples (Elman 2000).

Family migration is, of course, not necessarily female migration, but there has been a tendency to distinguish between primary, predominantly male labour migration and secondary, dependent, predominantly female migration. While much of the guest-worker migration in the 1950s and 1960s was by men, it was also the case that there were substantial numbers of female labour migrants too (Morokvasic 1984). The growth in family migration in the 1970s and 1980s did lead to an increased number of female migrants in EU states, but also to increased numbers of children and older people too. As the character and composition of migration flows changed then so too did the type of engagement with the institutions of the countries to which these migrants moved. As a result:

- There was reduced economic participation because of the changed age profile of the family migrant population.
- Where economic participation did occur it was often in particular types of economic activity with evidence of gendered segmentation of the labour market across skills levels (that is, higher- and lower-skilled work) with female migrants more likely to be found in lower-skilled paid or unpaid reproductive work (Kofman 2004; Kofman and Raghurman 2006);
- Engagement with welfare state institutions, such as education, healthcare and housing, increased.
- Unemployment increased.
- Service sector employment increased, particularly in care work.

What is the family?

The EU Directive on the right to family reunification seeks to define what it means by family reunification and defines it as:

The entry into and residence in a Member State by a family member of a third country national residing lawfully in that

Member State in order to preserve the family unit, whether the family unit arose before or after the resident's entry.

This provides a legal definition of the family, but there are understandings of the family in the economic and sociological literatures too. Economic analysis of migration has been criticized for focusing on decision-making by individuals rather than thinking about the family units within which these decisions can be made and where their effects are seen. Some economists have sought to factor in the family as the decision-making unit, assuming that family units act in an economically rational manner and migrate when the expected future earnings arising from migration exceed the expected earnings in the country of origin, taking into account the costs of movement (Sandell 1977; Mincer 1978).

These perspectives have been challenged by those who point to the relative distribution of power and resources within families and gender-based inequalities as highly relevant factors (Halfacree 1995; Smith 2004). Additional important insight has been provided by those who point to the 'cumulative causation' of migration and its strong internal momentum as one form of migration leads to another. Notions of 'cumulative causation' draw from Gunnar Myrdal's (1957) work to develop 'the idea that migration induces changes in social and economic structures that make additional migration likely' (Massey 1990:4–5). In such cases, household and family structures contribute to recurrent migration, with one form of migration instigating further migration flows. The result is that primary and secondary flows cannot be easily distinguished. To refine this point and emphasize the social and economic basis of migration, Bailey and Boyle (2004:231) argue that:

> Economic issues may be the key force driving migration but the resources of the power base on which people draw in migration decision-making are not necessarily synonymous with neat monetary calculations for the family as a whole [and dominated by the] hegemonic, ungendered brute economic logic of net family income [with the family little more than] an aggregation of individual utility functions.

One result of a 'brute' logic could be that women become 'invisible agents' (p. 232) in migration. This would mean that they are present, but we don't see them or their centrality to the process and thus may misunderstand it.

The demand for family migration

There is a significant supply of family migrants, and states have developed complex legal frameworks as part of their attempt to deal with it. The supply of family migration as well as the structuring of family units and relations between family members does, however, need to be put alongside the demand for other forms of entry and the capacity of EU states to manage these various entrance and admissions channels. Only one EU state, Austria, imposes a quota on family migration (4540 in 2007, according to Adam and Devillard 2008:60) and also introduced restrictive family migration laws, as part of the 2006 immigration legislation, that require the sponsoring partner to have an income at or above the minimum wage (OECD 2008:228).

In the absence of decisions by states to greatly increase overall levels of immigration, an increase in migration for employment 'comes at the expense of the family and refugee classes and would seem likely to lead to sharp conflicts among the groups supporting each migration class' (Freeman 2006:233). This creates real and compelling dilemmas. If there are admission limits then should asylum-seekers fleeing persecution be given preference over family migration? Gibney (2004) argues that asylum-seekers should be given consideration at least equal to that given to members of the more extended families of migrants (that is, beyond spouses and children to include, for example, parents). In contrast, Honohan (2008) makes the case for family reunification, particularly when this is linked to provision of care. She argues that family migrants can offer vital support for family structures, that EU states value these structures and that, consequently, family migration can facilitate greater social cohesion.

These tensions between migrant categories can also be illustrated by statements made in 2007 by the then French interior minister, Nicolas Sarkozy, who addressed the French *Comité Interministériel de Contrôle de l'Immigration* (Interministerial Committee on Immigration Control). He expressed his preference for '*migration choisie et non subie*' (migration that is chosen and not endured). In light of the fact that 59 per cent of new migrants entering France in 2006 did so as family migrants, this marked a preference for 'productive' labour migration rather than 'unproductive' family migration. In 2006 the French immigration and integration law (no. 2006-911) tightened rules on family migration by imposing an 18-month waiting period for sponsors, and requiring non-EU migrants to wait for a probationary or conditional between 2 and 3 years to be joined by their spouse. The 2007 law (no. 2007-1631) was even more controversial because it introduced for an 18-month trial period voluntary DNA tests for children of migrants, with parents also obliged to sign a good-behaviour contract for their offspring (Kofman and Meetoo 2008: 160)

Denmark too has notably tightened its family reunion laws. The entry into government of the anti-immigration Danish People's Party in 2003 led to a toughening of immigration rules. For instance, a foreign spouse cannot be brought into Denmark unless both partners are over the age of 24. Developments in Denmark also provide evidence of another type of issues linkage: between family migration and integration capacity (Groenendijk 2004). In Denmark, applicants for family reunion have to sign a declaration of integration 'which obliges the applicant to actively participate with his/her children in Danish language courses and integration into Danish society' (Kofman and Meetoo 2008: 161).

When we analyse the EU's family reunification Directive later in this chapter we see in more detail how EU member states can specify 'integration measures' for family migrants (such as linguistic abilities), but that there is also some terminological creepage as 'integration measures' can seemingly become 'integration conditions' (Groenendijk *et al.* 2007).

To sum up, four narratives of debate about family migration can be identified. First, a gendered element has led to a legacy of distinctions between male-and- primary and female-and-secondary migration. These have been influential in structuring understandings of migration, but such distinctions do not hold. A temporal element means that this makes even less sense when we extend the analysis to newer immigration countries in central, eastern and southern Europe (King and Zontini 2000; Castles and Miller 2009). The distinction between primary and secondary migration can also lead to a further unhelpful distinction between men producing and women reproducing (Kofman 1999: 272). Family migration may also be important in sustaining family structures that could be weakened by international migration and thus be a force for cohesion.

Second, the continuation of family migration after the supposed immigration stop contributed to the politicization of family migration in the 1970s and led to the issue being identified as one of control. Family migration was (and is) complex and diverse, but political debate about family migration was strongly focused on control and on specific manifestations of family migration, such as marriage and the notion that sham marriages or marriages of convenience could be a new, illicit migration route. In Denmark tests are now required prior to the marriage that both parties are able to communicate with each other in the same language. Suspicions may be aroused if there is a large age-gap. Potential marriage partners might also be quizzed about how well they know each other. In the UK, a 2005 provision requiring short-term non-EU migrants to request permission to marry was struck down by the High Court because it breached article 12 of the ECHR on the right to marry. The challenge was brought by a Muslim Algerian irregular migrant and a female, Polish Catholic migrant. The High Court also found there to be discrimination on the grounds of religion, as marriage in the Church of England was regarded more favourably (Kofman and Meetoo 2008:161). There has been debate too about arranged marriage and forced marriage. In the UK, Kofman and Meetoo (2008:162) point to the Home Office's rather ambiguous reference to 'those communities that continue the practice of forced marriage', but point out that 'those communities' means Asian communities.

Third, the specific focus on gender and migration imparts a key dynamic to the debate about family migration with a body of work challenging the relative neglect of female migration, but also specifying more closely the interactions between female migrants and the institutions of the society they move to, with a particular focus on the paid and unpaid work done by female migrants (Morokvasic 1984; Andall 2000; Kofman *et al.* 2000; Bailey and Boyle 2004).

Fourth, since the 1970s, the limits on immigration control that EU states have encountered have led to an intensified emphasis on specification of integration measures for family members (Groenendijk 2004). It may be the case that family migration enhances rather than detracts from integration by helping to avoid problems of isolation (Honohan 2008:5), but this has not been the underlying policy narrative except in certain, limited circumstances in high-skilled migration policies. As we saw in Chapter 2, the German 'Green Card' scheme was targeted initially at individuals but was modified to include families. In the UK, 'Tier 1' (highly skilled migrant workers under the points system) also includes the right of spouses to work. We see a differential approach to family migration linked to the perceived productiveness of migrants.

Political debate

Family migration is at the heart of what some have seen as a key puzzle for students of European migration. How and why did governments that in the 1970s proclaimed their desire to 'end immigration' end up presiding over increases in their immigrant populations? This kind of disjunction is central to the policy failure thesis – that is, states specify policy objectives, but do not attain them. In the case of family migration what happened was that national governments expressed a desire to impose tight controls on family migration, but seemed unable to do so. Instead of migration falling after the 'immigration stop' it continued to rise. An influential body of work has developed that focuses precisely on this question and shows how the restrictive objectives of governments (or to be more precise, the executive branches of these governments) were ameliorated by the decisions of courts that ruled to protect the rights of migrants to family life (Hollifield 1992; Lahav 1997; Guiraudon 1998).

This does not mean that European states did not pursue restrictive policies or that they were unable to exercise some degree of control, but it does mean that they encountered constraints when seeking to implement these policies. From where did these constraints emanate? The answer to this is that they emanated principally from judicial arenas within which the harsher and restrictive content of the executive branch of government was mitigated by the decisions of judges to offer protection to the rights of labour migrants to be joined by their family members. This again emphasizes the importance of specifying the venue or arena within which decisions about migration are made. In his account of the development of forms of rights-based politics in France and Germany, Hollifield (1992) draws from Ruggie's account of the embedded liberalism of the postwar period to analyse the impact of 'rights-based politics' on the continuation of family migration in France and Germany (Ruggie 1983; Hollifield 1992). In her account of the effects of judicial and bureaucratic decisions on family migration in France, Germany and the Netherlands, Guiraudon (1998, 2000b) specifies the importance of decisions made behind 'gilded doors'. By this she means that venues such as courts that were 'shielded' from open public debate and governed by judicial procedures and method, were capable of delivering more liberal migration policy outcomes that created some space for the protection of the right to family life for TCN migrants, and created scope for an openness and expansiveness in migration policies that was not intended by the governments of these countries. As we have also seen, the struggle continues as the executive branch seeks new routes to control – the UK case referred to earlier, of requiring requests for permission to marry, is a good example – while the courts can intervene to strike down those deemed excessive – as they did in the UK case just mentioned.

Others have similarly explored how the liberal norms that underpin liberal-democratic states can act as a constraint on their ability to control immigration. Joppke analyses how European states have sought to distinguish in their policies between 'wanted' and 'unwanted' forms of immigration (Joppke 1998; see also Bhabha and Shutter 1994). Family migration was not solicited; as Joppke (1998:281–2) puts it: 'They [European states] had to accept family immigration, recognizing the moral and legal rights of those initially admitted. In this sense, European family immigration is unwanted immigration.' Comparison of Germany with the UK also shows how different forms of both constitutional and judicial politics in Germany and the UK impacted on family migration – more positively in the German case and more negatively in the UK case. In both Germany and the UK family migration was an unintended consequence of primary flows in European countries that had employed temporary, guest-worker modes of recruitment and did not see themselves as immigration countries. In Germany, for example, family reunion was officially discouraged because it would encourage permanent settlement. The Turkish and Yugoslav cases of 1977 allowed for family migration albeit with an 8-year residence qualification for the spouse and a 1-year waiting period for the partner. The UK was subject to rulings in 1985 in the ECHR that challenged the discriminatory basis of family migration by requiring female migrants to prove that the 'primary purpose' of family migration (for example, by a potential spouse) was for family reasons and not to acquire permanent residence (that is, that it was not primary immigration by another route). In the *Abdulaziz, Cabales and Balkandali* case before the ECHR in May 1985 it was found that UK legislation amounted to sex discrimination (Bhabha and Shutter 1994). The UK government responded by applying the rule to both male and female family migrants; as Joppke (1998:291) puts it, 'one must admire the cleverness of turning a European court indictment into a means of even firmer immigration control'.

The EU's role

This section looks more closely at the resonance of family migration in debate and decision-making processes and, in particular, analyses the role played by the EU through the 2003 Directive on the Right to Family Reunion. Denmark, Ireland and the UK are not covered by this Directive, as they opted out of its provisions.

We have already identified why and how certain types of 'venue' such as courts were particularly important in securing the rights of migrants to be joined by their family members. To reiterate, this did not constitute a positive right to family migration, but EU states did develop legal frameworks that contained provision governing when and how migrants could be joined by their family members.

We also encounter an interesting twist to our focus on 'decision'. We see scope for disjuncture between decisions made by families, on the one hand, and decisions made by governing authorities in EU member states, on the other. When considering decision-making about family migration we can thus consider the family as a decision-making unit and also the institutional setting within which decisions about family migration occur.

EU states have encountered constraints because of cumulative causation linked to migration dynamics and the role of the family in those dynamics. They have also experienced constraints because of their constitutional commitment to respect for family life. This did not mean that EU states ceded all capacity to regulate these flows or that they have somehow ceded a right of family migration. Rather, the liberalness of these liberal states constrains them; but liberal states have sharp edges and engage in illiberal practices in order to protect their liberal identities. Joppke represents these constraints as 'internal' – that is, related to the legal and political constitution of EU states – and is dismissive of external constraints such as international human rights standards. Guiraudon (1998, 2000) also points to the limited reach of the 'post-national'.

How then do we account for the growing EU role in this area and, more specifically, the 2003 EU Directive on family reunification? We have already discussed why and how European integration should not be understood as some simple transfer of power and sovereignty loss. We have also seen that EU responses to international migration are highly differentiated, with more activity in some policy areas than in others.

The EU Directive on family reunification was agreed in June 2003 after a negotiating period of three years and after three different Commission proposals. Denmark, Ireland the UK are not covered by its provisions. The long negotiating period indicates that the Commission encountered resistance from member states and was forced to temper some of the more progressive aspects of the original proposals that would have impinged more directly on member states' admissions policies. Throughout the negotiation it became clear that a core group of states – with Austria, Germany and the Netherlands to the fore – would insist on EU measures that did not place additional constraints on their capacity to regulate admission of family members.

During the 3-year negotiation process of the family reunion Directive there was a movement away from the Commission's more liberal initial proposals to a stronger emphasis on integration by migrants and their families. The Commission's original proposals had conceptualized 'integration' in relation to the promotion of social stability through, for example, access to training and education for family members. During the negotiation, the Austrian and German governments were insistent on the inclusion of integration provisions in accordance with national laws. As noted earlier, these were integration *measures* and not integration *conditions*, but they are sometimes represented as the latter and as a means of stemming family migration flows.

The EU's Family Reunion Directive

The EU Family Reunion Directive determines:

- the right to family reunification of TCNs who reside lawfully in the territory of an EU member state;

- the conditions under which family members can enter into and reside in a member state;
- the rights of the family members once the application for family reunification has been accepted regarding, for example, education and training.

The Directive also recognizes the rights of member states to impose conditions on family migration and gives them a margin to do so in relation to factors such as the definition of the family, waiting periods and integration measures.

The EP has often intervened in debates about immigration to advocate a more progressive EU stance. Under the powers given to the EP by the Treaty of Nice it sought annulment of the Directive. The EP argued that certain articles were not in line with fundamental rights, such as those specified by the ECHR (specifically article 8 on the right to family life and article 14 on non-discrimination on grounds of age) and a number of other international agreements. The Council responded by pointing out that the EU is not actually a party to these agreements. Specific problems were as follows:

- Article 4.1 of the Directive specifies that member states are to authorize entry and residence for dependent, unmarried children below the age of majority in the member state they move to. There is a derogation that allows member states to require that children aged over 12 who arrive independently of the rest of his/her family may be required to satisfy the integration conditions set down in national law in the country they move to.
- Article 4.6 specifies a derogation that member states may require that applications for family reunification for minor children be submitted before the age of 15.
- Article 8 states that member states may require the sponsor to have been legally resident for 2 years prior to family members joining him or her. There is then a derogation that allows a member state to take into account its 'reception capacity' and extend the waiting period to 3 years.

The ECJ was then called upon to make a ruling. This could mark the development of what Hollifield (1992) referred to in his analysis of France and Germany in the 1970s and 1980s as 'rights-based politics', but the ECJ rejected EP calls for annulment of the Directive on the grounds that, while member states must have regard to a child's interests, the EU's framework of fundamental rights does not create an individual right for family members to enter the territory of a member state. This goes back to a point that has already been made, namely that the right to enjoy family life does create scope for courts to intervene to protect the family rights of migrants, but does not create a right to family migration. It was established that EU member states have a 'certain margin of appreciation' when examining applications for family reunification. Similarly, the court held that member states would still be obliged to examine requests made by children of more than 15 years old in light of the interests of the child and with a view to promoting family life. The ECJ also ruled that integration was a legitimate factor to be taken into account, but not as the base for a quota system or a 3-year waiting period imposed without regard to the particular circumstances of specific cases. As already noted, Austria is the only EU member state that has a family migration quota, but the Austrian quota requirement no longer applies 3 years after submitting the application, so this does not appear to breach the Directive. It is an indication of the discretion that member states possess that harsh Austrian standards still fell within the margin of appreciation allowed by the family Directive (Adam and Devillard 2008).

In such circumstances, it seems that the development of EU capacity in the area of family migration fits with an understanding of the EU as sovereignty-enhancing rather than sovereignty-denuding. We see resistance from member states to intrusion on their admissions policies. We see too a manifestation of contemporary concerns about integration capacity. This tends to cast the EU as a new venue or arena within which member states seek to cooperate in order to reinforce attainment of their domestic policy priorities. The picture, however, is somewhat more complex. Competence has been established. There are groups pushing for enhanced competence and challenging the lowest common denominator basis of current policy. The 'move' to Europe does raise the possibility of unintended or unexpected consequences in the future for member states. Thus far, however, we have seen it to be clearly established that EU member states have a certain margin of appreciation, that is, EU states clearly encounter national, EU and international legal constraints on their actions, but also can still exercise significant discretion over this form of admission to their territory.

Administrative practice and implementation

So far in this chapter we have explored the framing of family migration, the narrative constructions of migration in academic and policy debate, and the venues and arenas within which decisions about migration are made. We have seen certain forms of 'talk' about family migration, but when the analysis shifted to the realm of decision-making we saw the importance of specifying the venue within which decisions about family migration are made and some constraints placed on the executive branch of governments by judicial arenas. We now move on to analyse implementation of family migration laws and policies across the EU.

EU states may seem to be convergent, but this may be for different reasons. We can identify in France, Germany and the Netherlands an increased emphasis on integration measures for family migrants and could see this as a form of horizontal convergence, but would also need to unpick these national cases in order to get a full picture of the comparative dynamics.

Similarly, we can also assess implementation and practice through analysis of a vertical dimension associated. We can then seek to identify whether or not the EU has helped induce change in family migration laws and policies. Here too there are analytical complications as we need to disentangle the various causes of policy change that may or may not be related to European integration. Indeed, change may occur that is in conformity with EU requirements, but the linkage is more apparent than real as it may not have been the EU that caused this change.

If we were to contrast family migration with labour migration then we could say that regulations for family reunification:

> are more harmonized in EU Member States than for other important areas, such as employment. Whilst there are still important differences in how EU Member States are regulating family reunification for TCNs residing in their territory, some minimum standards have been set and, as a result, several

countries have developed clear and detailed regulations on the issue. (Adam and Devillard 2008:66)

At the same time, EU member states still possess significant discretion when regulating family migration. There are four main areas in which we can see this discretion being exercised. These are:

- The definition of the family unit for those members that do not belong to the nuclear family, such as parents, adult children and unmarried partners. EU member states tend to focus their family migration policies on the nuclear rather than the extended family.
- The imposition of age restrictions for spouses and children. Spouses and minor children are admitted in all member states, although some countries insist on a maximum age (this is 18 in the UK, the Netherlands and Germany, but 15 in Denmark.
- Waiting periods before family members can join their partners. 11 member states have a waiting period of usually around 2 years. Spain is the shortest at 12 months while Denmark requires at least 3 years.
- The specification of integration measures. The EU family reunification Directive does allow member states to specify integration measures. France, Germany and the Netherlands all require integration conditions that include linguistic competence and, in the case of France and the Netherlands, some knowledge of French and Dutch societies.

What sorts of competences are required? Germany requires a language test as the basis for family reunion. France requires foreigners between 16 and 64 to take a test in their country of origin on the French language and French values. Family migrants seeking to enter France must also confirm their respect for the fundamental principles of the republic including equality between genders, secularism and the rejection of discrimination on the basis of origin. The Netherlands requires foreigners between 16 and 65 to take a civic integration test at a Dutch consulate or embassy before they can move. The exam is taken orally in Dutch and consists of two parts. In Part 1, knowledge of Dutch society is tested, including Dutch geography, history, political organization, parenting and education and the Dutch health system. Part 2 tests knowledge of the Dutch language. Only when they pass this civic integration exam are migrants eligible for a provisional residence permit necessary to enter the Netherlands (OECD 2008:112).

The question that arises is whether these measures are designed to promote integration or to control immigration. Moreover, does this kind of testing and emphasis on educational settings favour some kinds of migrants and discriminate against others? If, for example, a migrant comes from a less-developed country and has had little access to formal education then these kinds of tests are likely to be quite daunting while someone from a more economically developed country who has enjoyed greater access to education may feel less intimidated by the measures. As with the notion of 'skill' in labour migration, there may be cultural biases in integration measures linked to family migration. Groenendijk *et al.* (2007) also point out that article 7.2 of the EU's family reunification Directive provides for integration measures and not integration conditions. A family migrant may be required to attend a course, but not to pass an exam.

There remains some diversity in the frameworks governing family migration and some margin for the interpretation of the requirements for family migration in bureaucratic and administrative settings within member states. The EU Directive does, however, play some part in reframing the debate. Its 'harder' legal effects may be constrained by the margins for appreciation that it gives to member states, but it may create other kinds of resources around which mobilizations can occur.

Conclusion

Family migration raises important issues for students of international migration. It is a key flow and a substantial proportion of Europe's migrant population entered via the family route. We see too that family migration has been viewed as integral to a core problem in European immigration politics, namely the continuation of migration even after the proclaimed 'immigration stop' of the early 1970s, which can be linked to the decision-making venues within which decisions about family migration are made. Restrictive measures governing family migration have developed, but courts have intervened at times to protect the right to family life for migrants. This has not created a right to family migration for TCN migrants, but has sometimes constrained the executive branch of government in EU member states. This emphasis in law on the conditions under which family migration can occur does not mean that all objectives are attained – this would be remarkable in any policy area, never mind one as complex as family migration. It does however show how, why and when family migration demonstrates core tensions and ambiguities at the heart of the migration policy process and it reflects what could be called a 'necessary mal-integration' of liberal and illiberal tendencies evident in the politics of migration.

Chapter 6

Irregular Immigration

At the end of March 2009 a boat capsized off the Libyan coast killing most of the 200 people on board; it was believed to be en route to Italy. Meanwhile, the Agency for the Management of Operational Cooperation at the External Borders of the Member States of the EU, or FRONTEX as it is known, was reporting that attempted illegal crossings at EU member states' land and sea border rose by 20 per cent between 2007 and 2008 (*European Voice*, 16 April 2009). In another incident in April 2009, around 120 people were stranded in the Mediterranean on the Turkish cargo ship the *Pinar E*, which had retrieved them after the small inflatable boats in which they had been travelling had sunk. Following their rescue the governments of Italy and Malta argued for four days about whose responsibility they were. According to the United Nations High Commissioner for Refugees (UNHCR) the boats were carrying 129 Nigerians, 3 people from Niger, 5 from Ghana, 4 Somalis, a Liberian and a migrant whose country of origin was unclear (*New York Times*, 20 April 2009). By journey's end a pregnant woman had died and many of the other travellers were ill.

These incidents exemplify the very real and pressing human dimension to debates about illegal and/or irregular immigration. They could also lend credence to 'the myth of invasion' (de Haas 2007) and the idea that Europe is besieged by irregular migrants seeking to clandestinely cross its borders. In fact, most irregular migrants enter in a regular fashion and overstay. This chapter shows the complexities of irregular migration and the basic difficulties that are encountered when seeking to understand the causes and effects of such complex flows. It shows that the pressures arising from irregular migration have been particularly focused on EU states such as Greece, Italy, Malta and Spain that are on the southern edges of the EU. We see too that the EU has played a growing role in this area, seeking to:

- build capacity at member state level;

- ensure that new member states accord with EU border control requirements; and
- export EU border control and security practices to non-EU member states.

In 2008, for example, the European Commission proposed a European border surveillance system (EUROSUR) focused on the EU's eastern land and southern maritime borders aiming to reduce irregular migration flows.

The dark side of admissions policies?

Irregular migration is the other side – or dark side – of admissions policies. As immigration controls across the EU have got tougher so the quest for evasion has intensified. For example, when Spain and Italy introduced visa requirements in 1991 as a result of the requirements of the Schengen system, there was an intensification of smuggling activity across their land and sea borders. Another recent and very evocative image was the plight in May 2007 of 27 people clinging to a tuna net for 3 days and nights while the Maltese and Libyan governments argued about whose responsibility they were.

This human tragedy – and many others such as those already recounted – has prompted debate touching upon the key themes that will be central to this chapter's analysis, namely:

- the continued resonance of borders;
- poverty as a 'push' factor;
- the importance of 'pull' factors in relatively wealthy EU states; and
- the persistence and creativity of an irregular or illegal branch of the 'migration industry' supporting and sustaining people-smuggling and human trafficking.

In this policy area we also see a lot of tough talk about borders and border security, but little to suggest that this tough talk has diminished the demand for entry. Moreover, there are significant pull factors at work here too because, as we see, there are some sectors of the economy in EU member states that provide employment for irregular migrants, such as construction work or family care services.

When the focus shifts to policy implementation, we see the kinds of ambiguities that can riddle what can be characterized as an 'institutional sector' where tough talk is difficult to translate into action in an area plagued by tensions, ambiguities and contradictions.

The salience of the issues cannot be disputed. Between 2000 and 2005 around 350 migrants a week were intercepted using Mediterranean routes to enter Europe (Carling 2007:4); how many actually got through is not known. It has also been estimated that 1200 people may have lost their lives between 1995 and 2005 trying to cross the Mediterranean to enter Spain (Carling 2007:5). *Patera* – wooden boats used by people-smugglers in crossings between from Morocco to Spain – became part of the vocabulary of the international migration literature. Similarly, in Italy, high-powered dinghies driven by people-smugglers crossed the Adriatic from Albania to land on the Puglian coast of Italy.

In its 2007 annual report, FRONTEX identified the main external border areas in Europe affected by irregular migration according to the number of detections and apprehensions of migrants as:

- land borders in south-eastern Europe, especially the Greek-Albanian and the Greek–Turkish borders;
- air borders in north and west Europe, especially in France;
- sea borders in south and south-eastern Europe, especially the Greek–Turkish sea border and the Italian coast (FRONTEX 2007:14).

The top three sourced countries were Albanian nationals trying to cross land borders into Greece, Iraqi nationals at Greek borders and at air borders of a number of EU states, and Moroccan irregular migrants often detected at sea borders, but also at the land border between Spain and Morocco (FRONTEX 2007:16). Nationals of Afghanistan, Algeria, Egypt, Eritrea and Somalia were detected at the sea borders while migrants from Pakistan, Palestine and Serbia were detected at land borders. Chinese nationals were mainly detected at air borders, followed by Brazilian nationals. Reports such as the one just cited by FRONTEX and media coverage of irregular migration can be important in dramatizing the issues, conveying images of Europe under threat, but also capturing some of the extreme circumstances and life-threatening situations encountered by migrants.

Narratives

The term 'irregular migration' is broad-brush and disguises a more complex reality that can include variation by modes of entry, residence status, employment status and type of employment. This absence of a clear definition could be a cause of frustration, but it can also help us understand the ways in which quests to define contentious issues such as irregular migration are actually central to the political process. Processes of issue definition necessarily involve making claims about – and thus seeking to attach meaning to – a particular problem or issue. On the basis of a particular definition then it is likely, too, that proposals will be made for the best way to resolve it.

It is also the case that choices about terminology and issue definition have implications. Attempts in academic work to theorize and classify can have what Bourdieu (1991) calls a 'theory effect', whereby the knowledge claims that are made are also interventions in the social conditions that are simultaneously object and subject. Put another way, interventions in debates about controversial issues such as irregular migration can have effects and be constitutive of the problems that they seek to address. This is a particularly acute issue in the area of irregular migration where there is fundamental uncertainty about causes, drivers and effects, but a strong desire that 'something should be done'. As Stone (2002:9) notes, 'political reasoning is metaphor-making and category-making, but not just for beauty's sake or for insight's sake. It is strategic portrayal for persuasion's sake, and ultimately for policy's sake.' The ways in which issues are understood, or framed, has important implications for the policy responses that develop. This is particularly the case for irregular migration where there are knowledge gaps and contestation about the nature of the issues.

These insights into political reasoning and claims-making and their effects are relevant for researchers and policymakers alike, particularly with the strong focus on what is often called 'evidence-based policy-making'. In relation to academic research into human trafficking, Kelly (2007:236) argues that publications and research can be 'a claims making process, vying for influence over how the issue is understood and where it is located intellectually, symbolically and materially'. Laczko (2007:14) notes that one effect of this has been a:

tendency to focus on studying the 'victims' [of trafficking with] less attention . . . given to studying the traffickers, the clients, and law enforcement agencies who may be involved in different ways in creating the conditions under which trafficking can flourish.

The policy relevance of issue definition becomes clear when we consider the EU's strong focus on its 'fight against illegal immigration'. This 'fight' represents irregular migration as a threat to EU member states, and irregular migrants as victims of ruthless criminal gangs operating smuggling and trafficking networks. Exploitation is without question an important aspect of the issue, but as Koser (2007) notes, people-smuggling may actually pay and not just for smugglers. A narrative framing of irregular migration as the exploitation of helpless, passive migrants may well not capture the reality of the situation. Koser's work is based on interviews with 50 smuggled migrants to the UK from Pakistan and Afghanistan. He found that the 'ticket' from Pakistan to UK on a direct flight cost between $13,000 and $14,000, and to the EU mainland between $9,000 and $10,000. The USA and Canada were the preferred destinations, with a 'ticket' costing between $17,000 and $20,000. Indirect flights cost between $6,000 and $12,000 depending on the destination country. The cheaper option was a flight to a point outside the EU, then overland travel to the UK ($4,000) or to the mainland EU ($3,000) (Koser 2008:12). This research is based on movement to one state and looked at only 50 migrants, but the figures provide fascinating insight into the modes of transportation and its costs. Migrants and their families may benefit from irregular migration and make a conscious choice to use this migration route (in the absence of alternatives) because of the benefits that they think it may bring. Others who benefit may include the employers of irregular migrants. There are also likely to be costs of irregular migration such as those borne by 'native' lower-skilled workers who may find increased competition in the labour market from irregular migrants and the costs of the enforcement of immigration controls borne by the general population. This helps us understand that the distribution of costs and benefits arising from irregular migration may be complex. It also shows that it is somewhat problematic to think in rather absolute terms of policy success or failure because these are likely to be distributed across the political process with costs and benefits at the stages of talk, decision and action.

The contest to define the issues

Irregular migration is a troubling issue because, as Willen (2007:2) notes, 'it is placed outside the conventional bounds of the state'. It is often portrayed within European countries as a threat, but, given that most irregular migrants come from less-developed countries then it also seems fair to assume that global inequalities, conflict and environmental calamities play a role in stimulating these flows to wealthy EU member states.

If we try to specify what we mean by irregular migration then the first point to note is that it is epiphenomenal. By this is meant that it is closely linked to the definition of regular or legal migration because without regular immigration there would be no such thing as irregular or illegal immigration. It is also nested within more general debates about work and welfare that are 'internal' to EU member states. Irregular migration is not something that 'just happens' to EU member states. Certain types of employment such as agriculture and construction rely on cheap and flexible labour. Migrant workers employed regularly or irregularly can help to meet demand for workers in such sectors. This helps us to understand how and why migration generally – and irregular migration as a form of it – is spatially and sectorally specific: migrants tend to move into particular places and into particular types of employment. This is analogous to the discussion of labour migration in Chapter 4.

To re-emphasize this point about the general resonance of the issues, irregular migration has been seen as 'an enduring manifestation of traditional modernity – the ostensibly rational bureaucratic state regime – continues to play a fundamental role in structuring "illegal" and "irregular" migrants' experiences of space, time, personhood, collectivity, and embodied subjectivity', yet supposedly 'rational bureaucratic processes may be experienced as contingent, unjust, violent or haphazard' (Willen 2007:2,3).

Following Düvell and Jordan (2002:15) we understand irregular migration in broad terms as crossing borders without proper authority, or violating conditions for entering another country. The EU Return Directive (article 36) agreed in June 2008 – analysed more fully later in the chapter – defines illegal stay as the presence, on the territory of a member state, of a TCN who does not fulfil or no longer fulfils the conditions of entry as set out in article 5 of the Schengen Borders Code or other conditions for entry, stay or residence in that member state. If we turn to article 5 of the Schengen

Borders Code (EC Regulation no. 562 of 2006) we can see that these conditions include:

- possession of a valid travel document;
- possession of a valid visa, if required;
- justification of the purpose of stay and means of subsistence for stay, return or onward travel;
- no alert on the SIS;
- no threat to public policy, internal security, public health or the international relations of any member state.

Any person of whatever nationality can cross the internal borders at any point without checks. These EU definitions provide formal clarification of the documents and resources that are needed to validate or legitimate migration, but they actually tell us little about how irregular migrants actually enter, reside, work and live in EU member states.

Terms and their consequences

Choices of terminology have consequences. In much of the public and policy debate reference tends to be made to 'illegal immigration' to describe people in breach of immigration laws. Despite its widespread usage, this could be seen to have pejorative connotations as it criminalizes migrants that may actually have entered legally and are undertaking useful work but have fallen foul of immigration rules (sometimes through no fault of their own).

Other terms sometimes used in these debates can have shortcomings. They may be inaccurate and not capture the phenomena they seek to capture. For instance, reference is sometimes made to 'clandestine immigration', but most irregular migrants have entered an EU state perfectly legally on, for example, a tourist or time-limited work visa, but then overstayed. Focusing on clandestinity gives the misleading impression that this is only a debate about people smuggled across land in trucks and trains or sea borders in little boats.

Similarly, the term 'undocumented migration' may not capture the issues in which we are interested because migrants may well possess various valid documents that may also have been appropriate at one time to secure entry to a particular country, but may not allow continued stay, residence or employment.

Table 6.1   *Detections of illegal entry in 'frontline' EU states 2007*

	Total	Land	Air	Sea
Cyprus	5,883	5,743	140	n/a
France	5,748	690	4,149	909
Greece	73,194	62,475	1,377	9,342
Italy	21,650	n/a	1,195	20,455
Malta	1,702	n/a	n/a	1,702
Spain	27,910	4,080	12,088	11,751
Total EU27	163,903	82,371	20,748	48,696

Source: Adapted from FRONTEX (2007:15).

Our view is that the use of the term 'irregular migration' in the analysis that follows can best help us to capture aspects of the fluidity, dynamism and diversity of this particular type of migration without perjorative connotations of illegality and criminal activity and without giving the impression that these migrants are necessarily clandestine or without documents.

Table 6.1 shows the numbers of reported detections of irregular migrants at land, air and sea ports in 2007. It also shows that 83 per cent of these detections occurred in just 6 of the EU's 27 member states.

Most irregular migrants enter regularly. This means we need to think about entry, residence and employment to get a picture of irregular migration in the EU. In an extensive analysis of irregular migration, four variables were specified that affect a migrants' status (REGINE 2009). We can take each in turn:

• Was entry regular or irregular?
• Is the migrant's residence status regular or irregular?
• Is the status of employment regular or irregular (is the person entitled to work)?
• Is the nature of the employment regular or irregular (are all necessary contributions such as tax and national insurance being made)?

If we think through each of these four variables then we get a sense of the complexity and diversity of the issues:

- An individual may enter regularly and may secure a regular residence status, but then may work irregularly – for example, not pay tax.
- She could enter regularly, overstay, have an irregular residence status and work irregularly.
- She may enter irregularly, have an irregular residence and employment status and undertake employment in the informal economy.
- She may be irregular but able to benefit from a scheme to regularize her status.

Thirteen different forms of irregular migration can be derived from four categories listed above, ranging from an irregular migrant transiting a country to a situation where there are children of irregular migrants who were born in the country of residence.

Another important distinction is between people-smuggling and human-trafficking. At a basic level, smuggling is assumed to be voluntary while trafficking involves coercion. In 2000, the United Nations General Assembly defined trafficking as:

> The recruitment, transportation, transfer, harbouring or receipt of persons, by means of the threat or use of force or other forms of coercion, of abduction, of fraud, of deception, of the abuse of power or of a position of vulnerability, or of the giving of payments or benefits to achieve the consent of a person having control over another person, for the purpose of exploitation.

Even with this definition, there is still a lot of disagreement about what is to be measured or included. Can the distinction between smuggling (voluntary) and trafficking (forced) hold? Could a migrant be smuggled (assumed voluntary) and then coerced in the workplace as their vulnerability is exploited? Are all migrant sex workers trafficked? Do the definitions and administrative practices that have developed in response to the problem of human trafficking prove better able to deal with the exploitation of women and children but find it harder to deal with trafficking and forced labour as it affects men?

Thus far we have seen that irregular migration in its various forms is closely linked to admissions and residence policies, has both a state and supranational resonance, is clearly embedded in broader patterns of global inequality and has induced an EU response that focuses on the 'fight against illegal immigration'. We have suggested that it is important to interrogate the terms that are used because these involve knowledge claims about the causes, drivers, effects and consequences of irregular migration and these claims can play an important role in shaping how we understand the issues and how policies develop in response to these understandings.

The migration industry

Attempts have been made to capture the dynamics of irregular migration and its relationship to state authority that identify a 'migration industry' or 'business'. This allows us to understand that there may be a wide range of public and private actors involved in this business and that while some may be acting legally others may be operating on the margins or in full breach of the law. The business metaphor was developed by Salt and Stein (1997:468), who saw it as a 'system of institutionalized networks with complex profit and loss accounts'. This understanding draws from a long tradition of migration research that emphasizes underlying economic drivers. Herman (2006) says that the migration business is less like a global conglomerate and more like a family business with strong influence from relatives, friends and acquaintances.

There is a strong presence of public authority and private action in the migration business. This returns us to the point about multi-level governance made in Chapter 1. Multilevelness implies the distribution of authority across levels of government, but also means the distribution of authority between public and private actors. It is important to see the role played by private actors operating both legally and illegally in the 'migration industry'. Migrant agency is embedded within networks composed primarily of private actors that encounter the public authority and organizational presence (usually) of states. It is important to identify migrant agency within debates about irregular flows in order to correct notions of migrants as passive victims of forces beyond their control. It is true that some migrants are horribly exploited. Many, however, are making a conscious decision to use irregular routes in order to seek a better life for themselves and their families. Smuggling networks then develop to meet this demand. Heckmann (2007:302) notes how the:

dynamism in the social organisation of smuggling evolves from the relationship between law enforcement and smugglers' networks. The basic pattern is an interaction process: the actions of one actor should provoke a reaction from the other, which in turn leads to another actor.

He then likens this to an arms race ending, he surmises, with 'the exhaustion of one of the competitors'.

The business metaphor captures the fluidity and dynamism of migration to, within and across Europe. It also allows us to see the array of organizational types and forms within this 'industry' and to understand how controls and restrictions can generate evasions and creativity on the part of migrants, smugglers and traffickers as they seek to dodge these controls. In the next section we explore the relationship between the narrative of the 'migration industry' and structures of political authority within the EU. By doing so, we see how much of the debate in the EU has been framed in terms of the threat posed by irregular migration and the consequent need to fight against this threat.

The fight against illegal immigration

In its paper entitled *Policy Priorities in the Fight Against Illegal Immigration* (CEC 2006), the European Commission specified the central elements of the EU response to irregular migration. These were:

- cooperation with non-EU states, particularly in sub-Saharan Africa and the Mediterranean;
- integrated management of external borders and secure travel and identity documents, including the development of e-borders that require carriers such as airlines to communicate data contained in passengers' passports to the immigration authorities;
- fight against human trafficking;
- combating illegal employment connecting with the European Employment Strategy and its attempts to reduce informal work;
- return policy and the Returns Directive;
- improving information exchange; and
- carriers' liability.

As can be seen, the focus of these measures is mainly on border security and the external dimension of migration policy. This external dimension has become an increasingly important component of EU action and is indicative of the 'global approach' to internal security issues and, thus, to the blurring of the distinction between internal and external security and, hence, to the roles of interior and foreign ministries (CEC 2007a, 2008). The EU now seeks to co-opt neighbouring states and regions into its migration and asylum framework. This can occur quite directly through the accession process. Croatia and Macedonia, for example, both have candidate status and are seeking to comply rapidly with the requirements of EU membership – that is, adaptation to the Schengen framework (CEC 2006c, 2009). Things become trickier when the EU seeks to secure compliance with non-member states in front of whom the 'carrot' of eventual membership cannot be dangled. The issue then is how to integrate migration and asylum within a broader negotiating framework that allows the EU's migration and internal security objectives (that could be seen as an unwelcome imposition by non-member states) to be accompanied by deal-sweeteners, such as development aid and economic assistance. This has been evident in relations with Libya, within which Italy has played a key role, and which have led to a warming of the relationship between the EU and the Libyan government, and to Libyan efforts to regulate movement across its land and sea borders.

If we also think about the terms that are used then we see words like 'fight' and 'combat'. This fight is evident in the growing emphasis on the external dimension of policy as part of the EU's 'global approach' to migration management, with attempts to include non-member states such as Morocco in EU control efforts. Morocco is often understood as a 'transit' country, by which is meant that migrants move across Morocco from sub-Saharan Africa en route to the EU. De Haas (2008:14) argues that the term 'transit' is also value-laden. Many migrants in Morocco, for example, are essentially settled, but are labelled as in transit, with Morocco seen as a transit country rather than an immigration country. This understanding is likely to elicit a particular type of policy response, but this 'casts serious doubt on the added value, usefulness and desirability of using "transit" as an analytical category'. The term 'transit migration' is, however, in widespread use, may capture some aspect of migration, and informs understanding of the policy issues and thus helps shape responses.

Measures at EU external frontiers will encounter the dynamics of the migration business described above. Massey and Capoferri (2007:57) argue that controls create evasions that lead to new controls and to further evasions and that the '[t]he imposition of tighter restrictions in the face of a persisting supply of and demand for immigrant labour has led to the emergence of undocumented migration as a universal phenomenon throughout the developed world'.

It is worth looking beyond Europe for comparison. In particular, there are some parallels with the USA, where there are estimates of between 11.5 and 12.3 million irregular migrants. Many of these enter across the US–Mexico border (Wöger 2009:142). In the USA too there has been an intensification of border security and controls, with militarization of the US–Mexico border and many deaths of migrants seeking to enter the USA (Cornelius 2001).

In both the US and EU it is possible to identify what Purcell and Nevins (2005) call 'boundary build-up', by which they mean the ways in which concerns about security have prompted 'a territorial strategy to achieve that security and assuage those concerns'. The result is that freer movement for goods, services and capital does not necessarily lead to free movement for people. Indeed, it may actually lead to greater efforts and expenditure to tighten controls on movement by people, or at least certain people from certain countries falling into the category of 'unwanted migrants'. The comparisons can be taken further if we factor in the 'internal' element and don't simply focus our analysis on external frontiers. In the US there is strong evidence of the sectoral and spatial specificity of irregular migration and the key role that labour markets play in driving both regular and irregular migration (Krissman 2005). This is an 'internal' factor that must be analysed alongside external pressures on EU borders.

The US has also undertaken regularization schemes, most notably following the Immigration Reform and Control Act (1986) that saw 1.6 million undocumented migrants benefit from a general amnesty and a further 1.1 million regularized as 'special agricultural workers' (Wöger 2009:142; see also Tichenor 2002:ch.9). After 2000, however, a number of proposals for further regularization made by the administrations of George W. Bush did not secure legislative approval, which illustrates the contention that can surround regularizations – a point we discuss in the EU context in more detail later in this chapter.

We have seen that a powerful organizing narrative at state and EU level is that of security. This sees irregular migration as a challenge to territorial borders and is grounded in the exploitation of migrants by smugglers and traffickers. The solution according to this narrative is tougher measures focused on reinforcing borders to fight against and combat smugglers and traffickers. The emphasis is then placed on implementing agencies in EU states – with some help from the EU – to develop appropriate controls at external borders. However, as we have seen already, this particular narrative construction of the immigration issue may fail to capture some of the characteristics of the migration industry, such as migrant agency, the complex and diverse forms of networks that facilitate migration and how these networks have a spatial dimension linking countries of origin with countries of destination and have strong roots in the labour market conditions of destination countries. The security narrative is powerful and compelling, but may not capture the dynamism and fluidity of irregular migration.

Political debate

If states continue to use admissions policies to decide who can enter their territory, on what basis and for what duration then it is likely that there will continue to be irregular migration. This then leaves EU states with three policy options:

- *Tolerate irregular migration.* This may be because the costs of enforcement are too high or because irregular migrants perform useful tasks. The other side of toleration may be exploitation of irregular migrants.
- *Regularize irregular migrants by offering them a legal status that no longer conflicts with immigration laws.* Migrants thus become full, contributing members of society, but there is some concern in EU member states that a 'bus stop queue' theory operates – that is, irregular migrants will continue to enter because they know that another regularization will be along soon.
- *Expel irregular migrants,* which is the most draconian, time-consuming and expensive measure, but is consistent with the logic of border controls, admissions policies and 'managed migration'.

EU member states usually employ some combination of these three policy options. They do so in the context of variations between them in relation to: labour market and welfare state organization; administrative capacities; legal and political traditions; timing of exposure to migration flows; and interrelations between irregular migration and other migration flows, such as regular migration and asylum.

By definition, it is not possible to know the number of irregular migrants in EU member states. After all, irregular migrants are hardly likely to advertise their presence because to do so could be to invite deportation. We do know that between 1996 and 2008 an estimated 4.6 million people in the EU 27 had their status regularized. The vast majority of these were in 3 member states: 1.4 million in Italy, 1.3 million in Spain and 1.1 million in Greece (REGINE 2009:32). In other member states, there have been estimates of the numbers of irregular migrants.

The sound of cannons in Italy?

A fascinating example of the ambiguities of policy responses to irregular migration can be seen in Italy between 2001 and 2006. We see a distinction between tough talk at election time, the complexities of intra-coalition decision-making and the difficulties of implementing tough controls in a country that neighbours key sending regions and has a sizeable informal economy.

Italy is a country at Europe's sharp edge. It has been a keen advocate of EU-wide migration and asylum policies that it thinks will help resolve domestic issues. Between 2001 and 2006 Silvio Berlusconi's *Casa delle Libertà* coalition governed Italy. This disparate centre-right alliance included the regional populists *Lega Nord* (LN) led by Umberto Bossi, the 'post-fascist' *Alleanza Nazionale* (AN) led by Gianfranco Fini and a smaller Christian-Democrat party, *Unione dei Democratici Cristiani e di Centro* (UDC) led by Marco Follini.

During the 2001 election campaign, Bossi and Fini were particularly active in proposing a much tougher line against immigration and as portraying the incumbent centre-left government as weak on immigration and on security issues generally. Yet, in power, the centre-right coalition, within which both Bossi and Fini played a prominent role, sought to introduce tougher immigration laws but also presided over the largest ever increase in the legally resident foreign population in Italian history (from around 1.3 million to 2.67 million) and the most generous regularization in European history (650,000 people who could prove 3 months' pension contributions and continuous employment were entitled to have their status regularized).

How could this apparent policy failure happen? It seems to be a perfect representation of the gap between the rhetoric of restriction and the reality of continued immigration; but to understand how and why this gap emerges we need to explore dynamics within the Italian coalition government. We can see how there are some payoffs at the 'talk' stage in terms of votes, but that the dynamics of intra-coalition negotiation allowed for key societal interests, particularly employers and the church, to exert influence. As soon as the centre-right coalition took power and mooted tougher immigration law, there was pressure for regularization of irregular workers – many of them women – in sectors such as domestic work and care (known as *colf* and *badanti*) who were delivering important services to Italian families. The employers' confederation, Confindustria, then argued that it was unfair that irregular workers in some sectors should be favoured when such workers were also present and performing valuable roles elsewhere in the economy.

The resultant situation saw tougher rules on admission, entry and residence in the form of the Bossi-Fini immigration law (2002), but also saw a large-scale regularization. This can be seen as an example of deliberate malintegration, as policymaking was subject to the influence of a range of competing interests with the result that policy was a fudging of priorities – the needs of employers for migrant workers, the needs of centre-right parties to appear tough on immigration and the need for the Church to emphasize the human dimension of migration. To this can be added the need of Prime Minister Berlusconi – successfully realized – to manage and maintain for a 5-year period a disparate and potentially fractious coalition government. Of particular importance was the role of the UDC, which was the key bargaining element within the coalition and brought powerful business and church interests to bear on negotiations. Even as the decision was being made to embark on a large-scale regularization, Bossi maintained his rhetorical commitment to strong anti-immigration measures when he said he wanted to hear '*il rombo dei cannoni*' (the sound of gunfire) (Geddes 2008a).

Gangmasters and irregular migrants in the UK

The UK has a formal opt-out from Title IV of the Amsterdam Treaty covering free movement, migration and asylum and has only partial compliance with the Schengen system. The UK has, however, opted in quite extensively to measures on asylum and border policy (Geddes 2005). We can also see in the UK how regular and irregular migration connects with key labour market dynamics. In 2009, it was estimated that there were between 524,000 and 947,000 irregular migrants in the UK with a midpoint figure of 725,000 (GLA Economics 2009). This updated a 2001 study by the Home Office (Woodbridge 2001) that put the number at between 310,000 and 570,000, with a central estimate of 430,000 people living irregularly in Britain.

The UK government, like those of several other 'northern' EU member states, has opposed any regularization on the basis of the 'bus stop' principle: one regularization is seen to encourage more irregular migration. The UK has, however, enacted regularizations to tidy up the consequences of changes in immigration law or judicial decisions or in relation to specific types of irregular migration, such as domestic workers (Guild and de Bruycker 1996; Anderson 2002). In 2009, the mayor of London, Boris Johnson, announced his support for an earned regularization, but this was not the policy of his own Conservative Party or the then Labour government. A particularly radical change in the UK was the redefinition of the issue as a result of EU enlargement. This led to a *de facto* regularization for nationals of the new member states who were living in the UK prior to their country joining the EU in May 2004 or January 2008.

If we look more closely at the UK case, we see the importance of spatial and sectoral factors – that is, migrants move into particular places and particular types of economic activity. They also encounter specific forms of labour market organization. This point was demonstrated in the most tragic circumstances by the death in February 2004 of 23 people from China who were employed as cockle-pickers in Morecambe Bay on the north-west coast of England. These workers may well have had an irregular entry and residence status. They were also employed by a 'gangmaster' (a temporary labour provider) who furnished them with neither adequate protection nor equipment for the dangerous work that were doing. The gangmaster in question, Lin Liang Ren, was reported to have connections with Chinese people-smuggling 'snakehead' gangs and was sentenced to 14 years imprisonment for manslaughter in 2006.

In response to the Morecambe Bay tragedy the UK government set up the Gangmasters Licensing Authority (GLA) to operate a licensing scheme for labour providers in agriculture, food processing, forestry and shellfish. All these sectors are difficult to regulate, have a large presence of migrant workers from within and outside the EU, and exhibit the importance of looking at the ways in which labour market intermediaries play a key role linking migrants with employment. In fact, the role played by agencies is central to the understanding of labour recruitment and deployment in the UK. Of particular importance in the UK is the structure of modern retailing and the power of large supermarkets; these latter have major effects on sectors such as agriculture and food processing, with downwards pressure on price leading to efforts to reduce costs by suppliers and increased demand for flexible, just-in-time production. Migrants employed both regularly and irregularly have been used to meet the demand for flexible workers. This dimension of labour migration cannot be understood as an 'external' issue, as a matter of border controls and security. Rather, it is closely related to the organizational borders and boundaries of work and welfare in the UK and in other EU member states (Geddes *et al.* 2007).

The EU and the issue of return

There has been the usual plethora of EU policy documents, conferences and reports, but, as we have also seen, these have tended to coalesce around the issue of border security, closer relations with non-EU states to secure implementation, and the development of a common approach to 'return' – that is, migrants with an irregular status being sent back to their countries of origin. The Commission's specification of policy priorities in the 'fight against illegal immigration' emphasized engagement with Europe's neighbours, such as ex-Yugoslavian states. The attainment of objectives does depend on the resources that are made available and the kinds of leverage the EU can exert. The EU has worked through various programmes such as MEDA for Mediterranean countries, TACIS for Soviet-Union successor states, and CARDS and SAP for the Western Balkans. EU budget resources devoted to the creation of an area of freedom, security and justice rose from €29.5 million in 1998 to €56 million in 2003, with much of this devoted to the asylum issue. In addition, between 2001 and 2004, a specific budget line (B667) devoted €42.5 million to cooperation with non-EU member states. Between 2004 and 2008, a further €250 million was channelled through the AENEAS Programme to provide financial and technical assistance to non-EU member states. The 5-year budget framework to take the EU from 2008 to 2013 allocated €4020 million to 'Solidarity and Management of External Migration Flows', including €1820 million to external borders, €676 million to a return fund, €699 million to the European Refugee Fund and €825 million to an Integration Fund (Geddes 2008:181–2). We can see that more than half of this financial allocation was dedicated to irregular migration and asylum in the form of border security and return measures.

Box 6.1   The EU's Return Directive

The 'Return' Directive is important because it was the first time the co-decision procedure was used and the EP participated on an equal footing in decision-making with the Council on migration and asylum issues.

The Return Directive is based on the Hague programme's 5-year plan for development of immigration and asylum within the EU's 'area of freedom, justice and security'. The final Directive went through 3 years of negotiations following the original Commission proposals and was finally adopted by the European Parliament on 18 June 2008. The EP passed over 70 amendments via the co-decision procedure.

The objective is to standardize the procedures regulating the expulsion of irregular immigrants. The Directive stipulates that EU member states cannot adopt harsher rules than the ones laid out in the Directive, but can retain more liberal rules or adopt more-permissive rules new.

Key aspects
Once a decision is taken to deport an individual who cannot claim asylum or refugee status, then a voluntary departure period (7–30 days) follows.

➡

In terms of formal competence, we can see the development of supranational governance involving enhanced cooperation, but also more substantive measures. Of particular significance is the Return Directive (2008), which was the first piece of legislation in this policy area to be decided using the 'co-decision' procedure. Co-decision is not just some arcane aspect of EU procedure. It means that the EP now has a much stronger say in decision-making on some immigration and asylum issues that were previously the domain of the member states. Box 6.1 outlines the key features of the Returns Directive.

There was a strong reaction from outside the EU to the proposed measures. Venezuelan President Hugo Chavez called the rules 'shameful' while Brazilian President Lula da Silva said that 'the cold winds of xenophobia are once again blowing from Europe'. Ecuadorean President Rafael Correa said that trade talks between

---

If the deportee does not leave, national authorities will issue a removal order, which can include an entry ban of up to 5 years.

If judicial authority in a member state has serious grounds to believe that the deportee might go into hiding, the person can be put into custody.

Article 15 of the Directive sets a maximum period of custody at 6 months, with a possible 12-month extension (adding up to a total of 18 months).

Families and children can be held in custody only as a last resort and for up to 6 months. Unaccompanied minors will only be repatriated if they can be returned to their families or to 'adequate reception facilities'.

The Directive states that legal aid will also be provided to immigrants without resources and a return fund was set up by the Commission with €676 million for the period 2008–13 which could be used to cover the costs of legal aid.

Member states are obliged to be consistent with international laws that forbid the return of people to unsafe countries where they are at risk of persecution (the *non-refoulement* principle); procedural safeguards for asylum-seekers are left unaffected. The Council of Ministers and the European Parliament drafted a list of 'unsafe' countries.

the EU and the Andean Community could be in jeopardy because, as he put it: 'What do we have to talk about with a union of countries that criminalises immigrants? It will be very hard to talk business and ignore human rights.'

This international reaction is interesting because it shows the importance of issue linkages. Within the EU we see complex negotiations between member states in the Council with the Commission and EP. We see too the framing of issues in a way that emphasizes member states' concerns about border security. This does leave open the issue of how the EU can secure its objectives in non-member states. It may well be the case that countries with a membership perspective such as Croatia and Macedonia may seek to do the EU's bidding because they can link these measures to the broader benefits of membership. What incentives are there for countries that will not become EU member states? President Correa of Ecuador hit the nail on the head when he made a basic issue linkage between measures on migration and the trade issue. If, for example, the range of issues to be discussed were to be broadened to include trade, aid and development, as well as EU concerns about irregular migrants and their return, then would there perhaps be more chance of successful realization of the external aspect of the EU's policy on irregular migration?

There is also recognition within the EU that a focus on external borders may not be sufficient. In 2007, the European Commission proposed a Directive that would introduce sanctions for employers of irregular migrants (Carrera and Guild 2007). Were it agreed by the Council then the Sanctions Directive would have three main elements:

- Employers would be subject to a number of new administrative obligations that would need to be fulfilled before recruiting any TCNs.
- Non-compliance would lead to punitive measures, financial sanctions and criminal penalties with harmonized procedures.
- Each member state would be required to inspect the employee records in 10 per cent of its registered companies.

Carrera and Guild (2007) note the potential difficulty of using immigration rules to tackle exploitation in the workplace. Sciortino (1999) in an earlier analysis of policy implementation noted that measures targeted at irregular migrants may be preferred because irregular migrants cannot vote, whereas a regime of tough labour market inspection may be more costly in the sense that it hits employers who may resent becoming the agents of the immigration control authorities, do have the right to vote and may be well-organized in business federations and the like.

The Return and proposed Sanctions Directive raised implementation issues, which we now move on to explore. This is in the context of our analysis of political debate, which has shown the complex domestic, European and international factors that impinge on the debate about irregular migration. We have seen that the costs and benefits of irregular migration are quite widely distributed and that it may not be helpful to analyse this complex form of migration in terms of absolute notions of success or failure.

Administrative practice and implementation

Irregular migration conforms closely with the characteristics of an 'institutional sector', as discussed in Chapter 2. We see a strong rhetorical commitment to controls but a highly complex and, at times, contradictory politics of irregular migration. Moreover, the nature of the phenomena associated with irregular migration introduces a fundamental epistemological uncertainty into the debate given the lack of clarity about numbers and about underlying dynamics. We also see that there is divergence among EU member states about the appropriate policy tool to deal with irregular migration. In southern Europe there have been a number of regularizations while northern European immigration countries may have undertaken smaller-scale regularizations, but do not favour the large-scale amnesties that have occurred in countries such as Greece, Italy and Spain.

There are some pressures for convergence in administrative practice and implementation. This could arise because EU member states face similar pressures and respond in similar ways to them (horizontal convergence), although we do see differences about the utility and effectiveness of regularizations. It could also be the case that the EU now intervenes more directly in this policy area and thus creates vertical convergence pressure. Or it may be that both horizontal and vertical pressures coincide – that is, member states face similar issues and do so in the context of European integration. We could also suppose that these pressures may be unevenly distributed across the EU with more emphasis on adaptation in newer member states and candidate countries.

Research has debunked the idea that irregular migration is driven by tightly controlled international criminal organizations running smuggling and trafficking operations into the EU. Pastore *et al.* (2006) analysed Italian court files to challenge the idea of 'hierarchically integrated, centralized, sophisticated, worldwide active, criminal cartels' controlling the smuggling and trafficking of migrants. In Italy they show that entry tended to be legal (with a visa) rather than clandestine (for example, on a boat). They also show that irregular migrants tended to be east-European rather than African. They then go on to argue that: 'the idea of a few sophisticated cartels controlling the world's immigration flows is good for screenplays. However it is radically at odds with theoretical wisdom and empirical evidence' (Pastore *et al.* 2006:97). Carling (2007:22) similarly identifies use of the term 'Moroccan mafias' to describe smuggling into Spain, but shows that the migration business is much more diverse, ranging from 'internationally organised criminal cartels to individual fishermen-turned-smugglers' and argues that: 'The bulk of smuggling is usually not organised by tight-knit criminal organisations, however, but in fluid networks of individuals.'

It is possible to identify five factors that could influence the level and extent of convergence between laws and practices on irregular migration in EU member states (REGINE 2009:44). These are:

- Labour market structures and size of the informal economy. The greater the extent of informality then the larger can be the space for insertion of irregular migrants into this type of economic activity.
- The respective influence of 'sanctity of the law' versus policy pragmatism.
- The timing of immigration – that is, whether the receiving state is a new country of immigration and the capacity of the administrative infrastructure to deal with the issues.
- Interaction with asylum policy and the position of failed asylum applicants, as rejected asylum-seekers may remain on the territory of a state and become irregular migrants.
- The size of admissions channels – that is, whether admissions policy chokes off some of the demand for irregular migration.

Across these five variables we see variation between EU member states that can help us understand the horizontal, comparative dynamics of the politics of irregular migration across Europe and the scope for and limits upon the development of vertical structures of policymaking at EU level.

Much of the implementation effort that has developed within the EU in response to irregular migration has been focused on external borders, on reinforcing capacity and on cooperating with non-EU states, such as Morocco and more recently Libya. Morocco also has strong bilateral ties on the issue with Spain, as Libya does with Italy. This provides a point of similarity with USA border controls and relations with Mexico, as well as economic cooperation through the North American Free Trade Agreement (NAFTA). There are, however, also important differences. Heckmann (2007:289) points out a key difference between the EU and the USA which relates to the density of internal controls. In Europe there tend to be more stringent internal controls, including the use of ID cards and of population registration.

While we do see a growing EU role, we should note that the EU is not responsible for implementation. Implementation is a matter for member states and their administrative authorities. The EU does, however, seek to coordinate these responses both through 'hard law' such as the Return Directive and also through FRONTEX (see Box 6.2), which, as Neal (2009) demonstrates, plays a key role in the development of a risk-oriented approach to the governance of migration centred on the identification of future challenges.

FRONTEX seeks to reinforce existing developments in member states. Greece, Italy and Spain have been keen to argue that this is a common European issue that requires a common European response. Spain has invested heavily in an Integrated System of External Vigilance (SIVE) along the coastline of the Canary islands of Fuerteventura and Lanzarote and its Andalucian coastline. Carling (2007) argues that SIVE led to diversion and landings in Granada or Almería and that it cost €150m between 1999 and 2004, or around €1800 for every migrant intercepted.

Measures to exert tougher external frontier controls have also been accompanied by regularizations or amnesties for irregular migrants, although there are divisions between EU member states on their utility. Some see them as pragmatic recognition of forms of migration that are unlikely to be reversed and that usher irregular migrants from the twilight world of irregularity, where they

Box 6.2   The role of FRONTEX

Set up in 2005 by Regulation 2007 of 2004, by 2008 the body had about 130 personnel and a budget of €70m.

According to its 2007 annual report, 'FRONTEX's principal activity is to strengthen border security by ensuring the coordination of the Member States' activities in the implementation of Community measures relating to the management of the external borders.'

It specifies 6 roles:

- Carrying out risk analysis.
- Coordinating operational cooperation on external border management.
- Offering training to national border guards,
- Disseminating research relevant to border control and surveillance.
- Technical and operational assistance to member states.
- Supporting joint return operations.

FRONTEX works with other relevant agencies such as EUROPOL, CEPOL and customs authorities.

Regulation no. 863 of 2007 established rapid border intervention teams (RABITs) composed of national border guards having the right to act on the territory of other member states.

FRONTEX has finalized a Common Core Curriculum offering basic training content for border guards. This involved collaboration with experts from more than twenty countries and international organizations such as UNHCR and IOM to set common principles in training for border guard officers in the EU.

may be open to exploitation, to the 'regularized' world of rights and duties. Others see regularizations as giving a green light to new migrants and thus serving as a 'pull' factor. Both views are, in a sense, correct because regularization address the consequences and not the causes of migration.

An overview of policies in EU member states suggests the following distinction (REGINE 2009:43):

- The UK and France have been reluctant regularizers. France has had exceptional regularizations. The UK used regularizations to clear up the consequence of new immigration law in 1971, with the effect that between 1974 and 1978, 1809 mainly Pakistani people had their status regularized after falling foul of tougher new immigration rules. Other special schemes have been developed, targeted at, for example, domestic workers (Anderson 2002).

- Germany and Austria are ideological opponents of regularization.
- There are also a group of non-regularizing new member states that include Bulgaria, Cyprus, Czech Republic, Latvia, Malta, Romania and Slovenia.
- There are the countries such as Greece, Italy and Spain that have used regularization as a key part of their response to irregular migration, which we now analyse.

Regularization programmes

A regularization gives a legal status to TCNs who are not citizens of the state in which they reside or of another EU member state, who are otherwise in breach of national immigration rules in their current country of residence. Greece, Italy and Spain are the 'big three' regularizing EU states. Practices do, however vary.

Implementation and its dilemmas in practice

Any attempt to regularize a large irregular population will encounter difficulties, given the scale of the task and the need to establish criteria as the basis for which regularization can occur. This can place significant pressure on administrative systems in those countries that do undertake regularizations. Baldwin-Edwards (2009) provides an overview of the implementation of the first Greek regularization in 1997. By 1994 there were estimates of between 500,000 and 600,000 irregular migrants in Greece. The first regularization occurred in 1997. Under this scheme, irregular migrants were entitled to apply for a Provisional Residence (White) Card and a Temporary Residence (Green) Card. These schemes were meant to be 2 steps in a single process, but in fact operated independently of each other. In total, 371,641 people applied for the White Card, of which 65 per cent were Albanian. A total of 219,000 White Cards were issued according to the Greek Interior Ministry. There were major implementation problems. These

Table 6.2   **Regularizations in Greece, Spain and Italy 1982–2007**

Greece	1997	1998	2001	2005	2007	
Applicants	371,941	282,000	367,504	no data	no data	
Accepted	no data	219,000	341,278	185,800	20,000	
Italy	1982	1986–88	1990	1995–6	1998	2002
Applicants	5000	113,349	234,841	258,761	250,747	702,156
Accepted	5000	105,000	222,000	246,000	217.000	650,000
Spain	1985	1991	1996	2000	2001	2005
Applicants	38,181	130,406	17,676	245,598	351,269	691,655
Accepted	34,832	109,135	21,382	199,296	232,674	578,375

Sources: Data from Baldwin-Edwards (2009:68); Ruspini (2009:81); Arango and Finotelli (2009:87).

included lack of communication between ministries (Justice, Health and Public Order) and practical administrative problems such as a lack of information and the failure to translate into migrants' own languages. Also, power was given to the local commissions to scrutinize applications on a case-by-case basis, and this could lead to a Janus-faced approach at local level as seasonal needs for migrant workers in sectors such as agriculture were balanced with anti-immigration sentiment. As a result there were significant local variations in approach.

As the Greek case demonstrates, it is important to bear in mind administrative structures and processes in EU member states when exploring debates about implementation. It can be difficult for any bureaucratic organization to secure its objectives, given the many factors that can intervene between the making of a decision and its implementation on the ground by 'street-level bureaucrats'. Greece may well be a particularly intense or difficult case given the relatively large number of irregular migrants on its territory and the ways in which interests played out at national and local level, but it can help to illustrate the general problem of implementation within the EU across national boundaries.

Conclusions

This chapter has analysed the EU politics of irregular migration. We see that there is a significant divergence between tough talk and continued high levels of irregular migration. We saw too that this can be linked to the tensions, ambiguities and contradictions within the decision-making process. We saw that it can be difficult to translate talk into decision and then into action, given the ways in which irregular migration is not simply an external issue linked to border controls, but also has an important 'internal' dimension linked to the organization of work and welfare in EU member states. The EU now plays a much more significant role in this area through laws, funding and technical cooperation. FRONTEX has also been established to facilitate attainment of EU objectives. Our analysis suggests that irregular migration demonstrates characteristics of an institutional sector with dislocation between talk and action. Strong rhetorical commitments to 'control', can pay off for political actors in, for example, electoral campaigns, as was the case in Italy.

A key driver of policy development has been the perception that these are Europe-wide issues that require an EU response and that the member states most exposed to irregular flows require some help and support from other EU member states. This has also prompted efforts to include non-EU member states within the EU's 'Global Approach' to migration management.

Chapter 7

Asylum

In April 1999, when the refugee crisis in Kosovo was reaching a head, EU governments met in Luxembourg to discuss how they would handle a potential mass influx of Kosovar refugees into the EU. The idea was to learn from previous experience during the conflicts in the former Yugoslavia (1991–5), when coordination between states had been haphazard and some countries, particularly Germany, ended up receiving far more refugees than others. This time, the aim was to establish some sort of 'burden-sharing' arrangement, whereby countries would pledge to admit and protect refugees in a more equitable fashion. Yet the EU was unable to impose any binding arrangement for distributing refugees, and all pledges were made on a strictly voluntary basis. There was no real or effective EU response. In the end, Germany ended up absorbing around 28 per cent of all those evacuated from the region to EU countries, France taking 12 per cent, Italy 11 per cent, Austria 9.6 per cent and the UK 8.2 per cent (van Selm 2002).

This episode captures well some of the key challenges and limitations of EU cooperation on asylum and refugee policy. Member countries often face quite similar problems and recognize the usefulness of coordinating their responses. Those countries admitting a larger number of refugees are especially keen to cooperate, to ensure an equitable balance of cost between different countries. There is by now a strong expectation that the EU will pursue common, coordinated approaches to dealing with refugee problems. There have also been steps taken to try to address some of these weaknesses or deficiencies. This has meant attempting to increase and improve the level and extent of EU action. Thus we can point to 'progress' made in developing EU legislation, but the question that remains open is whether this progress is progressive, or reactionary and regressive. What we can note immediately is that the Amsterdam, Nice and Lisbon treaties have provided a base for significant development of asylum policy. The Stockholm Programme – setting the agenda for EU migration and asylum policy between 2010 and 2014 – aims to develop a common

150

European asylum system, with a target date of 2012 for its enactment.

This chapter accounts for development of this EU framework as well as the impediments that have been faced. Much of the controversy has been linked to the sharing of responsibility for refugees, or burden-sharing as it is also known. The Stockholm Programme makes reference to the development of redistribution of refugees between member states, albeit in a voluntary system. We begin by unpacking some of the key features of EU cooperation on asylum, and critically reviewing prevalent approaches to explaining this cooperation. In contrast to most accounts, we challenge the idea that the EU has acted as a 'fortress' against asylum, or that European countries have favoured EU cooperation as a means of smuggling in more restrictive approaches. To the contrary, while the EU has contributed to the rolling out of restrictive approaches in some areas, in many instances it has influenced countries to adopt more liberal approaches. Many of the more restrictive and controversial approaches have been adopted by individual states, sometimes with Commission disapproval. Moreover, even when states in the EU 'talk tough' about asylum, there are numerous ways in which they can and have decoupled restrictive rhetoric from more lenient practice.

EU cooperation on asylum: key themes

Building on the framework developed since the Amsterdam Treaty and the Tampere and Hague Agreements, both the Lisbon Treaty and the Stockholm Programme express the intention to create a common EU-wide asylum system with a single procedure, a uniform international protection status, mutual recognition of decisions and a European Asylum Support Office. We can call this the 'post-Amsterdam framework'; it has four main elements:

- The so-called Dublin II Regulation, which specified a one-stop EU asylum procedure that means that a claim must be made in the first EU member states through which an applicant passes.
- The Reception Conditions Directive, which introduced minimum standards for reception, including detention.
- The Asylum Procedures Directive, which specifies minimum standards in procedures governing the processing of claims made by asylum-seekers.

- The Qualifications Directive, which seeks minimum standards on procedures in member states for granting or withdrawing refugee status.

An aspect of all these provisions that has been strongly criticized is the emphasis on minimum standards, which has been seen as a levelling-down of provision and lowest-common-denominator policy-making, which reduces standards rather than improving them. Moreover, these provisions cannot be detached from the EU's 'fight against illegal immigration', which aims at tougher border controls that have the effect of making it harder for would-be asylum-seekers to enter the territory of a member state. In turn, this is then linked to the external dimension of EU policy, which seeks to build cooperation with third countries, such as Libya, to reduce migration flows across these countries. The purpose of the remainder of this chapter is to explain how we got from 'there' to 'here' – that is, how, why, when and with what effects did cooperation and integration on asylum develop.

The rise of asylum as a major political issue in many west European countries largely coincided with the emergence of EU JHA cooperation after 1993. Table 7.1 shows the numbers of asylum applicants in EU member states between 1996 and 2007. We can see the differential nature of the asylum issue, with countries such as Germany and the UK having large absolute numbers of asylum-seekers while 'newer' immigration countries in southern Europe have much smaller numbers of asylum-seekers (but relatively large numbers of irregular migrants, as discussed in the previous chapter).

Table 7.1 shows that asylum is a pan-EU issue, but there is an uneven distribution of asylum-seekers with particular concentrations in Belgium France, Germany, Sweden and the UK, with significant growth in Greece and Italy.

We can now look at the development of legislative responses. From the 1980s onwards, a number of European countries were beginning to change asylum rules in response to rising numbers of applications. The early 1990s also saw concerted efforts to reform asylum systems. Similarly, EU cooperation on immigration and asylum saw some tentative first steps in the second half of the 1980s, but was given more clout by the Maastricht Treaty of 1992, which established a legal basis for cooperation in JHA. Given this overlap in timing, it is not surprising that there was a high degree of mutual influence in the formulation of national and EU

Table 7.1   *Asylum-seekers in EU member states, 1996-2007*

	1996	1997	1998	1999	2000	2001	2002	2003	2004	2005	2006	2007
Austria	6,990	6,720	13,805	20,130	18,285	30,125	39,355	32,360	24,635	22,460	13,350	11,920
Belgium	12,435	11,790	21,965	35,780	42,690	24,505	18,800	13,585	12,400	12,575	8,870	11,575
Bulgaria		370	835	1,350	1,755	2,430	2,890	1,320	985	700	500	815
Cyprus			225	790	650	1,620	950	4,405	9,675	7,715	4,540	6,780
Czech Republic		2,110	4,085	7,355	8,790	18,095	8,485	11,400	5,300	3,590	2,730	1,585
Denmark	5,895	5,100	5,700	6,530	10,345	12,510	5,945	4,390	3,235	2,280	1,960	2,225
Estonia		0	25	25	5	10	10	15	10	5	5	15
Finland	710	970	1,270	3,105	3,170	1,650	3,445	3,090	3,575	3,595	2,275	1,405
France	17,405	21,415	22,375	30,905	38,745	47,290	51,085	59,770	58,545	49,735	30,750	29,160
Germany	117,335	104,355	98,645	94,775	78,565	88,285	71,125	50,565	35,605	28,915	21,030	19,165
Greece	1,640	4,375	2,950	1,530	3,085	5,500	5,665	8,180	4,470	9,050	12,265	25,115
Hungary	1,260		7,120	11,500	7,800	9,555	6,410	2,400	1,600	1,610	2,115	3,420
Ireland	1,180	3,880	4,625	7,725	10,940	10,325	11,635	7,485	4,265	4,305	4,240	3,935
Italy	680	1,890	13,100	18,450	15,195	17,400	16,015	13,705	9,630	9,345	10,350	14,055
Latvia			35	20	5	15	25	5	5	20	10	35
Lithuania		240	160	145	305	425	365	395	165	100	145	125
Luxembourg	265	435	1,710	2,930	625	685	1,040	1,550	1,575	800	525	425
Malta		70	160	255	160	155	350	455	995	1,165	1,270	1,380
Netherlands	22,855	34,445	45,215	39,725	43,895	32,580	18,665	13,400	9,780	12,345	14,465	7,100
Poland	600	3,580	3,425	3,060	4,660	4,480	5,170	6,810	7,925	5,240	4,225	7,205
Portugal	270	250	355	305	225	235	245	115	115	115	130	225
Romania	585	1,425	1,235	1,665	1,365	2,280	1,000	885	545	485	380	660
Slovakia	415	645	505	1,320	1,555	8,150	9,745	10,300	11,395	3,550	2,850	2,640
Slovenia	35	70	335	745	9245	1,510	650	1,050	1,090	1,550	380	660
Spain	4,730	4,975	4,935	8,405	7,925	9,490	6,310	5,765	5,365	5,050	5,295	7,195
Sweden	5,775	9,680	12,840	11,220	16,285	23,500	33,015	31,355	23,160	17,530	24,320	36,205
UK	29,640	32,500	46,015	71,160	80,315	71,365	103,080	60,045	40,625	30,840	28,320	27,905
EU 27			313,645	380,450	406,585	424,180	421,470	34,800	276,675	234,675	197,410	222,635

Source: Data from Eurostat.

approaches to asylum. The EU asylum policies that emerged in the 1990s were very much shaped by the approaches being favoured by major countries of asylum such as Germany, the Netherlands and the UK; while the resulting EU policies significantly influenced the (often nascent) asylum policies of other EU states. Perhaps more so than in any other area of migration policy, then, the EU has been and remains at the heart of evolving national approaches. This can happen through the 'twinning' that occurs during the accession process, as potential member states receive advice from officials in existing member states. A range of international organizations, such as the UNHCR, the International Organization for Migration (IOM) and the International Centre for Migration Policy Development (ICMPD), are also active in providing advice to new and potential member states on migration policy.

Policy aims

Approaches to asylum that emerged in the early 1990s – at both national and EU level – were based on two core assumptions and goals:

- The perception that many asylum-seekers were abusing generous European systems, and that policies and procedures should therefore be tightened to screen out or deter 'non-genuine' applicants. This was to be achieved through impeding entry to EU countries, streamlining application procedures, tightening some of the criteria for recognition as a refugee, and reducing social support for asylum-seekers.
- Restrictive measures should be adopted across EU states and beyond. The EU and its neighbours should cooperate to ensure there was a level playing-field across the EU, and no easy route to access EU territory. Countries on Europe's borders were also expected to play their part in controlling movement into the EU. Both the impulse towards harmonization of asylum systems and the so-called 'external dimension' of cooperation in JHA are key components of EU policy (Guild 1999; Lavenex 1999; Noll 2000; Byrne *et al.* 2002; van Selm 2002; Noll 2003; Hailbronner 2004).

Given the close links between EU and national policies, it is mistaken to conceive of the EU as an especially malignant force in asylum policy. EU cooperation does provide a forum for countries to exchange ideas and 'good practice', allowing for some degree of norm diffusion. The EU also had some useful instruments at its disposal to export its preferred approaches to non-EU countries, in the form of the accession process and various external relations tools. In this sense, the restrictive paradigm that crystallized in the 1990s was perhaps more consistently and widely applied in and beyond Europe than might have been the case had the EU had no competence in this area. Moreover, as some scholars have argued, EU cooperation may have provided a venue for policymaking that in some cases allowed states to adopt more restrictive approaches, evading the judicial and parliamentary scrutiny of domestic policymaking venues (Guiraudon 2000a).

However, a key argument of this chapter is that the notion that EU states use cooperation as an excuse for greater restriction has been overstated. We challenge this account in four ways:

- We question the assumption that the EU has produced measures that are more restrictive than national approaches would otherwise have been. Common approaches have in many cases worked the other way, with the EU setting standards on asylum that have raised the level of protection or assistance in some member states. Indeed, some EU countries have used harmonization as a way of justifying more liberal approaches.

- We challenge the claim that states have used the EU as a secretive venue for adopting more stringent measures. On the contrary, most governments have gained political mileage precisely from demonstrating their willingness to introduce measures to curb asylum numbers. Cooperating at the EU level is often a way of sending a clear signal to their electorates that national governments are getting tough on asylum through international cooperation. As such, EU cooperation can be another opportunity to 'talk tough', rather than a covert way of bringing in more restrictive measures.

- We suggest that in many instances the EU is depicted as the source of domestic control problems – a convenient scapegoat for national governments' inability to meet public expectations.

- We argue that the picture is more nuanced, as member states can play a two-level game using domestic constraints as a pretext for uploading their preferences at EU level, and invoking EU constraints to justify domestic reforms.

Meanwhile, in national discourse, the EU may be depicted as the 'good cop' or the 'bad cop', depending on the dynamics of national political debates on asylum.

A second major issue we address in this chapter is that of the different institutional interests at stake in EU asylum policy. One reason why EU asylum policy lends itself to good-cop–bad-cop labels is that there are different institutions involved in shaping policy, with conflicting interests. The Commission, the EP, the Council of Ministers, the Council presidencies and national interior ministries often have quite different agendas in this area of policy. The ECJ role is also likely to grow post-Lisbon.

The outcome of policy deliberations will vary considerably, depending on the institutional venue or the constellation of interests around a given issue. For this reason, there is often what appears to be a pendulum movement between bold, expansive pledges to develop common approaches, followed by disappointingly slow progress in agreeing on the details of legislation. This can create the impression that EU asylum policy is inconsistent, fluctuating between quite enlightened and forward-looking approaches on one hand, and more niggardly and piecemeal measures on the other. We suggest that this may be seen as an example of quite useful 'malintegration' or fudging of policy goals and measures, with these different signals offering something to please each of the different actors involved.

The third main issue we deal with is the question of implementation. Unlike in other areas of immigration policy, states appear to have ample means at their disposal to chart the implementation of asylum policies and monitor their impact. Statistics on asylum applications, decisions and removals are regularly gathered and tend to be fairly reliable (at least in comparison with many other types of migration statistics). However, there are many ways that state and non-state actors have found to decouple discourse from practice, ensuring that the latter is often more tolerant than the former. One of these is the broadening of categories of protection or 'leave to remain', meaning that many more asylum-seekers get to stay than are granted asylum. Public services and NGOs also play a huge role in cushioning asylum-seekers from the worst consequences of restrictive measures, often with the tacit agreement – or at least acquiescence – of governments. Again, this is not a deviation from state interests, but a way of reconciling conflicting claims. States want to demonstrate they are acting to reduce asylum numbers, but they are also committed to support people facing destitution, and may also be concerned about the impact of highly discriminatory policies on ethnic relations. They often have to juggle conflicting interests and narratives about asylum-seekers, and about what sorts of duties countries of asylum owe to those seeking protection.

Narratives

Asylum is an area rife with conflicting claims about the causes and scale of asylum-seeking, the legitimacy of asylum claims and the impact of policy responses on asylum-seekers. Perhaps more than in any other area of migration policy, much is at stake in how one views the background circumstances and motives of those seeking protection: Are asylum-seekers victims of persecution seeking refuge in European countries? Are they economic migrants motivated by the desire to improve their standard of living? Not surprisingly, policy, NGO and academic narratives on these questions tend to be sharply divided.

Since the late 1970s when asylum first emerged as a real issue for European countries, policy narratives often emphasized supposed abuse of asylum and welfare systems. Indeed, the first country to experience a significant rise in asylum applications, West Germany, quite quickly developed a narrative about *schein* (bogus) asylum-seekers. One reason for this was the increased proportion of asylum-seekers from countries that had traditionally been a source of labour migration, rather than associated with persecution. For example, of the roughly 108,000 asylum-seekers applying for protection in West Germany in 1980, over half were from Turkey. This perception of abuse was heightened by legislation in 1983, which forbade asylum-seekers from accessing employment, serving to underpin perceptions that asylum-seekers were a burden on West Germany's generous welfare system. When the asylum question surfaced in other west European countries from the mid to late 1980s, similar ideas about abuse dominated political debate. The notion that asylum-seekers were somehow 'non-genuine' and thus not deserving of assistance and protection helped legitimize the range of restrictions introduced to asylum systems. In the first instance, these restrictions centred on new visa requirements, as well as reductions in the level of welfare assistance or employment rights. By justifying these restrictions as efforts to stop supposedly abusive behaviour, governments hoped to ward off accusations of discrimination or infringement of human rights.

Perhaps just as importantly, by narrating the problem as one of 'abuse', governments could demonstrate their capacity to clamp down. If the source of the problem was that asylum-seekers stood to benefit from generous welfare systems, employment opportunities and legal rights, then this was a domain in which states could take action, through removing the opportunities and incentives for asylum-seekers to access these perceived benefits (Bommes and Geddes 2000). Governments had effectively isolated the one aspect of the phenomenon that was open to manipulation through domestic policy reforms. In effect, the narrative about supposedly bogus and abusive asylum-seekers can be seen as a case of constructing a policy problem to match a preferred solution and can be understood as a top-down process. So rather than view the policy cycle in terms of problem definition (asylum abuse) followed by proposed solution (tighten asylum systems), it may be more pertinent to see the cycle as reversed: feasible solutions (restricted access to welfare benefits) encouraged the construction of the problem in terms of abuse. There is, however, little empirical evidence to suggest that asylum-seekers are motivated in their choice of destination by their deep knowledge of comparative European social security systems and benefits levels (Koser and Pinkerton 2002).

Not all European countries developed this sort of discourse about asylum abuse. Countries with less-developed asylum systems and lower numbers of applicants often focused attention more on problems of controlling irregular migration and labour than on the modalities of asylum procedures and assistance. In Italy, for example, asylum numbers have been low, and comprehensive protection for refugees was introduced only in 1990, with the Martelli Law. Provisions for welfare assistance remain patchy and refugees may prefer to live and work as irregular migrants (and await a regularization), rather than registering as asylum applications. Given the absence of any real tradition of protection, centre-right parties have felt little compunction to defend their harsh policies against criticisms from more human-rights-oriented left-wing parties, church groups and NGOs. Greece has also received only very low numbers, usually well under 10,000 per year. The issue has remained very low-profile, with little domestic pressure on the government to introduce reform (Sitaropoulous 2000). Until the late 1990s, Greece lacked legislation on key aspects of asylum reception and protection, and still has arguably the least-developed welfare support for asylum-seekers of the original EU-15 countries – that is, prior to the 2004 and 2007 enlargements (Schuster 2000).

Other 'new' immigration countries, such as the 'A8' central and eastern European countries that joined the EU in 2004, have even less of a history of receiving asylum-seekers. These are countries from which people sought to defect to the west, rather than countries people moved to in order to seek asylum. Asylum legislation is very much seen as an imposition by the EU, rather than a home-grown tradition of protection. In Poland, for example, a large proportion of asylum applications are lodged by people using the country as a transit to western Europe. Large numbers of asylum-seekers in Poland have arrived from Chechnya and around half of the claims have typically terminated before the end of the process because people have left Poland to head further west.

In contrast to policy discourse, academic and NGO narratives of asylum tend to be sceptical about the notion of abuse, and are typically more sympathetic to the plight of asylum-seekers. Academic literature on asylum has tended to focus on three main factors influencing trends in protection-seeking:

- the causes of refugee flows;
- interactions between sending and receiving countries that encourage or facilitate movement; and
- the impact of restrictive entry policies on asylum.

Scholarship on the causes of flight has typically sought to understand the pressures that force people to flee, including new forms of civil and ethnic violence, and failed and imploding states. In contrast to predominant policy discourses, scholars are often at pains to emphasize that a large proportion of asylum-seekers are fleeing from very real risks of persecution and human rights abuses (Kushner and Knox 1999; Helton 2002). Most of these actually escape to neighbouring countries in Asia, Africa, Latin America or the Middle East, or are internally displaced within countries, rather than making the longer journey to Europe (Zolberg *et al.* 1983; Hyndman 2000). Indeed, as Table 7.2 shows, the three main countries of origin for asylum seekers in Europe in 2009 were Afghanistan, Iraq and Somalia, all countries wracked by civil conflict and generalised violence.

Table 7.2   *Top 10 countries of origin of asylum applications lodged in Europe, 2009*

Country of origin	Number of asylum applications	Proportion of total applications (%)
Afghanistan	25,310	8.9
Iraq	23,332	8.2
Somalia	21,697	7.7
Russian Federation	19,194	6.8
Serbia	18,305	6.5
Nigeria	12,307	4.3
Georgia	10,812	3.8
Islamic Republic of Iran	10,398	3.7
Pakistan	9,843	3.5
Eritrea	9,498	3.4

Note: 38 European countries, including the EU.
Source: Data from UNHCR (2010).

Where scholars have focused on the (albeit limited) choices made by asylum-seekers about countries of refuge, they have explored the influence of historical, linguistic or cultural ties between countries of origin and asylum, or the role of migrant or smuggling networks in directing flows (Morrison and Crosland 2000; Koser and Pinkerton 2002). In fact, research has debunked the notion that knowledge of asylum legislation has much impact on asylum-seekers' decisions to flee, or their choice of country of asylum (Koser and Pinkerton 2002; Sasse and Thielemann 2005). Instead, many authors have been more interested in exploring the detrimental impact of asylum reform on human rights, including the difficulties faced by refugees in finding protection in the current restrictive climate (Tuitt 1996; Nicholson and Twomey 1999; Koser 2002). Others have discussed the difficulties faced by asylum-seekers during the application process, especially given their reduced access to social benefits and (in the case of most countries) the ban on being employed. These problems can result in increased stigmatization of asylum-seekers, as well as numerous psychological, social and health problems.

This more liberal discourse is common to scholars of refugee movement in most European countries (Lavenex 2001). Indeed, this is an area of research that is quite internationalized, with numerous Europe-wide networks of researchers and lawyers adopting a similar discourse. It is further bolstered by international organizations and NGOs such as UNHCR, the Council of Europe, Amnesty International and the European Council for Refugees and Exiles (ECRE), which interact closely with researchers working in this area and draw on their work. The upshot is a polarization of positions, between, on one hand, researchers, international organizations and NGOs, and, on the other, European governments, public debate and mass media, which often adopt a more restrictionist discourse.

This division can create some tensions between policy and academic accounts of asylum dynamics. For example, in 2000 the UK Immigration and Nationality Directorate (IND) commissioned independent academic research on the factors influencing asylum-seekers' choice of country of destination, fully expecting it to demonstrate the significant impact of legal provisions on asylum. On the contrary, the report found that other factors, such as historical ties and language, or migrant networks, had more influence (Robinson and Segrott 2002). The research was quickly sidelined by the operational division of IND, which cast doubt on the methodology employed by the study, preferring to stick with its own organizational narrative about asylum dynamics (Boswell 2009). This is a good example of how policymakers can effectively choose what sort of knowledge to embrace, based on their existing beliefs and policy preferences.

Political debate

Divergent ideas about the causes of asylum flows to Europe and the impact of policy also shape understandings of the EU's role. Again, the debate tends to be normatively laden. Academic literature in particular has been critical of the EU 'fortress Europe' project, with lawyers and political scientists emphasizing the negative impact of harmonization on asylum-seekers and refugees (Joly 1996; Guild 2001; Byrne *et al.* 2002). Perhaps somewhat unfairly, the EU was equally criticized for its lack of influence, especially prior to the Amsterdam Treaty. Thus EU asylum policy was castigated for the weak legal basis of its instruments (Guild 1999), or its general ineffectiveness (Noll 1997; Hurwitz 1999). Arguably,

Box 7.1   EU cooperation on asylum: key developments

1990: *Dublin Convention* on determining the state responsible for examining asylum applications lodged in one of the member states.

1992: *Treaty on European Union* (Maastricht Treaty)
Established cooperation on Justice and Home Affairs as the 'third pillar'.

Asylum became an 'area of common interest'.

1992–6: *EU Resolutions, Decisions or Joint Positions* on:

- Asylum procedures (1992).
- 'Safe countries' to which asylum-seekers could be returned (1992).
- Minimum guarantees for asylum procedures (1995).
- Burden-sharing of those in need of temporary protection (1995).
- Joint position on the interpretation of 'refugee' (1996).

1997: *Treaty of Amsterdam*
Asylum policy switched to the 'first pillar' – in principle.

Article 63: established 5-year deadline for adopting policies on:

- Standards for asylum reception.
- Refugee recognition, asylum procedures.
- A new Dublin Convention (Dublin II).
- Standards for giving temporary protection.

this implies that one of the sources of dissatisfaction with EU asylum policy was a disappointment that the EU did not do more to engender a more liberal approach. It implies somewhat idealized expectations about the potentially benign and liberalizing tendencies of European integration in this area, but can also take a somewhat naive view of the potential and scope for EU action detached from the difficult political context for decision-making in a complex international organization such as the EU.

By the late 1990s, the 'fortress Europe' critique had largely given way to analyses of the perceived 'securitization' of EU immigration and asylum policy. Much of this literature was informed by the seminal work of the Copenhagen School, which argued

---

➡

1999: *European Council on Justice and Home Affairs, Tampere*
Committed states to a 'common European asylum system', including a common asylum procedure and 'uniform status' for those who are granted asylum.
Set out a 5-year programme of legislation (1999–2004).

2000–2004: *EU adopts Directives on*:

- Minimum standards on granting temporary protection (2001).
- Minimum standards for the reception of asylum-seekers (2003).
- Dublin II (2003 – this was a Regulation).
- Minimum standards for qualification as a refugee (2004).
- Minimum standards on asylum procedures.

2001: *Treaty of Nice* shifted asylum into the 'first pillar' (subject to qualified majority voting, greater role for Commission, Parliament and ECJ).

2004: *Hague Programme* (2005–9) reaffirmed the aim to create a common asylum system and set out a new 5-year programme (2005–9).

2009: *Stockholm Programme* set the agenda for 2010–14 and called for:

- A common European asylum system.
- Uniform international protection status.
- A voluntary system for sharing responsibility for refugees within the EU.

The aim has been to establish a common asylum system by 2012.

---

that immigration was becoming a 'new focus for insecurity' in Europe (Waever *et al.* 1993). By constructing immigration and asylum as a threat to European societies, politicians were able to legitimize practices that had traditionally been reserved for responding to military threats (Huysmans 2006). In the wake of 9/11 and the subsequent attacks in Madrid and London, EU officials were able to introduce supposedly 'exceptional' measures that would normally have been considered unacceptable infringements of civil liberties. Other scholars focused less on public discourse, instead charting how experts and professionals attempted to expand their power by applying securitarian practices and technologies to migration control (Bigo 2001; Huysmans 2006).

Interestingly, this Foucauldian approach has found less support from scholars with a background in migration studies, who tend to see migration policy as also driven as much by market considerations as by a restrictive securitarian logic (Favell and Hansen 2002; Boswell 2007).

Policy discourse in the EU has tended to be variegated and complex. Political debate in some countries, especially those receiving a high number of asylum-seekers, has often depicted EU cooperation as a possible means of adjusting these imbalances between member states. Thus political elites in Germany in the early 1990s, and the UK later in the 1990s, both saw EU asylum policy as a possible venue for securing agreement for some sort of burden-sharing arrangement. Such an arrangement might take the form of a more balanced distribution of refugees or resources between states, as proposed by Germany in 1994. Or it could imply more indirect measures to ensure a 'level playing-field' of asylum provisions across the EU, through the harmonization of reception and protection standards, as favoured by the UK and Sweden. Arguably, such expectations about burden-sharing created a strong impetus to develop a common EU policy, with Germany at the forefront of initiatives in the first half of the 1990s.

These ideas about EU cooperation as the solution to large numbers of asylum-seekers were not necessarily shared by opposition parties or the mass media. In the UK the idea remained largely restricted to government officials; the generally Eurosceptic media rarely picked up on the idea, preferring to stick to the notion that EU cooperation and Europe in general undermined the UK's capacity to control inflows of asylum-seekers. Moreover, as has been argued elsewhere, these expectations about achieving a 'level playing-field' were generally disappointed. EU legislation on reception conditions for asylum-seekers (2003), on who qualified for protection (2004), and on asylum procedures (2005), were all based on minimum standards. Beyond this minimum, there remained substantial differences in conditions between member states. Ultimately, most countries have relied on domestic reforms to try to reduce numbers of asylum-seekers, rather than EU harmonization.

Indeed, countries that feel they have a good grip on asylum numbers have often viewed EU cooperation as a constraint. One reason may be fears about lax migration controls in neighbouring countries which allow migrants or refugees to transit without valid documents to the country concerned. A case in point is the UK media furore about migrants seeking to crossing from a Red Cross camp near Sangatte in France to the UK. Germany and Austria have both been concerned about possible weak links in the EU border because of EU enlargement to the east, which would allow irregular migrants to cross via Poland, the Czech Republic or Hungary.

In other countries, there have been concerns that EU harmonization might require the introduction of more liberal measures. Thus by the late 1990s, when numbers of asylum-seekers in Germany had significantly fallen, political discourse became more sceptical about EU asylum policy, which many feared would imply unravelling the restrictive constitutional and legislative arrangements that Germany had introduced since the early 1990s. In the early 2000s, Germany was under pressure in EU negotiations to introduce a number of more liberal provisions, such as a broader interpretation of the concept of 'refugee' to include those with a well-founded fear of persecution on grounds of gender, or by non-state actors. Negotiations on 'safe third countries' to which asylum-seekers could be returned also threatened to undermine the stringent measures introduced by Germany's constitutional reform of 1993. (See Box 7.2 for an explanation.) Germany managed to play a clever 'two-level game' on these provisions, using the EU as an excuse to introduce a broader definition of refugee at home, and using domestic constraints as a reason to tighten proposed EU measures on safe third countries. Thus elements of Germany's domestic asylum policy were Europeanized, while aspects of EU policy became 'Germanized' (Post and Niemann 2007). This is a good illustration of the complex interactions between levels of governance in this area.

In sum, we can say that while the EU has exerted a restrictive influence in some cases – notably in imposing its asylum *acquis* on new member countries – it may well have also exerted some more benign influences. This includes those that did not have an effective protection system in place to deal with the asylum-seekers they were receiving and countries with well-established systems that were obliged to broaden provisions in line with EU legislation. Nonetheless, it has not, as yet, been able to introduce any robust form of burden-sharing between countries, and it is doubtful how far harmonization of policies in itself can produce a 'level playing-field' of the kind favoured by some countries.

Box 7.2   Safe third countries and readmission agreements

The concept of 'safe third country' or 'host third country' was developed in order to justify denying certain asylum-seekers access to asylum procedures in European countries. The grounds for this denial was that the asylum-seeker in question already enjoyed protection in another country, or at least that she or he had access to such protection. Thus the asylum-seeker's country of origin, or the country through which they had travelled before arriving in Europe, was considered 'safe'. On this basis, an EU country could justify returning the asylum-seeker to that safe country, without violating the principle of non-refoulement.

An EU Resolution adopted in 1992 specified that in order to qualify as a safe third country, only three criteria must be fulfilled:

- The life or freedom of the asylum applicant must not be threatened, within the meaning of Article 33 of the Geneva Convention.
- The asylum applicant must not be exposed to torture or inhuman or degrading treatment in the third country.
- It must either be the case that the asylum applicant has already been granted protection in the third country or has had an opportunity to make contact with that country's authorities in order to seek their protection, before approaching the member state in which they are applying for asylum, or that there is clear evidence of their admissibility to a third country.

In order to implement this concept, the EU has signed a number of bilateral agreements with third countries, termed 'readmission agreements'. These agreements oblige countries to readmit their own nationals, and in many cases also to readmit non-nationals who have transited through their territory to enter the EU illegally. The first readmission agreements were signed with countries in central and east Europe that had a border with the EU (and are now EU members, so the agreements no longer apply). The EU currently has readmission agreements with 16 countries: Albania, Algeria, Bosnia-Herzegovina, China, the Former Yugoslav Republic of Macedonia, Hong Kong, Macao, Moldova, Montenegro, Morocco, Pakistan, Russia, Serbia, Sri Lanka, Turkey and Ukraine.

Administrative practice and implementation

EU asylum policy has been the object of a range of different critiques, as we have seen. It has been criticized for being too restrictive and too liberal; for lacking legal clout and for imposing provisions ill-adjusted to specific national contexts. One reason for these divergent perspectives may well be the often ambiguous nature of EU objectives and policy programmes in the area of asylum. Commentators can read very different things into EU asylum policy, depending on which documents they care to consult. So it is worth considering the sources of this ambiguity. One obvious candidate is the rather different priorities and goals of the various organizations involved in policymaking, which, as we will see, can generate rather contradictory messages about policy objectives. The European Council, the Council of Ministers, the EP and the Commission all have rather different goals and strategies in this policy area, which can mean that policy proceeds in a rather disjointed and inconsistent fashion.

A case in point was the Tampere European Council of October 1999. The Tampere Conclusions came as quite a surprise to commentators at the time. They committed member states to the quite far-reaching development of migration and asylum policies, far beyond what had been agreed in the Treaty of Amsterdam in 1997. Thus member states agreed to establish a Common European Asylum System which, in the longer term, would lead to a common asylum procedure and a uniform status for those who are granted asylum valid throughout the Union – quite a bold aspiration. Perhaps even more significantly for many observers, the conclusions included a lengthy introductory statement about the EU's commitment to human rights and humanitarian assistance in forging policy in this area, and especially its commitment to 'full and inclusive' application of the Geneva Convention. This was greeted with near euphoria by organizations such as UNHCR, Amnesty International and ECRE.

As is typical for such Conclusions, the Commission was requested to follow up on what had been decided, through drafting relevant proposals and preparing Communications outlining possible programmes or legislation. It was also to keep track of progress in implementing the Tampere goals, through a so-called 'Scoreboard' which assessed progress every six months. These tasks were duly carried out, with the Commission preparing a raft of proposals on options for a common asylum system, but then experiencing frustration in the face of opposition and foot-dragging in the Council. Levy (2002) suggests that this confirms the intergovernmental nature of EU cooperation in this area as member states retain sovereignty and that, notwithstanding the more supranational impulses of the Commission or the declaratory aspirations of European Council meetings, restrictionist and control-centric approaches will always prevail.

This intergovernmental approach may, however, overlook the more subtle ways in which the Commission has nudged states towards integration. Such tactics include laying the ground for harmonization through gathering data that expose apparent anomalies or inefficiencies in current national approaches, for example through cross-national legal comparative studies and the collection of comparable data. Indeed, the Commission has been able to capitalize on its role as having privileged access to data on all member states, enabling it to get the sort of cross-national comparative perspective that is unavailable to national governments (Stevens 2001; Boswell 2009). It has also been clever in gradually introducing ideas about possible harmonization to member states in an incremental, non-threatening way, for example through discussing ideas in less formal subcommittees of the JHA Council. This can be seen as a form of 'softening up' (Majone 1992), whereby the Commission introduces controversial ideas, but, on encountering resistance from member states, it puts these ideas on hold, effectively biding its time. In the meantime, it continues to gather evidence or data, or work on technical aspects of the problem. Over time, member states become accustomed to these ideas and may be gradually convinced by the technical arguments and data that the Commission has collected (Cini 1996).

Even though Treaty goals and European Council Conclusions are not always implemented to the letter, they frequently set up timetables for action which put pressure on member states to deliver. Indeed, the Commission is constantly pushing the pace of reform, arguing that a loss of momentum or a failure to reach stated targets could jeopardize the whole process of harmonization. European Council presidencies may also feel under pressure because of concerns about presiding over a period of inertia, or failing to provide the necessary leadership to meet specified deadlines. Of course, national governments operate according to rather different timetables and these EU deadlines may be seen as an intrusion. Thus in 2007 the UK government complained about the

Commission's rigid following of a 10-year timetable for adopting a common asylum system, arguing that an over-hasty move to a common system would not allow sufficient time to identify those aspects of harmonization that were working and those that were not (House of Commons 2006). The Commission agreed to push the deadline back two years, but members states were still clearly constrained by this rather rigid timeframe.

These various institutional interests and constraints might explain why EU asylum policy appears to display the pendulum tendency already identified. Walker (2004) argues that there also appears to be a polarization between two types of commentators on JHA: the 'structural fatalists', who are pessimistic about the possibility of real progress, and the 'naive separatists', who have unrealistic expectations about integration, divorced from any real understanding of political context. The failure to realize naive-separatist projects can generate frustration, encouraging a retreat back into fatalistic mode. We suggest that these 'naive-separatist' declarations – typically made by European Councils – may be reflecting more than the vague aspirations of an ambitious presidency. In a sense, they embody precisely the type of 'malintegration' we referred to in Chapter 2. Whether deliberately or not, such statements provide something to suit all stakeholders: a commitment to humanitarian and human rights principles, and ambitious goals for EU integration; but they also contain sufficiently woolly targets to pose little threat to those who are sceptical about EU integration. It is only in the follow-up phase that these contradictions are clarified and begin to pose problems. But member states are by then at least partially locked into timetables, or open to a phase of subtle steering and softening-up by the Commission.

This implies the need for caution in reading too much into these documents issued by EU institutions such as the European Council or, at the very least, to try to locate them within the wider political context. EU documents are not definitive statements about social or political reality, but are interventions in a process of policy formulation and deliberation by institutions with their own stake and role in it. Similarly, the apparent lack of implementation can be seen as a sign of EU policy failure, but it may offer a useful fog that keeps different parties committed to a common project, while ensuring that the contours of the project remain sufficiently vague so as to suppress intergovernmentalist qualms. Different parties are thus kept on board in an area full of risks and uncertainties.

Dilemmas of implementation in practice

It would be tempting to think that asylum is an area in which it is quite easy to observe the success or failure of policy goals. In comparison with labour migration, it would appear to be relatively straightforward to chart relevant trends in asylum, and to assess policy impacts. National governments and international bodies such as Eurostat (the EU statistical service) and the UNHCR keep systematic data on asylum. These data typically include numbers of asylum-seekers, the proportion of those recognized, what sort of status they were granted, and how many rejected asylum-seekers have been deported or returned of their own accord. Moreover, facilities and systems for accommodating asylum-seekers often enable governments to keep an eye on the whereabouts of asylum-seekers – through dispersal to specified locations, housing in reception centres, or, increasingly, imprisonment in detention centres. All this would imply that policy impacts and the success of measures can be kept track of quite effectively.

There is, however, still scope for the decoupling of government rhetoric from practice, meaning that there may be more to asylum policy implementation than meets the eye. Indeed, a closer look reveals immense problems. Two main ways can be identified in which tough rhetoric on asylum may be decoupled from more lenient practice. The first is in terms of practices regarding the recognition or toleration of different types of asylum-seekers. And the second relates to the ways in which both asylum-seekers and those whose applications have been rejected can access support in host countries.

Decoupling by changing categories

The first potential decoupling relates to the various ways in which governments can fudge the issue of how many asylum-seekers actually get to stay. One device in this respect has been to expand the categories of those who qualify for some form of protection. The Geneva Convention, which is now codified in the legislation or constitutions of all EU members, provides the most classic and generous form of protection, in the form of refugee status. Such status is typically open-ended, implying permanent residence and relatively easy access to citizenship. However, since the early 1990s European governments have introduced a range of protection statuses to allow for more provisional or temporary stay. Many of these statuses were developed in response to the influx of refugees triggered by conflict in the former Yugoslavia in 1990–1. Provisions on 'temporary protection', or 'temporary leave to remain' were designed to fulfil protection obligations to those fleeing civil war, while keeping open the expectation that people would eventually return. In many cases, people granted such status end up staying for prolonged periods of time, since for a variety of human-rights, welfare and logistical reasons it proved extremely difficult to return people. Thus most Bosnians who had been granted temporary protection in Europe eventually converted their status into that of permanent residents (van Selm 2002). However, in official statistics, such temporary statuses are not counted as positive decisions on asylum applications, since they do not confer refugee status.

Even more interesting are those cases where the presence of rejected asylum-seekers is tolerated on the grounds that they simply cannot be repatriated to their countries of origin. In these cases there may be various practical impediments to returning failed asylum-seekers. For example, they may have destroyed any documentation, making identification difficult – indeed, around 85 per cent of asylum-seekers arrive in Germany without identifying documents (Ellermann 2008). Alternatively, or in addition, their countries of origin may impede or slow down administrative processes for identifying them, because they are reluctant to take them back. Even where EU countries have managed to sign a 'readmission agreement' with the source country which commits it to taking back any failed asylum-seekers, the source country may still be reluctant to implement its commitment. In the case of the 1995 German readmission agreement with Vietnam, for example, the Vietnamese government effectively blocked implementation of return by creating various administrative barriers, meaning that by the end of 1996 only 24 per cent of the targeted figure for returns had been achieved (Ellermann 2008).

Finally, in other cases rejected asylum-seekers cannot be returned simply because they 'disappear' from the system. In Austria, for example, 62 per cent of asylum cases were closed without reaching any decision mainly because the applicants had absented themselves from the authorities (Jandl 2004). A large number of rejected asylum-seekers also tend to slip out of the surveillance of interior ministry officials responsible for migration control. This has been the object of considerable criticism from the media and opposition parties in many European countries, who lambast governments for failing to surveil those who have entered the asylum system.

For this reason, governments have introduced various measures to try to ensure people cannot slip off their radar. One such technique is to hold asylum-seekers or rejected asylum-seekers in detention centres, pending the conclusion of their case or their return to the country of origin. Although the ECHR only permits such detention in exceptional cases where non-custodial measures have been demonstrated not to work, it has become almost routine practice in a number of EU countries. Austria, Belgium, Germany and the UK have been particularly active in the use of detention, especially at the pre-deportation stage (Hughes and Field 1998). Another approach is the use of so-called 'dawn raids', surprise night-time or early-morning visits by the police or immigration officials to the home of a rejected asylum-seeker, so that they can be forcibly deported. Such raids are intended to deal with people facing a deportation order, but who, it is thought, may abscond or 'disappear' from the system. Despite these controversial measures, the number of those returned after disappearing from the asylum system or having their application rejected remains significant. When all else fails, governments can still fall back on fudging the statistics. Indeed, it has become increasingly difficult to obtain figures on deportations of rejected asylum-seekers or numbers of 'disappeared' asylum-seekers, with many interior ministries now cautious about publicizing such potentially compromising data (Schuster 2004).

Decoupling in the welfare system

The second main area prone to decoupling is asylum-seekers' access to social support in host countries. As we saw, states have been keen to send out a signal to voters about how they are limiting asylum-seekers' claims on public resources, to prevent perceptions of the 'abuse' of social or welfare services. Yet such practices of exclusion are very difficult to enforce in practice. For a start, states or local authorities may face judicial challenges if they seek to cut off social support for asylum-seekers. In the case of the UK, a government proposal to deny welfare benefits to asylum-seekers who had not lodged a claim within the first two weeks of arriving in the UK was overturned in 1997, on the grounds that local authorities have a duty to provide 'the basics of survival' to those in need (Moyes 1997).

Even where the legal situation is clear, however, there may be all sorts of reasons why states are unable or unwilling to enforce exclusion from welfare or social support. One factor is that it can be extremely difficult to oblige different parts of the welfare system to implement policies of excluding (rejected or current) asylum-seekers. Organizations delivering education, health or social assistance tend to operate on an inclusive logic, extending their services to all residents who are in need of them (Bommes and Geddes 2000). And such systems are often governed by an ideology that is sympathetic to the plight of asylum-seekers or irregular migrants. Moreover, in many countries, there is considerable scope for such organizations to exercise discretion on whom they consider as relevant recipients of support. The upshot is that most of the social and economic spheres relevant to welfare are quite accessible to migrants, whether their stay is authorized or not. Labour markets operate according to a logic that selects workers based on skills and price. Similarly, public health, education and welfare institutions adopt criteria of inclusion based on the life-stage or needs of individuals, usually only reluctantly imposing restrictions based on nationality, ethnicity or legal status (Boswell 2008).

Much of the impetus to introduce restrictive measures seems to be based on the need to reassure electorates that states are acting to protect their interests. In other words, restrictive asylum policies are often more about 'talk' than 'action' (Brunsson 2003). Indeed, governments may have rather limited interests in ensuring that such rhetoric gets translated into practical action. A systematic denial of social support to asylum-seekers or irregular migrants could create more problems than it solves: cases of serious destitution and harm; health problems that are not dealt with in time, thus necessitating more expensive emergency treatment; or the long-term exclusion of children from schooling. Not least, the consistent implementation of such measures would involve far more control of the systems delivering such services, and thus considerable investment in resources. Taken together, these points are likely to imply that governments will have an interest in some decoupling of rhetoric from practice: adopting tough talk, but tolerating more lenient – or more practical – approaches.

Conclusion

Cooperation on asylum policy is – along with irregular migration and border security – the most developed area of EU migration policy. The steady flow of measures adopted since the mid 1990s has focused predominantly on trying to standardize national approaches to the reception of asylum-seekers, the processing of applications, and the recognition of those in need of refugee or some other form of protection status. EU cooperation has also sought to circumvent duties of 'non-refoulement', through concepts of 'safe countries' and readmission agreements that enable EU countries to employ accelerated procedures or even return asylum-seekers. Finally, some attempts have been made to redistribute the costs of refugee reception and integration, through (albeit rather weak) instruments of burden-sharing.

Most commentators have depicted these measures as unashamedly restrictive, or 'securitarian', leading to a lowering of protection levels in EU countries, and by extension in countries bordering Europe that are involved in accession or pre-accession negotiations. Moreover, EU cooperation has been seen as a means for governments to 'escape' national scrutiny, enabling them to pursue far more restrictive measures than would otherwise have been the case.

This chapter challenged these accounts by unpacking some of the conflicting interests and processes at play in the area of asylum policy. The analysis has suggested that far from offering an escape from domestic scrutiny, EU cooperation has frequently been used as a means of demonstrating that a government is acting to address issues of public concern. In this sense, EU cooperation plays an important symbolic role for EU member states, signalling their readiness to employ international channels to address seemingly intractable domestic problems. Cooperation has also been used as a lever or pretext for introducing more liberal measures, on the basis that EU cooperation requires governments to ensure their legislation is in line with predominant European trends. Thus it can have liberalizing as well as restrictive impacts. The chapter has also argued that practices on asylum can be decoupled from restrictive rhetoric, so that even where EU and national measures appear tough they may be more lenient in practice.

In sum, asylum policy is an area in which states have by and large been keen to talk tough, at both the national and the EU level. They have also been adept in crafting discourse on the asylum problem to focus on causes or problems that are susceptible to government intervention: overly generous welfare provisions or rights to appeal, visa rules or requirements for travel documentation. Problems that are less susceptible to government control – such as enforcing returns – have been less prominent on the public agenda.

Governments have rarely shown any inhibition about being seen to pursue often highly draconian practices. Nor have they been particularly sensitive to criticism from human rights and refugee groups. Rather than hiding behind EU cooperation, member states seem to be keen to advertise tough measures. In many areas of practice, though, governments have had to grapple with factors that impede the implementation of restrictive approaches. Thus they have allowed some degree of leniency in areas such as leave to remain, developing categories of protection that fall short of refugee status; they have recognized they are unable to enforce returns; and they have often turned a blind eye to the extension of various forms of social assistance to asylum-seekers. This suggests that where they do face practical or resource barriers to implementing restrictive measures, they are quite willing and able to decouple tough talk from more lenient practice.

Chapter 8

Mobility, Citizenship and EU Enlargement

In this book we have argued that patterns of population movement in the EU cannot be understood without reference to people moving between EU states as well as those moving from outside the EU. We now analyse EU mobility, beginning with an example that illustrates some of the issues at stake. In 2000, Mrs Chen, a Chinese national who was living and working in the UK, travelled to Northern Ireland to give birth to a daughter, Catherine. At that time, the citizenship law of the Republic of Ireland had a rather unusual provision: it granted the right to citizenship to anyone born on Irish territory, including Northern Ireland. Thus the fact that Catherine was born in Northern Ireland – even though her parents did not live there – meant that she was entitled to citizenship of the Republic of Ireland. As an Irish citizen, she then had a right to reside in any EU state, provided she had adequate means of support. Thus her mother Mrs Chen was also entitled to residence in the UK as Catherine's primary carer. When the UK Home Office refused Mrs Chen a residence permit, she appealed to the ECJ, which upheld her right to UK residence in 2004. The only condition was that Mrs Chen be able to demonstrate she had the means to support herself and her family (which she was able to do), so would not be dependent on social or welfare services in the UK. Irish citizenship law was subsequently changed so that it would no longer be possible to acquire nationality simply by being born on Irish soil, but the right of EU nationals to mobility within Europe remains robust.

The fact that the ECJ was able to override the British government demonstrates that EU mobility rights can constrain national sovereignty. At the same time, EU mobility rights are not unconditional. They depend on a person being able to demonstrate that they have sufficient means to support themselves and their families, whether through employment or from other sources of income. We have also seen that states retain their prerogative for nationality and citizenship laws and that the Irish government was able to change its laws. In this sense, provisions on free movement are truly multi-level, comprising a complex mix of national citizenship laws (which determine who is a citizen), EU treaty provisions on rights to mobility, and a national prerogative to deny access to those who are not self-supporting.

Table 2.2 (p. 22) provided data on levels of intra-EU movement in 2006 and showed how it is a distinct and important component of population movement in contemporary Europe. To refresh our memories, if we take the case of Germany, we see from Table 2.2 that, of 661,855 immigrants in 2006, 320,727 came from another member state, which is almost 50 per cent of the total. Among these EU free movers were 152,000 people from Poland. In Ireland in 2006, the number of EU free movers (65,002 was far greater than the number of TCN migrants (19,363). In Belgium too, more than 50 per cent of migrants were, in fact, EU citizens moving from another member state (35,143 mobile EU citizens compared with 33,657 TCNs).

This chapter will explore the discourse and practice around EU mobility provisions, examining the various arguments advanced about the distinction between migration and mobility at both EU and national level. We will examine some of the controversies around free movement, especially in the context of EU enlargements. And we will consider how far EU aspirations vis-à-vis mobility are realized in practice. In fact, intra-EU mobility remains surprisingly low. Nonetheless, as we will see, mobility provisions have had, and are likely to continue to have, a subtle but important role in reconfiguring migration policies in spatial, temporal and social terms.

The EU framework

In April 2004 the EU brought together in one Directive (2004/38/ EC) the previous piecemeal arrangements (covered in 1 Regulation and 9 Directives) governing free-movement and mobility rights. This single Directive covered the rights of EU citizens and their family members to move and reside freely within the territory of the member states. The Directive specifies the conditions under which EU citizens can move freely and imposes only minor constraints on movement – linked, for example, to public-order or public-health concerns – and specifies a right of permanent residence for EU citizens exercising mobility rights.

In practical terms, this means that all EU citizens able to present a valid identity card or passport have the right to enter another EU member state. Family members have the same rights as the EU citizen they have accompanied. If residence is to be for longer than 6 months then certain conditions can be imposed. These are interesting because they reveal the economic impetus that underlies the mobility and free-movement framework. To acquire a right of residence for more than 6 months, an EU citizen must be:

- engaged in economic activity or be self-employed;
- have sufficient resources, including health insurance, so that they do not become a burden on the member state that they move to; or
- be following vocational training and have sufficient resources to support themselves; or
- be a family member of an EU citizen who falls into one of these categories.

EU citizens acquire a right to permanent residence following a 5-year period of uninterrupted, legal residence. This right is not subject to any conditions. This same rule also applies to family members.

The 2004 Directive also deals with important welfare and social security issues and provides for the transferability of social and welfare entitlements. It is obviously the case that were these not transferable then there would be significant impediments to mobility (Eichenhofer 1997). Essentially, the 2004 Directive affirms the principle of equal treatment, which means that EU citizens that are resident in another member state have the same rights and access to welfare and social services as the citizens of that state and cannot be discriminated against. In fact, the provision for non-discrimination on the basis of nationality was an important aspect of the Treaty of Rome (1957) and the principles of equal treatment that were specified in a 1976 Directive.

Narratives

The EU offers mobility rights within a Union of 27 member states to all EU citizens. This represents a major transformation of the constitutive principles of the European state system. EU member states are no longer able to control access to their territory by nationals of other EU member states. We have seen that mobility is an important component of overall migration to the EU, but, in absolute terms, the numbers that move remain quite low. Fewer than 2 per cent of EU citizens exercise their right to free movement. This presents us with a situation that is somewhat similar to more general debates about immigration: in relative terms migration remains relatively small and on the margins; but it is also at these margins that debates about issues such as access to resources and identity can be at their most intense.

The distinction between mobility and migration, and the free-movement provisions that underpin it, have important profound effects on member state immigration policies. By signing up to free-movement provisions, EU governments have ceded sovereign authority over the entry, residence and employment of nationals of other member states. Free-movement provisions have also impinged on other areas of national immigration policy, including the rights of TCNs in EU states. Arguably, the provisions have also reshaped discourse on immigration in European countries. Nationals of EU states now accept by and large that various categories of nationals from other EU countries – workers and their families, self-employed people, students and pensioners – have the right to live and work in their country. Of course, there are notable exceptions to this. As we will see later in the chapter, access to full mobility rights has been challenged in the context of EU enlargements, especially in the recent enlargements to central and eastern Europe in May 2004 and January 2007. The experience of southern enlargement two decades earlier suggests that initial concerns about admitting new countries into the 'club' of free movement could eventually subside as new members catch up economically, reducing the incentives for large-scale movement. The 'big bang' enlargement may also have had some chastening effects at EU level, with diminished appetite for further EU expansion and particular controversy about the longstanding Turkish application for membership. Were Turkey to join then it would be the largest member state. Austria and Germany have expressed concerns about the migration potential from Turkey, while the French government has indicated that it would hold a referendum on Turkish membership.

Transition measures have been used for new member states and were an important aspect of the agreement that brought 12 new member states into the EU in 2004 and 2007. For a period of up to 7 years after accession, restrictions were imposed on the right of their nationals to move freely. As already mentioned in Chapter 4, only Ireland, Sweden and the UK allowed immediate free-movement rights for nationals of the 10 states that joined on 1 May 2004. Other member states agreed to a 2+3+2 formulation, allowing them to look at extending free-movement rights to A8 nationals after 2 years, 3 years and then at the expiry of the transitional arrangements in 2011 (see Table 8.1).

Austria and Germany will wait until 2011, although as Table 2.2 (p. 22) showed, there are large numbers of citizens from A8 states issued permits to work in Germany, including 150,000 people from Poland who entered in 2006 alone.

The distinction between 'beneficial' mobility by EU citizens and 'threatening' migration by TCNs reflects two rather different paradigms for understanding international migration. On the one hand, the EU's mobility agenda reflects free market values, according to which migration is a means of enhancing the efficiency of labour markets and thus increasing Europe's competitiveness and growth in a globalized economy (Favell and Hansen 2002). By this account, migration is understood in terms of its economic benefits. On the other account, immigration from outside the EU is still treated as a potential challenge to the nation-state. In particular, it is seen as undermining the state's control over who accesses its territory, its labour market and other socio-economic goods and rights normally reserved for citizens or legal long-term residents

Table 8.1   *States allowing mobility rights to A8 nationals*

Date	State(s)
May 2004	Ireland, Sweden, UK
May 2006	Finland, Greece, Portugal, Spain
July 2006	Italy
May 2007	Netherlands
November 2007	Luxembourg
July 2008	France
May 2009	Belgium, Denmark

(Halfmann 2000). Not surprisingly, this rather neat way of distinguishing migration from mobility often becomes blurred in European migration policy and politics. In particular, the notion that intra-EU mobility is beneficial has tended to become contested in the context of EU enlargements, as well as for sectors of the labour market facing high levels of unemployment. Conversely, it is not always the case that the most economically desirable immigrants will originate from other EU countries. Many high-skilled immigrants come from third countries, while a substantial proportion of intra-EU mobility is low or semi-skilled. Thus the notion that migration is less economically desirable than mobility can and has been questioned in some national debates.

Mobility and the free movement of workers

As we suggested, two rival paradigms have tended to inform thinking on migration: a liberal, free-trade-oriented paradigm emphasizing the economic benefits of free movement; and a more state-centric, restrictive paradigm premised on concerns about the impact of migration and mobility on the state's capacity to allocate socio-economic and political resources. The free movement of workers within the EU has tended to be conceptualized in terms of the more liberal economic model. This free-market perspective dates back to the original 1957 Treaty of Rome, Article 3 of which committed signatories to 'the abolition, as between Member States, of obstacles to freedom of movement of persons, services and capital'. Title III of the Treaty set out provisions for ensuring the free movement of workers.

Free movement of workers was therefore at the heart of the vision of Europe as a free-trade area. This perspective is continually reiterated in both European Council and Commission documents. Free movement is represented as a means of creating a European employment market and of creating a more flexible and more efficient labour market. Labour mobility is represented as allowing individuals to improve their job prospects and employers to recruit the people they need from within a single European market (Guild 1998; Jileva 2002; Guild 2005; Pécoud and de Guchteneire 2005).

More recently, the benefits of mobility have also been embraced in the context of the Lisbon Strategy, which was adopted by the member states in 2000 to make the EU 'the most dynamic and competitive knowledge-based economy in the world capable of sustainable economic growth with more and better jobs and greater social cohesion' (Lisbon European Council 2000). This grand declaration was not realized in practice, but greater mobility within the EU has been seen as a key part of realizing these ambitious goals. The EU this provides a powerful market-oriented framework for understanding mobility and free movement. Until 2003, these various provisions on and for mobility have tended to evade the issue of TCN mobility. As we will see later, questions of free movement for TCNs who have been resident for a long period in EU member states became a real issue only from the late 1990s onwards and were included within the 2003 Directive on the rights of long-term residents, which we also analyse in Chapter 9.

Not surprisingly, this liberal, market-oriented view is warmly endorsed by many economists, for the sorts of reasons discussed in Chapter 3. The mobility of labour between EU countries is seen as a means of matching labour supply to demand, ironing out inefficiencies in national markets and reducing unemployment. Indeed, economists typically support the extension of free-movement provisions beyond the EU or the EEA (see Box 8.1). Many economists were strongly in favour of extending free movement to the nationals of newly acceding countries in central and eastern Europe, without the imposition of any transitional arrangements. This debate on eastern enlargement provides an excellent lens into discourse on mobility, so it is worth outlining the main lines of argument.

From the late 1990s, as the prospect of eastern enlargement began to appear more concrete, a plethora of studies sought to forecast the impact of accession on mobility from central and eastern European countries (Hars 1998; Bauer and Zimmerman 1999; Boeri and Bruecker 2000; Boswell 2000; Bruecker 2000; Hoennekop and Werner 2000; Dustmann *et al.* 2003). Most reports stressed the net economic benefits of increased mobility for receiving countries, flowing from increased productivity and growth; as well as fiscal gains through an injection of income tax but limited takeup of public services. Most studies sought to allay concerns about large-scale migration flows from east to west – doubtless reflecting the liberal leanings of many of the economists involved in preparing these studies. As Straubhaar concluded in his overview of estimates, most studies broadly converged on the view that east-west migration would reach about 3 to 4 per cent

Box 8.1 Free movement, the European Economic Area and Switzerland

The European Economic Area (EEA) extends provisions on free movement to three of the countries of the so-called European Free Trade Area (EFTA), namely Iceland, Liechtenstein and Norway.

EEA membership means that free movement provisions also apply to the nationals of these three countries, even though they are not EU members. In fact, these countries have signed up to the full Single Market package, including relevant aspects of the Treaty of Rome and secondary legislation. However, cooperation does not cover other areas of EU policy, such as the Common Agricultural and Fisheries Policies, the Customs Union, the Common Trade Policy, the Common Foreign and Security Policy or cooperation in Justice and Home Affairs.

Switzerland is the fourth member of EFTA, but its proposed accession to the EEA was rejected in a referendum in 1992. Instead, in 1999 the government of Switzerland negotiated a range of bilateral agreements with the EU, including one on the free movement of persons, which allows EU nationals access to residence and employment. In 2005 and 2009, Swiss voters agreed in referendums to extend free movement provisions to the nationals of new member states.

of the CEEC population within one or two decades after the introduction of free movement. Taking into account predicted high rates of return or onward mobility to other countries, the *net* migration figure would be only around 1 to 2 per cent of their population (Straubhaar 2000). Boeri and Bruecker (2000) similarly argued in their extensive study prepared for the European Commission that concerns about the EU being 'swamped by migrants from the CEECs' were 'ill-founded'. These studies lent strong support for those opposing any sort of moratorium on the introduction of free movement for the nationals of newly acceded countries.

The more tempered projections of east–west migration after enlargement also drew on the experience of the southern accessions of Greece (1981), and Spain and Portugal (1986). Greece, Portugal and Spain were all traditional emigration countries until around the 1980s, exporting large numbers of workers to northern European countries during the 1950s and 1960s. The nationals of Greece, Portugal and Spain all benefited from mobility provisions on joining the EU, once 6-year transitional restrictions on mobility had been lifted in 1987 (for Greece) and 1992 (for Portugal and Spain). In each of these cases, free-movement rights did not lead to any significant increase in mobility, and it actually decreased in the case of Spain (Dustmann *et al.* 2003). This was despite the persistence of considerable differences in per capita GDP and salaries between southern and northern European countries. Some scholars argue that potential migrants were deterred from moving because of growing optimism about improving economic conditions in these countries (Dustmann *et al.* 2003). Others have argued that possibilities for unimpeded mobility have facilitated the return of many migrants (Montanari and Cortese 1993), who could travel freely between countries without fear that their decision might be irreversible. These types of arguments were again marshalled to mollify concerns about the effects of European enlargements in 2004.

Even among the academic community, however, there were dissenting voices. Hans-Werner Sinn (2002) painted a bleak picture of an enlarged Europe with free movement creating extensive opportunities for welfare shopping between countries. He suggested that migrants from poorer acceding states with less-developed welfare systems would move to the west to access more generous provisions, placing pressure on existing welfare provisions and eventually leading to the erosion of welfare states. More populist parties and the media in many EU countries were similarly gloomy about the impact of mobility from central and eastern Europe. The German and Austria governments, in particular, were concerned about a potential mass influx of workers from neighbouring countries to the east, and were keen to impose transitional agreements to limit access to their labour markets. Indeed, the moratorium on free movement that was eventually imposed by most EU countries (the exceptions being the UK, Ireland and Sweden) echoed similar arrangements to deal with the southern enlargements of Greece in 1981 and Spain and Portugal in 1986. Concerns about mobility now appear to be one of the major stumbling-blocks to progress with Turkey's accession to the EU, which has a population of 70 million and a substantial diaspora already resident in north European countries, especially Germany.

Unlike most other EU countries, the UK took the rather unusual step of granting full labour market access for A8 nationals from 1 May 2004. There was some initial debate in the media and party politics about the potential for a large influx of workers or people seeking welfare benefits (Boswell 2009). However, migration was generally seen as economically beneficial, coming at a time of nearly full employment and acute labour shortages in many sectors. A study commissioned by the research department of the Home Office predicted relatively low levels of immigration from A8 countries, at 5000 to 13,000 per year. As it turned out, movement was far more substantial than projected, and contributed to a pronounced shift in UK public discourse on immigration from around 2005 onwards. Table 8.2 shows numbers of A8 nationals whose applications to the Worker Registration Scheme (WRS) were approved. This WRS data is not evidence of either flows or stocks of migrants because, for example, there was no requirement to deregister, but it does provide a good sense of the scale of A8 movement to the UK and of the large numbers of Polish people within these flows. Table 8.2 shows that 66 per cent of approved WRS applications between 2004 and 2008 were by people from Poland with the second-largest nationality being Slovakians at 10 per cent.

As levels of A8 migration to the UK rose, there were concerns about social costs, especially in terms of its impact on accommodation supply and social services in local authorities. WRS application data show downturn in numbers in 2007 and 2008, suggesting some sensitivity to changed economic conditions.

Table 8.2   *Approved WRS applications, UK, May 2004–08*

Year	WRS applications approved	Number from Poland
2004 (May onwards)	125,885	71,025
2005	204,970	127,325
2006	227,875	162,495
2007	210,800	150,255
2008	158,340	103,015

Source: Data from Home Office/UK Border Agency (2009).

Box 8.2   Posted workers in North Lincolnshire

In January 2009, workers at the Lindsey Oil Refinery in North Lincolnshire went on strike over the employment of foreign workers. The oil company Total had decided to give a £200m contract to build a desulphurization unit at the refinery to an Italian firm, IREM. It claimed that the previous British contractor had failed to deliver on time. IREM announced it would bring in 400 skilled workers of Italian and Portuguese nationality to carry out the work. IREM pledged to pay the workers at normal British rages, and said they expected no 'direct redundancies' as a result. Nonetheless, the decision came in the midst of growing unemployment in the UK and the onset of global recession. In reaction, 695 British workers went on strike, protesting that there were sufficient British workers with relevant skills who were available to do the work. They mobilized around the slogan 'British jobs for British workers', a phrase that had been used by British Prime Minister Gordon Brown at a conference in 2007. Spontaneous strikes in support of the workers broke out across the UK.

Problems of EU mobility

Concerns about the negative economic impacts of mobility have surfaced not only in the context of EU enlargement. They have also emerged in relation to what has been dubbed 'social dumping'. In the context of labour migration, social dumping refers to the practice of hiring workers or subcontracting firms from other EU countries to carry out work at a lower rate of pay, social protection or working conditions than are typically afforded to domestic workers. In fact, EU legislation in principle forbids companies from recruiting workers under less favourable terms. The Posted Workers Directive of 1996 stated that EU workers posted to another EU country should be paid the same wages as local workers from the first day of their employment, thus avoiding the problem of domestic workers being undercut by their cheaper EU rivals. The Directive was strongly supported by the German and French governments, who were under pressure to mollify trade union pressures about social dumping in the construction industry (Bilous 1999). The then Conservative UK government opposed the Directive on the grounds that it would hinder competitiveness – a position that came back to

➡

The issue drew media attention to EU provisions on mobility, and especially the 1996 posted workers Directive. Under the Directive, IREM was fully within its rights to employ EU nationals for the job. Nonetheless, the government was highly embarrassed at the claim that it was failing to prioritize the interests of its own unemployed labour force. At the same time, it was also concerned that the protests might trigger a backlash against British workers posted in other European countries. In fact, while there were only 15,000 foreign workers posted in the UK at the time, there were 47,000 UK workers posted in Europe.

The dispute was settled in February 2009 through a deal between unions and management. Total guaranteed it would give 102 of the 195 new jobs to British workers. Meanwhile, the employment minister, Pat MacFadden, reached a broader agreement with the engineering construction industry to ensure contractors from outside the EU would 'always explore and consider the local skills availability'. The incident demonstrates just how sensitive an issue mobility rights can be, especially at a time of rising unemployment.

haunt the Conservatives (by then in opposition) in 2009, when there was a public outcry over employment of workers from other EU member states at an oil refinery in North Lincolnshire (see Box 8.2). We will explore some of the political ramifications of discourse on mobility and migration the next section.

EU citizenship

While European integration was originally conceived as an economic project, since the 1992 Maastricht Treaty – although discussion dates back to at least the 1980s – free movement within the EU has been associated with a broader political goal: that of guaranteeing nationals of EU member states a common set of political rights, endowed by virtue of their EU citizenship. Article 17(1) of the amended Treaties of Rome states that:

- Citizenship of the Union is hereby established. Every person holding the nationality of a Member State shall be a citizen of the Union. Citizenship of the Union shall complement and not replace national citizenship.

- The rights associated with this status are set out in articles 18, 19, 20 and 21 of the revised Treaty, including:
  - The right to move and reside freely within the EU.
  - Various electoral rights, including the right to vote and stand for election in local and EP elections in one's country of residence.
  - The right to diplomatic and consular protection.
  - The right to out-of court methods for the protection of citizens' rights (including to petition the EP, and to apply to the Ombudsman).

In fact, this rather limited list of mainly political rights excludes some of the most important socio-economic rights achieved for EU nationals over the previous decades. These include the right of workers and self-employed people to equal tax and social security, to certain types of training, and to equal housing with other workers. Workers had the right to be joined by family members, who were also entitled to the same rights and provisions as the worker on whom they were dependent. Over time, these rights were extended to those who were not economically active, provided they could demonstrate they had adequate health insurance and were not dependent on the receiving state (Geddes 2008b). This meant that the new political rights accorded under the Maastricht Treaty were not particularly radical compared with the extensive set of entitlements already accumulated through the application of free-movement provisions. Nonetheless, the Maastricht Treaty did enshrine the right to free movement as a fundamental right to move and reside freely in the Union, and decoupled this right from economic activity (although, as before, there were in practice various restrictions on the exercise of the right by those without employment or an independent source of income).

Shaw's (2007) study of EU citizenship shows that this new codification of the right to free movement, and the various associated electoral and civil rights, implies a tension between the EU's economic and political–cultural aspirations. The EU was originally conceived as an economic arrangement, with mobility introduced to enhance the efficiency of labour markets and productivity. The Maastricht Treaty implied the aspiration to forge a common political identity, mimicking concepts of citizenship characteristic of *national* categories of membership. This discourse on citizenship can be traced to legal literature in the late 1960s, which had stressed the need to conceive of free-movement provisions in the context of the rights of European nationals, rather than in purely economic terms (Shaw 2007). It was also taken up in political discourse in the 1970s, in the context of a more general shift in rhetoric away from economic aspects of integration towards political ones (Wiener 1998). Arguably, this was very much a top-down project, devised by Brussels bureaucrats and national officials, in the absence of any real grass-roots movement to develop the concept of political membership. Not surprisingly, discourse on EU citizenship has remained limited largely to a narrow circle of officials, lawyers and academics. There is little to suggest that it has permeated national political discourse in any meaningful way, despite various attempts by the European Commission to highlight the significance of the concept, and the importance of its attendant rights.

Indeed, the gap between the Commission rhetoric and the takeup of these questions in national debates is quite striking. The Commission is keen to mobilize support among European nationals for the notion of a shared citizenship with certain fundamental rights, and sees this as an important area for the EU to demonstrate its 'added value' to citizens. This agenda is very much tied up with the EU's expressed programme of creating an 'area of freedom, security and justice', a phrase adopted in the 1997 Treaty of Amsterdam. The idea is that:

> Citizens of the European Union enjoy unparalleled freedom to travel, work and live anywhere in the EU. To benefit fully, people need to lead their lives and go about their business in security and safety. They must be protected against international crime and terrorism, and at the same time enjoy equal access to justice and respect for their fundamental rights across the EU. This is why the EU is creating an area of freedom, security and justice. (European Commission 2008)

Thus the notions of free movement, citizenship, and the 'area of freedom, security and justice' are closely bound in EU rhetoric. Free movement can be said to imply the need for certain political rights, as well as judicial and police cooperation to protect individuals as they live, work and move around in the EU. This way of linking up free movement with both citizenship provisions and police and judicial cooperation appears to be a classic case of matching solutions to problems. The European Commission is keen to bolster support for more extensive cooperation on justice and home affairs, and attempts to justify such cooperation through linking it to the goal of free movement, which has, of course, a much longer and more established vintage.

Little of this rhetoric has permeated the consciousness of EU residents. Arguably, the most significant shapers of a sense of shared identity have come about as side-effects of other measures and procedures: visa-waivers and provisions for passport or customs checks at European airports may help create a sense of commonality, at least *vis-à-vis* those from non-EEA or Schengen countries; while the availability of cheap European flights through a 'Ryanair effect' has greatly increased intra-European tourism. Not least, the common currency, the Euro, has undoubtedly contributed to a sense of commonality among nationals of its member states. The more high-flown discourse on citizenship emanating from the Commission and from various European Council Conclusions and treaties, on the other hand, shows little sign of impacting on firmly entrenched conceptions of political membership along national lines. Indeed, one prominent scholar of European citizenship has dubbed the EU citizenship project 'a dismal failure' (Bauböck 2005).

Political debate

Mobility within the EU really emerges only as a contentious issue where it is seen as running counter to national interests – whether because of concerns about competition for jobs with non-nationals, or as creating a burden on welfare and social provisions. There is also evidence of an elite category of higher-skilled mobility by 'Eurostars' congregated in 'Eurocities' such as Brussels, London and Paris (Favell 2007). While political resistance to free movement within the EU tends to be patchy and sporadic, there are many groups that strongly support the project. These supporters include most areas of business, economists, politicians with a liberal bent, and also more protectionist politicians espousing a federalist vision of Europe. In this sense, EU mobility is a classic case of a policy yielding a liberal outcome: the costs of mobility are diffuse, but its benefits are concentrated, implying strong incentives for advocates to lobby hard for reduced impediments to free movement (Freeman 1995).

Nevertheless, as was seen in the previous section of this chapter, where mobility *has* become politicized – for examples in debates on enlargement and on social dumping – governments have been prepared to make concessions to popular pressure. Such concessions do tend to be only at the fringes and involve imposing moratoria on free movement or attempting to mitigate the impact of free movement on local jobs or wages. Indeed, governments are highly constrained in their margin of manoeuvre in this area. Not only are they obliged to admit and grant full labour rights to EU nationals; they are also committed to prioritizing the claims of these nationals to jobs over those of non-EEA nationals. This has been a source of some embarrassment for governments with established ties to third countries or formal arrangements for recruitment from them. Thus the UK, for example, was severely criticized for favouring EEA recruits in the medical sector over nationals of third countries who had actually spent several years studying in the UK.

Moreover, in many cases, opposition parties have little sympathy for the constraints imposed on governments by EU provisions. There have been frequent cases of populist parties mobilizing support through their opposition to provisions that incumbents are simply unable to evade (and indeed, which opposition parties would also be obliged to embrace were they to win power). This can create a tension between the often unfeasible demands of opposition politics and the scope of action of governments, which has elsewhere been described as a 'populist gap' (Boswell 2003).

How do governments cope with these constraints? In fact, they can and have used the EU as a way of excusing certain unpopular provisions, such as provisions on mobility, or the lack of intra-EU border controls, along the lines that 'there is nothing we can do about it'. This tactic works best in pro-EU countries, where opposition parties largely accept the EU and the constraints it imposes on domestic immigration policy. It is less likely to work in countries with strong Eurosceptic opposition parties, where these can question the wisdom of signing up to such EU arrangements at all. Thus in Austria, Italy, the Netherlands and the UK, populist right-wing parties or anti-European sections of mainstream centre-right parties have all questioned certain aspects of EU provisions on free movement, implying that it would be possible for the government to opt out of EU arrangements (or leave the EU altogether). Again, it is questionable how far such parties can and will act on these positions once in power. Indeed, right-wing governments in Austria, Denmark, Italy and the Netherlands have continued on a similar course of embracing EU provisions on mobility, despite some contrary rhetoric.

At the same time, governments can attempt to wield influence on EU legislation, encouraging other countries to adopt measures that would mitigate any awkward domestic problems caused by mobility. A good example of this would be Germany, which has used its clout in the EU – and its tactical alliance with other countries such as France – to soften some of the more damaging political fallout from mobility. Thus, as we saw above, it was able to push for the Posted Workers Directive to limit the problems raised by social dumping in the German construction industry. Germany and other member states such as Austria and France have also been exercising their influence on the EU to try to block or at least postpone the accession of Turkey to the EU, mainly because of concerns about mobility by Turkish nationals. If Turkey were to join the EU at some point in the future – although when this point may be is far from clear – then there may also be significant constraints on movement by Turkish nationals in the form of transitional arrangements.

How have newer immigration countries in southern Europe responded to EU provisions on mobility? As we saw, Greece, Portugal and Spain all had temporary restrictions placed on mobility after acceding to the EU, because of fears about north–south labour migration. And until recently there was very little debate within these countries about questions of mobility *to* the southern countries from the rest of the EU. Migration in this direction has been mainly limited to small numbers of skilled migrants seeking a better quality of life (and a sunnier climate), or large numbers of northern European pensioners moving south, especially to the Spanish coast, to retire – so-called 'sunset migration' (King and Zontini 2000). That has changed more recently, with Italy and Spain both receiving large numbers of nationals from central and eastern Europe.

Spain, for example, has seen a massive rise in immigration with an increase in the migrant population from 2 to 12 per cent of the total between 2000 and 2010. Of these, the largest group has been Romanians. Indeed, Spain has become the most important destination country for both Romanian and Bulgarian emigrants (OECD 2008). Part of this immigration takes the form of so-called 'annual quota' migration, as well as bilateral agreements to recruit seasonal workers. However, much of it consisted of irregular migrants who subsequently regularized their status under one of the government's amnesty programmes (Balch 2010).

Interestingly, this immigration flow has not been affected by enlargement and mobility provisions, since Spain initially imposed a restriction on free movement for the nationals of accession countries in both waves of enlargement – 2004 and 2007. This restriction on free movement by A8 nationals was relaxed in May 2006. A work permit scheme was introduced for Bulgarian and Romanian nationals after the accession of these states in 2007, but this was dropped in January 2009. Indeed, these flows largely predated the accession of Bulgaria and Romania in 2007. Instead, the immigration of Romanian and Bulgarian nationals may well have been influenced by the waiver in 2002 of a visa requirement for nationals of these countries entering Schengen countries, which facilitated entry and subsequent overstay (Elrick and Ciobanu 2009). In this sense, concerns about excessive immigration from these countries cannot be laid at the door of EU free-movement provisions and enlargement, but probably has more to do with other factors: the high demand for low-skilled labour in Spain's agricultural, construction and tourism sectors; the signing of bilateral agreements for labour recruitment; and, in the case of Romanians, the linguistic similarities between Spanish and Romanian. In fact, while public opinion and debate has registered increasing concerns about immigration, Romanians and Bulgarians have not tended to be the main target of hostility. Instead, much of the public debate on excessive uncontrolled immigration focuses on irregular entry from northern Africa via Spain's coastline, and the large numbers of especially Moroccan immigrants in the country.

Spain has also been a recipient of 'sunset migration' by retired people moving from the colder climes of northern Europe to warmer weather in the south. Box 8.3 surveys this sunset migration.

In Italy, people from new EU member states, and especially Roma, have been the target of hostile and vitriolic media coverage and racial harassment. Following the rape of an Italian woman in November 2007 by an irregular migrant presumed to be of Roma origin, there was a massive popular and media backlash against Italy's 150,000-strong Roma community. Silvio Berlusconi's rightwing government responded with a heavy clampdown on Roma, declaring a 'Roma emergency', shutting down unauthorized Roma camps and deploying 3,000 soldiers around stations and tourist spots in Rome to crack down on Roma crime (Meo 2008). The

Box 8.3   Sunset migration

'Sunset' migration refers to pensioners relocating to another country for their retirement. In the European context, it is often associated with migration from northern countries such as Germany, the Netherlands and the UK to sunnier climes in the south. The main motivations for sunset migration appear to be the wish for a change in lifestyle and environment. Increased sunset migration since the 1970s has been made possible by increased longevity, earlier retirement, raised incomes and increased assets (King and Zontini 2000). Many destinations coincide with the most popular tourist destinations, such as coastal areas of Spain, implying a strong link between previous holidays and place of retirement.

Sunset migration has spurred an increase in housing developments along the Iberian coastline and the emergence of new settlement areas, such as the *urbanizaciones* in Spain. In turn, this has triggered debates in the Spanish media about an invasion of foreigners, rising house prices, and environmental effects of development (Dasado-Diaz *et al.* 2004). It has also raised social issues about health and welfare services in these areas, and concerns about the poor integration of many pensioners, who remain relatively isolated in their expatriate communities (O'Reilly 2007).

government also introduced a controversial measure, which involved photographing and fingerprinting all Roma over 14 years of age (Pisa 2008). The measures were roundly criticized by NGOs and international organizations including the Council of Europe and the UN Commissioner for Human Rights, and were the object of a resolution in 2008 adopted by the EP condemning the government for measures that violated numerous human rights and anti-discrimination provisions. The European Commission duly approached the Italian government to criticize the provisions, and received a report from the Italian government at the beginning of August reassuring them that the exercise would be carried out in conformity with relevant laws, which apparently satisfied the Commission (Barrot 2008).

The issue of free movement was thrown into stark relief in 2010. when France began to expel Roma (mainly from Romania, but also from Bulgaria) whom the French government claimed were illegally resident on French territory.The French immigration minister

Pierre Lellouche sought to blame the Romanian government for an influx of Roma to France and, at a Brussels press conference in September 2010, used the French verb 'se défausser', which means 'to get rid of a bad card', to describe the behaviour of the Romanian government in allegedly seeking to offload the issue on to the French. Around 8,000 Roma were sent from France to Romania and Bulgaria in the first nine months of 2010. Each received a small cash compensation of €300. In a remarkably strong attack on a member state government, the European Commissioner responsible for free movement, Viviane Reding, labelled the French government's actions 'a disgrace'. On 30 September 2010 the European Commission issued a letter of formal notice to the French government requesting full information on the transposition of the 2004 free movement directive into national law.

A leaked French government document had suggested that Roma were being specifically targeted for expulsion, which would be a breach of EU law. In its letter of formal notice, the Commission asked detailed questions about the practical application of French repatriation policy since summer 2010 and to explain whether or not there was the objective or the effect of targeting a specific ethnic minority. EU law requires that all EU citizens are treated equally.

Finally, we should consider how political debates in the new member states have dealt with mobility issues. In the runup to accession, the primary concern for governments of A8 countries was that their nationals should receive treatment equal to that of other EU citizens – including mobility rights. As we have seen, such rights were made subject to a transition arrangement in most EU countries, such that full access to the labour market was not permitted until 1 May 2007. While the central and eastern European countries joining the EU in 2004 accepted the imposition of moratoria on free movement of their nationals, they were far from happy with arrangements. The Polish government was especially vocal in its objections, with accession negotiator Jan Truszczynski expressing 'our view that there is no sufficient economic basis, nor demographic basis, for having an arrangement of that nature' (Jileva 2002). Indeed, there was a widespread perception of double standards being operated by the EU, which obliged Poland and other A8 states to adopt EU policies on immigration, asylum, visas and border control, while denying them the corollary benefits of mobility.

Interestingly, concerns about discriminatory treatment because of transition arrangements for Poland subsequently gave way to a rather different set of concerns: the risk of a major loss of labour, skills and social payments due to the large outflow of migrant workers from Poland after 2004. While emigration initially had benign effects on the Polish economy, triggering a reduction in unemployment, it soon became evident that most of those leaving were relatively young, skilled people. The departure of over 1.2 million Poles to the UK, Ireland and Sweden by late 2007 raised fears of a 'brain drain' and a 'youth drain', which could severely hamper the Polish economy and welfare provisions. In September 2007 the government introduced a range of incentives to try to encourage its nationals to return home, including measures to facilitate the launch of new businesses, job fairs to inform Poles about rising wages and job opportunities at home, and greater support for Polish language schools in other EU countries to facilitate the eventual return of migrants (Spiegel 2007).

Administrative practice and implementation

As we have seen, the EU exercises quite extensive influence in the area of free movement. This influence should be understood not just in terms of the broad parameters of free movement, but also in its effect on a number of policies at the margins of free movement. These tend to receive less attention in political debate. A combination of legislation and judicial intervention has, however, meant that, in practice, free-movement provisions have had knock-on effects in a number of related areas. One of these areas is in relation to the rights of EU nationals residing in another country. EU nationals who have relocated to another country are supposed to enjoy the same social advantages as national workers. Indeed, a series of ECJ rulings have successfully expanded the rights of EU nationals in areas of child support, education, employment, training, family and pensions (Allen 1999).

Free-movement provisions have also affected the rights of TCNs resident in member states, although the impact of the measures in these areas remains relatively limited. This relates to the rights of immigrants resident in a particular state to live and work in another one (see also Chapter 9 on integration). As we have seen, the right of free movement is in principle reserved for citizens of

EU member states, but a series of decisions has expanded certain aspects of the free-movement provisions to apply to TCNs. Under the Schengen Agreement, TCNs were allowed to circulate within the Schengen territory for short-term stays of up to three months, and in 1999 this provision was incorporated into the main European Community treaty framework following the ratification of the Amsterdam Treaty (Kostakopoulou 2002). In 2003, a Council Directive on the rights of long-term residents extended these provisions in two main ways. First, it defined a new *EU* status of 'long-term resident' to all TCNs who had been resident in a member state for five years or more, with a legal status comparable to citizens of that country. More importantly for free movement, it stated that long-term residents could reside in a second member state for *more than* three months, for the purpose of economic activity as employed or self-employed, to pursue studies or vocational training, or for other purposes. The gradual extension of free-movement provisions to TCNs is justified as a means of promoting labour mobility, and also in order to promote the effective integration of immigrants. As we see in Chapter 9 when we look at this measure in more detail, progress in this area is still relatively circumscribed. It does, however, have the potential for gradual expansion over coming years, despite – or maybe because of – its low political profile.

Another way mobility provisions can affect other areas of immigration policy is in terms of how individuals have used citizenship provisions to secure free-movement rights. Free-movement provisions apply to all citizens of EU states, but they ignore the question of *how* this citizenship status is acquired. Thus many countries (indeed seven of the 'old' EU member states and all those that acceded in 2004 and 2007) allow their emigrants to transfer nationality to subsequent generations. So Argentinians or Brazilians can 'discover' their Italian roots, and now have access to full mobility rights across the EU (Bauböck 2005). Professional footballers, for example, have been quite rigorous in their analysis of family trees in order to discover European ancestry that can then allow them to ply their trade in the more lucrative European leagues as EU citizens. Similarly, countries which permit those born on their territory to acquire citizenship – such as Ireland until it changed its laws recently – would permit those children and their primary caregivers to mobility within the EU. Indeed, as we saw at the start of this chapter, such a claim was upheld by the ECJ in 2004, when a Chinese national, Mrs Chen, whose child had been born in Ireland defended her entitlement to residence in the UK.

Thus there are a number of dynamics that have led to an expansion of free-movement provisions to cover perhaps unanticipated circumstances and arrangements. Part of this expansionist dynamic seems to be a classic instance of 'spillover' from different policy areas:

- from the realization of the common market to free-movement provisions;
- from free-movement provisions to social and political rights;
- from these rights to a concept of EU citizenship for member state nationals; and
- from the ongoing (if gradual) expansion of this scope of citizenship to long-term residents from outside the EU.

Some of this dynamic is driven by the European Commission and various treaties, while in other cases it is individual claims-making backed up by the ECJ that has served this expansion.

Despite these various provisions, in practice, mobility within the EU remains relatively low. The Commission has been keen to promote free movement and greater mobility as a way of attaining its ambitious economic reform objectives. The European Commission (CEC 2007b) has highlighted various obstacles that it considers are impeding higher levels of mobility:

- problems of legal and administrative obstacles;
- housing costs and availability;
- employment of spouses and partners;
- portability of pensions;
- linguistic barriers;
- problems with the acceptance of qualifications in other countries.

The European Commission has been active in seeking to overcome these barriers – indeed, the goal of promoting mobility has become one of the key tenets of its ideology, and a core part of its bid to promote European integration. It has launched a string of initiatives to try to increase levels of movement. In 1996 it set up the High-Level Panel on the Free Movement of Persons, chaired by the prominent French politician Simone Veil, to identify barriers to mobility. This produced more than eighty recommendations on issues of entry and residence, access to employment, social rights and family status, tax and pensions, many of which were incorporated into the Commission's 1997 Action Plan for the Free Movement of Workers. Clearly this did not have the desired impact, because in 2002 the Commission launched a new Action Plan for Skills and Mobility. This plan included further analyses and measures to promote mobility, including designating 2006 as the 'Year of Workers' Mobility', and allocating funding to a series of projects to raise awareness of mobility possibilities. Again, the action plan was succeeded by a further Job Mobility Action Plan for 2007–10, which aimed to improve existing legislation and administrative practice regarding worker mobility, and raise awareness of the 'possibilities and advantages of mobility' among the public.

One of the main obstacles highlighted in recent contributions from the Commission has been the problem of coordinating arrangements for social security between countries. Based on a survey of 'stakeholders' (mainly employers and trade unions), the Commission has argued that the complexity and divergence between different social security systems can deter people from moving to take up shorter-term employment. For example, a worker employed under short-term contracts in different countries would need to deal with several different social security schemes. Another disincentive seems to be problems with the portability of supplementary pensions between different countries. Some of these problems may stem from administrative practices in implementing European arrangements addressing the rights of mobile workers.

Clearly, the Commission will continue in its attempts to remove barriers wherever it is so able: factors such as lack of information on possibilities for mobility, the recognition of qualifications, or facilitating access to social security or pensions for mobile workers. However, it is unclear how far such impediments really account for the lack of mobility within the EU. Indeed, as Guild (2005) has argued, the removal of obstructions to free movement through abolishing residence and work permits has actually coincided with a reduction in intra-EU mobility. So the impact of such measures may be relatively weak, with other factors such as linguistic or cultural barriers to mobility proving far more intractable. Favell has argued that there are a range of more insidious social and cultural barriers to free movement, with Europe remaining 'an imagined landscape of national cities, national cultures, and national differences' (Favell 2003).

Conclusion

EU provisions on free movement exercise an important constraint on member states' national prerogatives in the area of migration policy. These constraints apply not just to national jurisdiction over admissions policy but also, increasingly, to the rights and status of EU citizens *and* TCNs resident on their territory. However, intra-EU mobility remains relatively low, and these provisions have proved relatively uncontroversial. The main exceptions to this are in the context of contentious episodes such as EU enlargements, as well as claims about native workers being 'undercut' by EU competition, or so-called social dumping. Public debate about mobility usually fades into the background in the absence of perceived competition for jobs or pressures on welfare systems. It will be interesting to see how far concerns about mobility surface in the context of the recent recession in Europe from 2008 onwards.

In an important sense, then, support for intra-EU mobility is very much dependent on the premise that EU nationals have similar socio-economic opportunities in their countries of origin, and thus will not use mobility rights to take advantage of higher wages or welfare benefits. This may be partly because mobility is generally only permitted once a member state's labour market and macroeconomic conditions are sufficiently propitious to discourage large-scale emigration. Moreover, various administrative, social and cultural impediments continue to provide disincentives to relocate to another EU country. This all implies that highflown talk about a common labour market supported by EU citizenship rights may be misplaced, at least for the time being.

Chapter 9

Immigrant Integration

This chapter shifts the focus to analyse immigrant integration. We have thus far concentrated on extra- and intra-EU population movement. We now look at 'what happens next' by analysing diverse responses to immigrant integration across the EU, their link to diverse models of nationality and citizenship and at how the EU now plays some role in these debates through, in particular, the two anti-discrimination Directives introduced in 2000 and a 2003 Directive on the rights of long-term residents as well as 'softer', non-legally-binding measures such as its integration handbook and funding instruments for integration projects (CEC 2004). We see integration as a two-way process involving adaptation by both migrant newcomers and members of the host society. The balance between the two and the associated expectations are, of course, central to the content of policy. We also show that, despite tendencies to overemphasize the cultural and ideological components of debates about integration, identity and citizenship, it is multiple adjustments in everyday life in relation to education, work, housing and health that play a key role in shaping identities and understandings of the effects of immigration. This means that we seek to avoid the risk of essentializing the identities of migrants – assuming that they act because of their status as migrants and that this crucially informs their social identities – and prefer to look at how identities are made, remade, shaped and reshaped in social and political contexts. In such circumstances, the key issue is to focus on these social and institutional contexts. When we do so at EU level, we see that this context is 'thin' in the sense that EU capacities are limited; but there have been significant developments and these do play a role in reshaping understandings of immigrant integration. We also see that member states have been keen to ensure that their own integration policy priorities are evident in EU measures too.

A good way to begin this discussion is to try to think what 'integration' might now look like for someone thinking of moving to an EU member state. In the Netherlands it is becoming a basis for entry – in the form of a pre-entry test. This means that non-EU migrants thinking of going to the Netherlands on a temporary basis with a view to a permanent stay there is now a 'Civic Integration Examination Abroad' taken at a Dutch embassy in the potential migrant's country of origin. The examination consists of a 30-minute film and then some questions in Dutch about it followed by a test of Dutch language abilities. Similarly, for those seeking to settle in the UK, there is a test that must be taken. The 'Life in the UK' website gives an idea of the kinds of questions that might be asked that provide fairly extensive coverage of UK society, history and institutions. In France and Germany too there are tests for would-be settlers.

These tests are supposed to examine the ability of migrants to adapt to life in the country to which they plan to move. These all mark a change in the direction of immigrant integration policies with a stronger emphasis on socio-economic integration and linguistic adaptation and a move away from 'multicultural' policies that emphasized group-based rights and own-language teaching. The obvious tension here is that societies in EU member states seem to be more multicultural, but official policy responses seem to place less emphasis on multiculturalism. Multicultural policies appear to be in retreat, as is marked by a growing emphasis on socio-economic integration and linguistic adaptation by migrant newcomers. In his analysis of France and Germany, Brubaker (2001) refers to a 'return to assimilation'. A key policy concern has been Europe's Muslim populations with, on the one hand, fears of alienation, radicalization and violence among a minority of (mainly) younger Muslims, but, on the other, hostility (sometimes labelled as 'Islamophobia') towards the peaceful and law-abiding majority of Europe's Muslim population.

When the focus shifts to EU action we see that this tends to derive its legitimacy from core market-making purposes. It is the status of TCNs as economic actors within the single market that informs the development of EU measures The EU role has developed since 2000 when the two Directives enacting EU laws to combat discrimination on the grounds of race and ethnicity were agreed. The Race Equality Directive of June 2000 provided for equal treatment for all people irrespective of their racial or ethnic origin, while the Equal Treatment Directive of November 2000 provided for protection against direct and indirect discrimination in employment, social protection and the provision of services. A

November 2003 Directive then extended to legally resident TCNs rights equivalent to those of EU citizens. These three measures are significant because they are binding and thus have implications for national law and policy as they must be implemented by member states. They do not represent lowest-common-denominator policy-making, as all three contain elements that mark a significant levelling-up in provision.

Narratives

In member states, not all migrants are subject to explicit policy interventions designed to promote their integration *qua* immigrants. EU states tend to worry far less about the integration of high-skilled migrants from the developed world and far more about lower-skilled migrants and their family members from less-developed parts of the world. They have also been far more concerned in recent years about Europe's Muslim minorities and their integration (or lack of it).

At a general level, we can distinguish between four groups that could be a reference for national or EU level immigrant integration policies.

First, citizens of EU member states (and thus EU citizens) who are immigrants or the descendants of immigrants. EU citizens can move freely, have been protected since the Treaty of Rome (1957) from discrimination on the grounds of nationality and gender and are now subject to protections offered by EU anti-discrimination and integration measures, including on grounds of race and ethnic origin.

Second, non-EU nationals (TCNs, in EU parlance) living in EU member states were formally excluded from the EU rights framework. The rights that they did have tended to derive from the laws of the member state in which they lived. We will see how since 2003 the EU has offered rights to legally resident TCNs and thus offers rights that derive from residence in a member state and not from holding the nationality of that state. Writing in the mid-1980s, Tomas Hammar coined the term 'denizens' to describe immigrants who were not nationals of the country they moved to, but who did acquire legal and social rights that fell short of full citizenship. By extending rights to 'long-term residents' the EU adds a supranational gloss to denizenship.

Third, EU citizens moving within the EU have long been protected by an EU mobility framework that, for example, allows transferability of social entitlements, including healthcare and pensions. This can at times be controversial, as we saw in the instance (Chapter 8) of UK Portuguese construction workers moving to Germany in the early 1990s to work on German building sites under EU provisions that guaranteed the right of establishment. They were seen to undercut the terms and conditions of German building workers and thus to threaten the German labour market and welfare system.

Fourth, non-EU citizens/TCNs moving within the EU were largely excluded from the EU rights framework, but have since the 2003 Directive on the rights of long-term residents acquired rights akin to those of EU citizens after 5 years' legal residence. The argument here is primarily economic – that is, that if the EU is to attain economic growth objectives then mobility of workers can be beneficial.

An additional complication is that it is not always easy to delineate statistically between these groups, as there is divergence in the ways data are gathered. Some countries such as France and Italy do not officially collect data on ethnic origin, which makes it difficult to view second or third generations of the migrant-origin population that have naturalized but may still experience disadvantages related to their migration heritage. Data on ethnic origin are systematically collected in countries such as the UK and the Netherlands, although this does not mean that these countries have necessarily been any more or less successful in integrating their migrant-origin populations.

Levels and dimensions

We now ask why the EU involves itself in immigrant integration policies. Aren't these primarily local and national issues where the principle of subsidiarity – decisions made at the lowest possible level – should apply? Moreover, is it not the case that the force and weight of national histories give meaning to immigrant integration? If so, then why have EU competencies developed? To what extent does this EU dimension differ in scope, form and content from national debates? Do the ideas and practices that animate action at EU level differ from those seen at member state level?

To start with, we can note that there is something new and distinct about the EU dimension that means it cannot be captured by viewing it as some kind of amalgam of 27 member states' responses or as some form of lowest-common-denominator response that indicates EU action but commits member states to very little that they are not already doing. EU action has not developed as a result of a desire to trample over national policies and to create a single Europe-wide approach to immigrant integration. Instead, its development is multi-causal and associated with a bundle of concerns:

- the dynamics of single-market integration;
- the perceived need to develop a rights framework for TCNs that extends the principles that support economic integration;
- a reaction against racist and xenophobic political movements;
- a necessary accompaniment to EU action on migration policies;
- a reflection of member states' concerns about the perceived failings of integration policies.

This means that there is no simple and straightforward narrative construction of the relationship between, for example, single-market integration and 'spillover' into the area of immigrant integration and migrants' rights. What we see later in the chapter is that a series of solutions to the 'incomplete membership' status of TCNs were already in circulation in the 1990s. The argument was that extending EU rights to TCNs could facilitate attainment of economic integration. To return to the framework established in Chapter 2, this could be seen as a set of 'solutions' that emphasized the potential economic contribution of migrants and these potential solutions, then sought to attach themselves to an EU 'problem' of the absence of EU protection for TCN rights.

Economic arguments did have some purchase at EU level, but the member states would need to see the logic of this or else nothing could be agreed. This meant that another powerful narrative exerted its influence over debates about immigration and this was primarily national and was linked to the perceived failure of multicultural policies. The theories and beliefs that inform debates about immigrant integration are strongly informed by historical and organizational memory, with significant divergence between EU member states in relation to different institutional settings and different understandings of national history in the face of immigration. Narratives about immigrant integration have been revised in line with a prevailing understanding that multicultural policies have failed to deliver integration. This means that we need to see how perceptions of failure fed back to influence the narrative framing of the issues.

There are also some rather basic disputes about terminology. We could get hopelessly bogged down in a rather tedious discussion of whether we should use words such as 'integration', 'inclusion', 'incorporation' or 'accommodation'. In the context of the analysis that we seek to develop throughout this book, it makes sense to use (and explore the usage of) the term that is most frequently used in national and EU policy debates – that is, 'integration'. The point is that it is important to understand the effects that particular conceptualizations can have, because the term 'integration' is widely used but deeply contested. Even the processes that might contribute to or detract from it are often unclear. Some basic questions are:

- Integration by whom (which groups)?
- How (what processes) and into what (which entity)?
- How would we know if it were achieved?
- How could it be measured?
- Would linguistic or cultural adaptation tell us something about integration?
- Would racist or xenophobic attitudes among members of the receiving state population provide evidence of barriers to integration?
- Could levels of educational attainment or types of employment also be signs of immigrant integration?

In fact, all (and many others) may tell us something about immigrant integration, or its absence.

Each of these indicators is also clearly linked to broader dynamics that go beyond the analysis of immigration. For example, measuring cultural adaptation would require some statement about which cultural norms or standards it is that immigrants are supposed to attain. In most EU states these are deeply contested, with scope for significant subnational variations.

Put another way, there are all kinds of 'intervening variables' that affect the relationship between migration and integration. For instance, educational or employment outcomes are linked to the highly complex organization of the education system and labour markets, and cannot simply be reduced to the immigration status or history of an individual, although these can and do also make a difference (Fleischmann and Dronkers 2007).

We also see that there is significant variation over time and between EU states in narratives about immigrant integration, with complex effects as the perceived results of past interventions feed back into current debates. Immigrant integration thus means different things in different places at different points in time. More usually, it is seen in its absence – that is, as the perceived failure of policy to secure immigrant integration that tends to be a salient public policy concern. Policy failure then becomes a resource around which mobilizations can occur. More particularly, it tends to be the failure of policy to secure the integration of certain targeted immigrant groups that is seen as emblematic of policy failure. Indeed, this is an issue area that is convulsed by perceptions of policy failure. The re-evaluations of integration policies that have occurred across the EU since the 1990s have been strongly driven by the perceptions that previous policies failed, that multicultural policies are in retreat and that civic integration has created a new Europe-wide framework for understanding core policy dilemmas and solutions to them (Joppke and Morawska 2001).

Narrative formulations of immigrant integration also tend to weave together a number of factors that, even on their own, would be rather complex. There are strong references to cultural adaptation on the part of either newcomers or those in the destination country (more usually both), and reference also to institutional factors that play a key role in mediating the relationship between newcomers and the societies they move to. It is in these terms that we can understand competing narratives of multiculturalism and civic integration.

Multicultural policies seek to reflect, represent and maintain the distinct cultural identities of migrant groups both because of the intrinsic value of these cultures and because this is seen as a vehicle for promotion of immigrant integration. Integration would thus not be a flattening process but equal opportunity accompanied by cultural diversity, as British Home Secretary Roy Jenkins put it in 1966. The Netherlands too followed a similar path with its 'minorities policy', which also sought to protect the cultural diversity of migrants through a group-based response to integration and measures such as support for education in the language of the origin country. Sweden too pursued a multicultural model. Other countries adopted wholly different responses.

Many nations eschewed such a multicultural approach. The French model – often labelled as a 'republican' approach – disavowed the group-based emphasis of the UK and the Netherlands whilst seeing integration as a process by which ethnic or racial differences would disappear as migrants were integrated into the French national community. France has, therefore, refused to collect data on the ethnic or racial background of its population because to do so would be divisive. Central to this French approach were expansive nationality laws that allowed foreigners to become French.

If we move to Germany we see another distinct approach to integration. Until the late 1990s Germany did not have formal mmigration or integration policies because there was no official acceptance that it was an immigration country. This meant that a social citizenship model was pursued where inclusion into the world of work and into welfare state membership was a route to integration.

We see significant diversity in all these countries as they pursue distinct 'philosophies of integration', as Favell (1998) put it. However, we see some evidence of convergence too. For example, France, Germany, the Netherlands and the UK have all adopted aspects of a civic integration approach marked, for example, by tests for migrant newcomers. This could be seen as indicative of convergence in the theories and beliefs informing policymaking. A note of caution does however need to be struck because ostensibly similar developments in various European countries may have different causes. What would seem relevant as a backdrop in all of these cases is EU membership, migration flows and settlement, plus the broader effects of welfare and labour market change. Obviously these work out in different ways because each of these countries has, for example, a different way of organizing their welfare state and labour market. However, we know that immigration policy is linked to economic performance. It seems plausible to link trends and patterns in integration policy to economic performance and to a key aspect of the identity of EU states – that is, their status as welfare states.

At EU level too we can see the influence of theories and beliefs that have informed the national turn to civic integration. At EU level also, however, we see a distinct twist to the debate because of the connections made in the narrative framing of the issues between immigrant integration and the rights framework underpinning European economic integration. The result is that the spatial relocation to EU level does create a distinct setting with its own forms of legal, social and political power; but, equally, the EU setting cannot be detached from national developments.

Political debate

This section explores the articulation of ideas about immigrant integration in political debate and decision-making at state and supranational level. If politics is centrally concerned with the questions of who gets what, when and how, then debates about immigrant integration can be seen as attempts to reframe the organizational and conceptual borders of a given community (usually a state) so as to develop the capacity to integrate or exclude migrant newcomers.

One of the more obvious arenas within which this reframing and reorganizing occurs is that of party politics. Radical, right-wing populist parties have been in government in Denmark, Italy and Austria while the *Front National* has had a significant presence in French politics at local and national level since the 1980s. In 2009, the British National Party (BNP) secured two seats in the EP and was able to join up with a small group of extreme-right and racist parties.

Have these extremist and racist parties had a strong impact on debates about migration? Have they managed to channel public hostility to immigration into the mainstream of party debate? What effects have they had on mainstream parties of the left and right? It could be the case that centre-right and centre-left parties have been caught like rabbits startled by the headlights of an oncoming car in the face of the rise or resurgence of right-wing extremists and perhaps have even meekly followed their agenda. Indeed, in 2008, British Prime Minister Gordon Brown seemed to draw from extreme-right discourse when he talked about 'British jobs for British workers'. Bale (2008) however is sceptical of the view that mainstream parties meekly follow the extreme-right agenda. After all, these parties have been key and powerful actors in European politics, but- if we follow this line of reasoning - then it would seem that they have been unable to make up their own minds on these important issues and simply followed the agendas of the extremists. This would be a strange situation because the kinds of issues that immigration and immigrant integration pose for the economy and wider society are important to centre-right and centre-left parties. They have consistently articulated their position on these issues. It may well be the case that we need to look elsewhere for the influence of extreme-right parties as they may not exercise this influence directly in government, but through an ability to frame issues and set the terms of debate. At the same time, we should also acknowledge the role and capacity of mainstream parties to take ownership of these issues and establish positions on what are clearly pressing social and political concerns.

If we focus on mainstream parties, can we see differences on immigrant integration issues between centre-right and centre-left parties? The evidence here is sparse. Givens and Luedtke (2005) analyse France, Germany and the UK between 1990 and 2002 and find that centre-right and centre-left parties are less likely to diverge on immigration control, but that there are sharper differences on integration, with right-wing parties more likely to be less favourable towards multicultural approaches and centre-left parties to be more favourable. Duncan and Van Hecke (2008) come to a similar conclusion in their analysis of the centre-right and centre-left transnational party federations in the EP. They find Christian Democrats and Conservatives to be less in favour of multiculturalism than are centre-left parties.

This insight into party behaviour can be placed alongside a prominent strand of work on policymaking that identifies the centrality of venue. Guiraudon's (1998) account of developments in France, Germany and the Netherlands does point to the importance of political opportunities at certain conjunctures. This again points to the importance of the temporal dimension – that is, opportunities created at particular points in time that have facilitated the emergence or development of extreme right-wing parties. One instance of this was the shift to proportional representation in France in the 1980s that helped the FN secure high levels of parliamentary representation. In the UK in 2009, it was 'second-order' EP elections fought on a PR basis with very low turnout and with Westminster MPs racked by scandal concerning their expenses claims that facilitated entry by two BNP MEPs in 2009.

The EU dimension

In this section we explore the EU's channelling of political debate through analysis of supranational institutions and the venues within which decisions about immigrant integration are made.

It is only really since 1997 and the Amsterdam Treaty that the EU has staked out a role for itself in the area of immigrant integration. More specifically, this has been marked by the increased presence of the Commission and EP in these debates. Until 1997 there was no legal basis for EU action. So, while the European Commission could push for immigrants to be part of the 'social inclusion' frame that it was seeking to strengthen throughout the 1980s and 1990s, the member states in the Council could always retort that there was no legal basis for such action to include TCNs. This began to change in the runup to the Amsterdam Treaty when there was concern about racist and xenophobic attacks across Europe and the damage that these caused to a Union founded on progressive and inclusive ideals. The Amsterdam Treaty introduced specific measures in article 13 that provided a legal base for EU action to counter various forms of discrimination (on the grounds of race, ethnic origin, age, disability, religion and sexual orientation).

The 'social inclusion' frame provided a powerful set of tools for mobilizations that sought to extend the EU rights framework to include TCNs. There are three interesting aspects to these mobilizations that also tell us interesting things about the EU setting.

A set of 'solutions' to the issues of deficient TCN rights were developed in the 1990s, which sought a 'problem' to which they could attach themselves. The problem that resonated most effectively with EU competencies was not nationality – that is, the EU intervening in nationality laws of the member states, but equal treatment for TCNs alongside EU citizens in the single market.

The mobilizations that were successful at EU level were not evidence of grassroots pressure from migrant organizations. Rather, they were based on the mobilization of expertise – particularly legal expertise by think-tanks and lobby groups. This was mobilization *on behalf of* migrants, not by them.

The ideas that were particularly influential within these mobilizations of expertise were drawn from the UK and Dutch settings, where legislation sought to tackle both direct and indirect discrimination and to target 'ethnic minorities'.

It is, however, one thing for member states to agree to a Treaty provision, but it is another to turn the commitment in article 13 of the Amsterdam Treaty into EU law. To do so would require the agreement of all the member states and, as we have seen, they have rather different understandings of these issues. Wouldn't the risk be a watered-down, lowest-common-denominator policy? In fact, what we do see during a rather remarkable negotiation between member state governments in the first 6 months of 2000 was a levelling-up process as EU anti-discrimination laws were agreed by the then 15 member states that led to common EU laws that were significantly more developed than those in many member states.

If we look at this negotiation more closely we see:

- The multilevel and multidimensional nature of EU politics, as state and European actors, including NGOs and think-tanks, sought to stake out a role for themselves in this policy area.
- The construction and articulation of an EU immigrant integration frame that drew heavily from existing EU laws related to economic integration, such as the principles of non-discrimination (nationality and gender were included in the Treaty of Rome) and the commitment to equal treatment contained in a 1976 Directive.
- The impact of contingent events, in this case the entry into the Austrian coalition government in January 2000 of the extreme right-wing Freedom Party. This event in Austria had a major impact on negotiation of the anti-discrimination Directive and on the narrative of immigrant integration that was to be consolidated at EU level in the form of anti-discrimination legislation.

A key question as the member states entered into negotiations on the basis of the Commission's proposal for anti-discrimination laws in the second half of 1999 was whether the French government would agree to proposals for EU anti-discrimination laws that drew heavily from UK and Dutch approaches that targeted both direct and indirect discrimination where explicit reference had been made to ethnic minorities.

The proposals made by the Commission in 1999 for anti-discrimination measures drew from the provisions of the Amsterdam Treaty and commitments in the Treaty of Rome to non-discrimination on grounds of nationality, gender equality and the principle of equal treatment. Non-discrimination, gender equality and equal treatment were linked more broadly to economic integration – that is, their attainment would help secure economic integration objectives. The Commission in the late 1990s argued that a stronger EU response that targeted discrimination experienced by a broader range of groups including migrants and their descendants could help with the attainment of EU economic and social objectives.

If we look behind the scenes, however, we can see how the specific contents of Commission proposals were influenced by ideas propagated by think-tanks and lobby groups in the 1990s that drew quite heavily from the UK and Dutch approach and sought to target both direct and indirect discrimination (Geddes 2008:ch. 7). The problem for the French government was that reference to indirect discrimination mirrored provisions in UK and Dutch law and would, it seemed, require some kind of monitoring to see whether or not discrimination was occurring. How could this be done without referring to the immigrant origin of migrants and gathering data about ethnic origin? During the negotiations in 1999 and 2000 the French government made it clear that they were not prepared to gather data on ethnic origin. This was a non-negotiable issue for the French in the negotiations, but did not mean that they would oppose the Directive or seek to water it down.

Events in Austria were to change the negotiating dynamic. For the French Socialist government, the Freedom Party were little more than Nazi sympathizers who had to be opposed for this reason and for the racist and xenophobic attitudes that they espoused. On the basis of this strong rhetorical commitment to anti-racism it would have been difficult for the French government to then veto proposed EU anti-discrimination legislation. This was so long as key issues, such as the aversion to gathering data on ethnic origin, could be accommodated. The French government did agree to the Directives on race equality (June 2000) and equal treatment on the grounds of racial and ethnic origin in employment and the provision of services (November 2000) with a proviso entered into the text of the final agreement that France would not be obliged to gather data on ethnic origin and would monitor the implementation of the Directive in other ways (Tyson 2001; Geddes and Guiraudon 2004).

By 2000 we see the development at EU level of progressive anti-discrimination legislation that was more advanced in terms of its content than legislation in most member states. It drew from a set of ideas and legal resources that were distinct to the EU context – that is, the legal framework of the single market and rights within it. Could this momentum be maintained? Could the EU offer a more progressive vision of immigrant integration that would somehow be detached from those prevailing in the member states? We now move on to examine the Directive on the rights of long-term residents (November 2003).

The Directive on the rights of long-term residents is important because we see that the concerns of some member states about the 'integration capacity' of immigrant newcomers had become more salient. Austria, Germany and the Netherlands were keen to see a greater emphasis within EU legislation on the capacity of migrants to integrate. This could be linked to a reaction to the terror attacks on the USA in 2001 and the shockwaves that these sent around Europe. This would, however, miss other aspects of this change in emphasis in integration policies, which had been developing before 9/11 and other terrorist attacks. Indeed, it is important to look at the broader dimensions of immigration policies in EU states at the time of the terrorist attacks, as many states were experiencing relatively large-scale immigration, but also seeking to refocus on socio-economic integration and linguistic adaptation in their integration policies. This had been a policy theme in the Netherlands since at least the beginning of the 1990s and cannot be explained by 9/11. In fact, the broader backdrop in the Netherlands and other EU member states was provided by new migration, economic restructuring, welfare state reform and labour market change.

The Netherlands began to re-evaluate its immigrant integration policies in the 1990s and had moved away from an ostensibly multicultural approach towards a stronger focus on socio-economic and linguistic factors. Germany approached the issues from a rather different direction. It was beginning for the first time to think about an immigrant integration policy, but was concerned that the reference in such policies to the national community remained strong. This did not disavow Germany's European identity, but meant that the EU approach that the German government favoured was also grounded in concerns about linguistic adaptation and socio-economic integration by immigrants. The German government thus supported the development of common EU measures on immigrant integration, but wanted to see some reflection in EU law of the domestic policy it was developing. This becomes clear when we analyse the EU's Directive on the rights of long-term residents.

The EU's long-term residents Directive

The rights of TCNs have long been a thorny issue for the EU. The EU is founded on mobility, but this was initially conceptualized as mobility for workers who were nationals of member states. Could legally resident TCNs be included within this framework? Some were, because their country of origin had an agreement with the EU, but this was not a generalized right.

What were the policy options?

- *At national level*
  - *Status*: legal and social rights acquired as a result of residence at national level with no associated rights at EU level.
  - *Process*: denizenship leading to national citizenship.
  - *Key mediating factor*: nationality laws.

- *At EU level*
  - *Status*: legal and social rights acquired as a result of residence at national level count towards the acquisition of rights at national level.
  - *Process*: denizenship leading to EU level rights.
  - *Key mediating factor*: agreement at EU level on the content of legislation.

If EU competencies in this area were to develop then it would challenge a nationally focused understanding of the acquisition of rights. It would also need to be supported by a strong argument. To understand the development of such an argument, we need to focus on the sources of power that have developed at EU level.

The economic integration and social inclusion frames had proven to be crucial legitimating strategies in the case of EU anti-discrimination. This economic focus did, of course, underpin the development of an EU mobility framework. TCNs did not fall within this framework as it developed in the 1950s and 1960s because they were not nationals of a member state and thus beyond the legal reach of the EU. The frame of reference for TCNs was thus the member state in which they resided. There were some special measures contained in agreements with associated states such as Turkey and Morocco, but there were no generalized rights for TCNs. There had been pressure for change in 1997 when the Commission proposed a convention that would in effect create rights of residence whereby TCNs would acquire legal and social rights equivalent to those of EU citizens after a certain period of residence (the Commission proposed that this should happen after 3 years residence). This 1997 proposal had no chance of being enacted. It did however set the scene and chime with arguments made by other groups. These held that the EU mobility framework discriminated against TCN long-term residents in a way that was injurious not only to the TCNs but also to the EU – which, they maintained, would benefit economically through an extension of its mobility rights in the context of a single market. The EU narrative centred on an economic framing of immigrant integration, with TCNs represented as a potential asset within the single market. The extension of rights to them was then consistent with long-established EU equal-treatment provisions. This argument acquired additional leverage in the context of the EU's ambitious Lisbon Agenda for economic reform, agreed in 2000 with the intention of making Europe the world's leading knowledge-based economy by 2010. Whether or not this was ever likely to occur – it did not, as it turned out – the point here is that this programme of economic reform sought greater mobility within the EU. This brought the situation of legally resident TCNs onto the agenda. In addition, the member states at the Tampere summit in 1999 had already agreed that they would 'approximate' the rights of TCNs with those of EU citizens.

On this basis the Commission brought forward new proposals that would effectively extend to legally resident TCNs the same rights as EU citizens after 5 years of legal residence. Denmark, Ireland and the UK exercised their right under the Treaty of Amsterdam to opt out of these discussions and have not been covered by the terms of the Directive. In effect, what was being created was a Europeanized form of denizenship, as non-EU nationals would enjoy social and legal rights backed and guaranteed by the EU legal framework without being nationals of a member state. Rights would be acquired by TCNs, in all member states except three, as a result of residence rather than nationality.

This was an important and, in some ways, radical departure for the EU as it began to legislate in areas (TCN rights) that had previously been closely guarded by the member states. However, the climate of opinion in 2003 had changed since the negotiation of the anti-discrimination Directives in 1999 and 2000. By 2003 there was greater concern to secure reference to 'integration measures' within the final Directive. This was particularly the case because the long-term resident's Directive created a right to move between member states and thus impinged on admissions policies. The Austrian, Dutch and German delegations were insistent on the inclusion of integration conditions in the final version of the Directive. Articles 5(2) and 15(3) allow member states to specify integration measures for TCNs in the member state that they move to.

As we saw in Chapter 5, similar integration provisions were included in the 2003 Directive on family reunion. This too was a radical departure from previous EU action that impinged squarely on a policy and legal domain that had previously been strictly a matter for member states.

Administrative practice and implementation

The purpose of policy measures is presumably to secure the integration of migrants, but we have seen that the meaning of integration is not clear, and there are also a wide range of variables that intervene in the relationship between outputs and outcomes (the education, training, housing and healthcare systems to name but four). It is important to note from the outset that policy outputs (the legal instruments) and outcomes (the effects of these instruments) are not the same things and may be informed by very different logics. In an area such as immigrant integration that is plagued by uncertainty and high levels of conflict we could expect to see quite a strong focus on the rhetorical and discursive content of policy outputs, but with a far more ambiguous relationship to policy outcomes (Matland 1995).

To understand why this gap between outputs and outcomes might emerge, and why it is significant, we need to explore the organizational context within which these policies are nested. This context reaches far wider than specific instruments or bodies designed to promote immigrant integration because, to understand the success or failure of policy, we need to relate our analysis to the broader configuration of key organizational boundaries, particularly those of work and welfare. Put another way, if integration is to be secured then it is likely to be delivered by education and training systems, by labour market interventions and by support for those excluded from the labour market. Such interventions need also to be sensitive to variations in age or gender. If we were to extract four key points from these observations then they would be the following:

- The attainment of immigrant integration is mediated by a wide range of factors – or intervening variables – that stretch far beyond formal immigrant integration policies.

- Rather than thinking about immigrant integration in broad terms, it is probably more useful to focus on specific locations or sites at which integration occurs (or does not occur).
- If so, our analytical focus would then be directed towards quite specific processes, often with a strong local or subnational focus, and towards the organizational characteristics of key social systems, such as those providing education, training, employment, housing and political participation.
- The EU cannot deliver integration. Rather it provides a rights-based framework that enables mobility and the portability of rights and entitlements within a single market. It does not necessarily change the content of integration policies, but changes the context in which their delivery (or non-delivery) occurs.

What would these perspectives on immigrant integration mean in practical terms? For one thing, they raise the analytical bar because they suggest that to understand immigrant integration we need to understand far more about the range of institutions, ideas and policies across a wide range of issues that could affect the attainment of immigrant integration. It could also mean that we need to rethink our focus on 'policy' in the sense of not assuming that it is immigrant integration policies that deliver or fail to deliver immigrant integration. It may actually be the case that immigrant integration policies are an effect of other processes (like, say, the perceived failure of previous policy) rather than a cause of immigrant integration. By this is meant that, if we consider the wide range of areas across which we might see evidence of immigrant integration, then it is likely that broader changes in welfare and labour market policies provide an important backdrop against which we can view immigrant integration. If we follow the logic of this argument then, as these broader labour market and welfare state processes begin to shift or change, we could expect to see changes in understandings of and responses to immigrant integration. This is what is meant when we refer to immigrant integration policies as an effect rather than a cause – that is, as an effect of changes in a broader institutional setting. The current focus on civic integration is thus an important component of a debate about immigrant integration, but is also closely related to a broader debate about how EU member states organize themselves and how immigrant newcomers 'fit' with these organizational models. Immigrant integration can thus be seen as a particularly intense component of a broader debate about integration, as it affects all citizens of EU member states.

We can now provide a practical example of what we mean by this. If we look at the employment rates of TCNs across the EU we can see some interesting patterns that could be seen as suggestive of policy failure in some member states, but that might also relate to broader institutional and organizational features of EU member states. One way of thinking about this is to bear in mind the observation made by Martin (2003) that migrants in Europe move into welfare, whereas in the USA they move into work. This is a stylized argument, but does capture something important in relation to the identity of EU member states as welfare states. These welfare state identities are often held dear by their citizens. Martin's observation does then need to be finessed by consideration of the different types and forms of welfare state organization in Europe and their relationship to labour market organization. Esping-Andersen (1986) distinguished between conservative (for example in Germany), liberal (for example in the UK) and social-democratic (for example in Sweden) welfare state types. Ferrera (1996) added to this a south-European type with a strong emphasis on provision of welfare in the home (by family members or migrants). We could suppose that interactions between welfare state organization and labour markets are likely to lead to different 'integration' outcomes. If we look at data on labour market outcomes then we can see how this might work out. Table 9.1 uses Eurostat data to analyse employment rates across the EU and distinguish between member state nationals, TCNs and other EU nationals. These data are quite broad. They do not distinguish between migrant groups, nor on the basis of age and gender. Indeed, it can be difficult to get hold of more nuanced data because not all member states collect them. What we can see from this table is some diversity in labour market participation by TCNs across the EU. We could suppose that this somehow relates to their immigrant integration policies, but actually it is far more likely to be related to their labour market and welfare state characteristics (with immigrant integration policies and frameworks such as civic integration an effect of these broader settings rather than a cause of immigrant integration, as argued above).

We see from Table 9.1 that, generally, TCNs have lower employment rates than nationals and that other EU nationals have employment rates that are not dissimilar from those of nationals.

Table 9.1   *Employment rates of nationals, TCNs and EU citizens, 2006 (per cent)*

	Total	Nationals	Non-EU 25 nationals (TCNs)	Other EU 25 nationals	Relative gap[a]
Austria	70.0	70.8	59.6	72.7	0.8
Belgium	60.4	61.5	33.1	56.5	0.5
Cyprus	69.5	69.0	78.3	66.1	1.1
Czech Rep.	65.3	65.2	74.5	75.4	1.1
Denmark	76.9	77.3	65.0	77.7	0.8
Estonia	68.8	68.7	69.1	n/a	1.0
Finland	69.9	70.2	48.0	71.7	0.7
France	63.0	63.8	42.9	65.5	0.7
Germany	67.0	68.5	47.9	66.5	0.7
Greece	61.0	60.6	70.8	51.3	1.2
Hungary	57.3	57.3	61.1	56.5	1.1
Ireland[b]	59.8	58.9	58.6	74.8	1.0
Italy[c]	58.4	57.9	52.9	53.9	0.9
Latvia	65.5	65.4	74.4	n/a	1.1
Lithuania	63.7	63.6	77.6	n/a	1.2
Luxembourg	63.6	60.9	47.3	69.1	0.8
Malta	54.3	54.3	46.9	68.2	0.9
Netherlands	74.2	75.0	46.6	74.0	0.6
Norway	75.3	75.5	56.9	83.0	0.8
Poland	53.9	54.0	47.7	41.3	0.9
Portugal	68.1	68.0	72.6	68.7	1.1
Slovakia	59.3	59.2	n/a	95.7	n/a
Slovenia	67.2	67.2	57.1	n/a	0.9
Spain	64.7	63.9	71.9	64.3	1.1
Sweden	73.1	74.0	46.4	71.4	0.6
Switzerland[d]	77.2	78.7	64.3	77.9	0.8
UK	71.3	71.7	62.3	74.1	0.9
EU 25	52.5	53.3	54.2	58.4	1.0

Notes:

[a] Relative gap = quotient of value for non-EU 25 nationals over the value for nationals.

[b] Based on Central Statistics Office Ireland, *Quarterly National Household Survey.*

[c] Annual data based on National Institute of Statistics (Istat), *Annual Report 2006.*

[d] Based on second quarter 2005 .

n/a = no data available.

Sources: Data second quarter 2006, *European Labour Force Survey*, Eurostat.

This would suggest that TCNs encounter stronger labour market exclusion than EU citizens whether they are nationals of a particular member state or mobile EU citizens.

If we look at the data more closely we see some interesting variations. Among newer immigration countries such as Italy and Spain we do not see strong differences between nationals, EU citizens and TCNs. This may well be because the TCNs in these countries are 'primary' labour migrants that is, younger men and women who move for work and have more limited engagement with welfare state institutions. In 'older' immigration countries such as the France, Germany, the Netherlands and Sweden we see quite stark differences. Indeed, it is precisely these kinds of figures that have driven perceptions of policy failure. But what kinds of lessons can be drawn? The preceding analysis would suggest that welfare state and labour market factors play a role in generating these apparent 'policy failures'.

In general terms, there seems to be a fairly substantial difficulty in the 'older' immigration countries in securing TCN labour market participation, while TCNs also suffer higher levels of unemployment (Table 9.2). The shift towards civic integration and its Europe-wide resonance in the 2003 Directive on the rights of long-term residents is a reflection of this. However, this framework for rethinking immigrant integration is nested within a broader debate about welfare state and labour market organization and the capacity of these powerful institutions to facilitate the integration of migrant newcomers. In their analysis of the labour market integration of TCNs in 13 member states, Fleischmann and Dronkers (2007) conclude that 'conservative' and 'southern' welfare state types have been less effective and that 'social-democratic' and 'liberal' welfare state types have been more effective. This obviously gives us more to ponder if we are to think about the factors that impact on implementation of immigrant integration policies.

Conclusion

In this chapter we have analysed the framing of debates about immigrant integration, and the articulation of these frames in debate at national and EU level and in the implementation of immigrant integration policies. As expected, we do not see some smooth and linear connection between talk, decision and action.

Table 9.2   *Unemployment rates of nationals, TCNs and EU citizens,*
2006

	Total	Nationals	Non-EU 25 nationals (TCNs)	Other EU 25 nationals	Relative gap[a]
Austria	4.8	4.2	11.7	6.6	2.8
Belgium	8.4	7.6	32.4	11.1	4.3
Cyprus	4.2	4.1	4.6	4.9	1.1
Czech Republic	7.1	7.1	6.4	4.3	0.9
Denmark	4.0	3.9	12.2	n/a	3.1
Estonia	6.3	5.5	10.3	n/a	1.9
Finland	9.0	8.8	29.2	n/a	3.3
France	8.8	8.3	23.2	8.0	2.8
Germany	10.4	9.5	23.0	11.7	2.4
Greece	8.9	9.0	7.4	n/a	0.8
Hungary[b]	7.5	7.5	10.8	0.5	1.4
Ireland[c]	4.3	4.1	8.1	5.9	2.0
Luxembourg	4.7	3.1	21.1	5.6	6.8
Netherlands	3.9	3.7	12.2	4.5	3.3
Norway	4.0	3.8	13.1	n/a	3.4
Portugal	7.7	7.6	10.4	n/a	1.4
Spain	8.6	8.1	12.2	10.5	1.5
Sweden	8.1	7.8	22.9	8.5	2.9
Switzerland[d]	4.5	3.3	14.1	5.5	4.3
UK	5.4	5.1	9.8	6.2	1.9
EU 25	6.4	6.5	18.5	10.2	2.8

Notes:
[a] Relative gap = quotient of value for non-EU 25 nationals over the value for nationals.
[b] Based on fourth quarter 2006.
[c] Based on Central Statistics Office Ireland, *Quarterly National Household Survey*.
[d] Based on second quarter 2005.
n/d = no data available.

Source: Data second quarter 2006, *European Labour Force Survey*, Eurostat.

Indeed, we identify different logics and dynamics at each stage, with a particularly strong focus on a reframing of the issues in the light of the perceived failings of multicultural approaches. This chapter has tried to show how this reframing of debate can be linked to broader changes in welfare state and labour market organization across the EU and had also been intensified by the recent stronger focus on concerns about the alienation and radicalization of some younger Muslims. We then saw that to understand debates about immigrant integration at national and EU level it is important to specify the relevant venues within which this debate occurs and decisions are made. This became particularly apparent when we looked at the development of EU action on anti-discrimination and the rights of long-term residents. We saw that the EU setting is related to but not simply derivative of national settings. At EU level, the core economic purposes of the Union have played an important role in providing legal, social and political resources for groups seeking to mobilize on behalf of migrants.

Finally, when our focus turned to implementation we saw the many difficulties of securing objectives in highly complex settings where a wide range of factors can impact on policy outputs. Even though the policy focus at narrative and decision-making stages is often on broad and rather abstract variables (the national community), these issues tend to play out in rather specific organizational contexts as immigrants encounter key organizational and conceptual borders and boundaries associated with work and welfare. To return to the framework sketched in Chapters 1 and 2, we see disjunction between talk, decision and action, but this is to be expected in complex areas such as immigrant integration and where notions of policy success or failure become problematic as we look across the policy process. What we do see in the area of immigrant integration are some of the characteristics of an institutional sector where fundamental uncertainties and ambiguities elicit a strong focus on talk and the discursive construction of the policy problem. There are, of course, technical outputs on the social position of TCNs, but underlying causes and drivers can be difficult to disentangle. What is clear, however, is that the perceived failure of multicultural policies has fed back into the narrative framing of the issues to help induce the new focus on civic integration.

The EU does not fundamentally reorder these debates. This is consistent with the argument throughout this book that spatial relocation to EU level must be understood in the context of national and subnational debate and not as somehow separate from them. We have seen that debates continue to resonate strongly at national and subnational level, given the spatial concentrations of migrant populations in EU member states. What we can say is that the EU now provides a rights framework that extends principles of non-discrimination, mobility and rights to legally resident TCNs. This is a significant development. Indeed, no account of immigrant integration in Europe could be complete without some account of the EU's role. At the same time, the role of the EU cannot be detached from developments in member states.

Chapter 10

Conclusions

At the beginning of this book we noted that it is something of a challenge to try to analyse various forms of migration across the 27 EU member states and account for the growing role that EU law and policy now plays. To undertake this task we needed to think seriously about the shape, scope and dynamics of the EU system and the types and forms of interaction that now occur within it. We established an analytical framework that focused on variation by migration type because we thought that this left us best placed to consider the ways in which power and authority were distributed across levels of governance in the EU system. We also developed a framework that sought to develop a non-linear approach to the policy process through which we specified the importance of looking across the policy process at 'talk', 'decision' and 'action' while leaving scope for deliberate malintegration or other inconsistencies whereby policymakers may say one thing and do another as they seek to appease competing – perhaps even contradictory – interests. This meant that we were sceptical about aggregate and undifferentiated notions of policy failure that didn't look at the more complex structures of winners and losers, costs and benefits within the process. We were particularly sceptical about extrapolating from the outcome of process to ascribe failure without actually looking closely at the nature of the process.

On this basis we have sought to analyse migration and mobility within the EU and the various frameworks that have developed to facilitate or constrain them. At the very core of our analysis is the claim that the contemporary politics of migration in Europe cannot be understood without accounting for the dynamics of both migration and mobility and, by doing so, thinking too about the role that the EU now plays in managing both. We also think it important that analysis of the EU stretches across all member states in an EU of 27 and does not just focus on a smaller group of 'older' immigration countries. Our framework was thus ambitious and we cannot claim that we have looked closely at developments in each and every member state, but we would claim that we have been able to develop a framework for analysis capable of application to all the key forms of migration evident in all EU member states. By doing so, we may fall into the typical academic trap of noting how things are all quite complex, multilevel and hard to pin down. This may appear a weakness compared with some of the more 'muscular' accounts of migration seen (predominantly in newspapers) as the problems of immigration and multiculturalism are neatly (and often simplistically) dissected. Our argument would be that a genuinely muscular account of the politics of mobility and migration in the EU offers little if it does not account for the diversity and complexity of flows and for the ways in which interactions now occur within the EU system.

The purpose of this concluding chapter is not to bombard the reader with new information or with additional facts and figures. Instead we seek to draw together the arguments developed throughout the book and focus on two important, underlying analytical issues:

- What do we mean by multilevel migration politics?
- Is there evidence of convergence between EU states, perhaps even Europeanization?

First, we seek to specify the key dimensions of multilevel migration politics in Europe and how we have tried to make connections between different types of migration, various stages of the political process in a political system and the EU political system within which powers are shared. We then look at whether the developments that we have mapped amount to convergence in European migration policies and politics; put another way, do policies and politics look alike in the EU and, if so, what role does the EU play in this?

Multilevel migration politics?

Multilevel politics is generally taken to mean the distribution of power and authority between a range of private and public actors located at various levels of governance (supranational, national and subnational). It is also often associated with new forms of politics that might involve novel types of decision-making and is typically applied to policy areas with a strong and well-established EU focus such as social cohesion and regional development (Bache 2008). Migration does not fit with the usual multilevel trope – not least because policy areas such as cohesion and regional development are redistributive types where resources are reallocated, while migration is a regulatory policy type governing access to those resources. That said, multilevel politics has a clear reference to the territorial basis of politics and migration policy is also fundamentally associated with issues around territory, territoriality and borders. In the areas of mobility and migration we do see certain manifestations of multilevelness – such as the growing role for EU institutions – and it is useful to specify what these might be. We can do this by returning to questions that we raised in Chapter 1.

Why have EU governance structures emerged?

How, why and when have EU governance structures emerged and to what extent do they impinge on state sovereignty? We have seen the steady development of EU mobility and migration structures. The clearest instance of EU competence is the highly developed free-movement framework that creates a right to movement for nationals of all EU states. Free movement (for workers, initially) was provided for by the Treaty of Rome and has been strongly associated with the economic impetus underpinning European integration, although there are clear and important political implications too, which also became clear as the EU citizenship agenda developed and became formalized in EU law after the Maastricht Treaty.

Development has been much slower in the areas of TCN migration and asylum because states have been more reluctant to cede authority in areas of high politics. Indeed, the very basis for the distinction made between 'low' and 'high' politics was that those areas most closely associated with state sovereignty would be precisely the ones in which states would be most reluctant to cede power. In fact, to do so was likened to playing Russian roulette with all of the chambers in the gun loaded (Hoffmann 1966).

How then do we explain common migration and asylum policies if we take it that they are not a collective suicide pact by EU states? We saw that market-related developments and the need for 'compensating' internal security measures was an important driver behind a renewed focus on TCN migration in the late 1980s. It was also the case that the end of the cold war and the dramatic geopolitical reconfiguration that followed provided a powerful impetus for the formalization of EU cooperation in the JHA pillar of the Maastricht Treaty. As we have seen, the Amsterdam, Nice and Lisbon Treaties have also contributed to the further development of migration and asylum policy linked to economic integration and a changed understanding of the meaning of security (and associated threats) in a wider EU.

We have shown how states struck sovereignty deals that led to legal and political developments at EU level that cover some, but not all, aspects of migration and asylum. We have also shown that there is more to it than this because these sovereignty deals need also to be understood as 'capacity deals' in the sense that EU migration and asylum policy has been strongly directed at reinforcing migration and asylum policy in newer immigration countries and new member states. This could then be understood as a state-driven force underlying the shift to European integration – that is, states have seen it as in their interest to develop common EU structures to resolve common problems. European integration need not diminish states: it need not be a collective suicide pact, but may be pursued as a means of strengthening states. We see this as a 'rebundling' of authority in the EU system. Clearly it is controversial that issues such as migration and asylum shift from their 'natural homes' at state level. We don't dispute that. But it is happening and is a key feature of contemporary European and EU politics.

What we have also shown is the longer-term effects of the shift to Europe – of the spatial relocation we identified in Chapter 2. The strategic context within which EU states operate has changed. It is now commonplace that national ministers and officials place their migration policy in the context of wider EU policy. There is a growing role for EU institutions too. We have shown the growth in the Commission's power and responsibility, of co-decision for the EP and greater powers post-Lisbon for the ECJ. One reason why these things have happened is that some key member states favour deeper integration. They want to see common migration and asylum policies and want to see a greater role for shared powers in this policy area. Put another way, on the basis of the history-making decisions for which national leaders tend to be responsible, there has been support for the initiation of day-to-day migration politics at EU level that encompasses mobility, migration, asylum and integration.

If powers are shared – and we have shown that they are – then what we have also tried to show is that 'Europe' does not just enter this multilevel setting as an objective set of external constraints, or some kind of checklist for what members have to do if they are to be 'good Europeans'. We also see that the meaning of Europe is contested (what role should it play?) and that political mobilizations have developed around these various meanings. In the same way that immigration is not a unified policy issue, the EU is not a unified field. We need to look, too, at interactions within the EU system and, as we have shown, explain the EU framework as both partial in terms of policy coverage and differential in terms of its effects on member states.

New actors?

Which actors have been strengthened within the EU system? Here we find that our approach is particularly helpful in picking out different dynamics across different policy types and seeing how the constellations of interests and actors can differ. We see different forms of politics for higher- and lower-skilled migration, for family migration, for irregular migration and for asylum. This is not to say that they are entirely distinct and bear no relation one to the other, but when we look closely at them we do see how there are different meanings attached to policy, different forms of political contestation, different venues within which decisions are made, different decision-making styles and different implementation dilemmas.

Bringing these together within the EU system is of course complex, but we do see a greater role for the European Commission as mobility, migration and asylum have ascended the EU agenda. As we have shown, the Commission is a particular kind of organization – a multi-organization, as we pointed out in Chapter 3 – divided between DGs. It is also an organization that often relies on the deployment of expertise for its legitimation. It tends to convey its action in technical terms and to seek to mobilize expertise and research to support its interventions in the policy process (Boswell 2009). This technical way of communicating immigration issues has been a key feature of EU action, but may be challenged by rights-based modes of politics associated with a growing ECJ role and a growing party-political role associated with the extension of co-decision to the EP. Time will tell. The EP has tended to be a pro-integration ally of the Commission, but there are growing numbers of anti-immigration politicians in the EP who combine this hostility to immigration with hostility to the EU itself.

Differences across policy types?

How does this multilevel distribution of power and authority play out across policy types? The analytical framework that we established was designed precisely to explore this issue. It leaves us well placed to analyse the different kinds of policy dynamics that become evident at EU level. We have shown that the EU framework is differential in that some types of migration are more closely associated with the EU framework than others. We have seen a strong focus in EU measures on asylum and 'the fight against illegal immigration'. The EU has extended mobility rights to all its citizens, but so far has avoided involvement in the admissions policies of its member states. The EU is, however, seeking to coordinate action on higher-skilled recruitment through its 'Blue Card' and sector-based proposals for greater coordination in other forms of migration such as seasonal workers and intracorporate transferees. One issue here can be seen as an extension of the multilevel framework in that the General Agreement on Trade and Services (GATS) already provides for what is called 'Mode 4' liberalization that facilitates movement by service providers. The European Commission needs to demonstrate the added value of its approach in a way that complements and is cognizant of both national and international frameworks.

Thus far, however, the EU has tended to focus on curbing unwanted forms of migration (unwanted, that is, from the point of view of state policies, not as some inherent characteristic of the migrants concerned). This is easier said than done and our approach has helped to demonstrate why this is the case as we have distinguished between talk, decision and action, explored the scope for inconsistencies and malintegration in the policy process and challenged linear accounts of policy and decision-making. This has direct relevance to EU action because the EU has made a strong rhetorical commitment to its 'fight against illegal immigration' but does so in the context of situations in its southern member states (long land and/or sea borders and large informal economies that provide employment for migrants, for example) that mean that it can be difficult to attain policy objectives. We have also shown that in sectors where there is relatively high ambiguity and contestation, more symbolic forms of action that seek to appease competing interests might be a more likely outcome of the policy process. This could be construed as policy failure, but if politicians secure votes at the 'talk' phase and employers secure cheap labour then is this a failure from their point of view? Is it a failure if migrants secure employment and send money home? This is not to claim that all is relative and that it is impossible to judge the success or failure of policy, but it is to suggest that success and failure are unevenly distributed across the policy process. At the very least, it is not possible to extrapolate from the outcome of a policy process – supposed failure to achieve objectives – without looking at the process itself. In this book we have tried to pay close attention to the policy and decision-making process and to the constellations of actors and interests that can intervene in the relationship between policy 'inputs' and 'outputs'.

Shaping and reshaping of policy

To what extent do member states shape policy and to what extent are they shaped by it? We have argued that the EU has differential effects in that some member states have played a greater role in shaping it and others have been more shaped by it. For example, the Schengen Agreement, which began as a smaller arrangement outside the Treaty, has provided the template for policy development in the area of internal security policy. The traditional pro-integration states that initially comprised Schengen (the Benelux countries, France and Germany) have played a key role in shaping the EU system, and indeed have often been advocates of its further development, or 'maximalism' as it is sometimes referred to in discussion of member states' attitudes to economic and political integration. At the same time, other member states have been much more marginal to policy development. A notable example here would be the UK, which has not joined Schengen and has the right to opt out of measures on migration and asylum. The UK has however been keen to opt back into those measures that it sees as consistent with domestic policy, which means that it has signed up to asylum Regulations and Directives but has not been party to rights-extending measures such as the Directives on the rights of long-term residents and family reunion.

In terms of countries that have been shaped by the EU context, then, we can make a distinction between newer countries of immigration such as Greece, Italy, Portugal and Spain where the development of policy was closely associated with EU membership. It may well have been the case that these countries would have adopted similar measures under their own volition, but EU membership provided at the very least a policy template and pressure for an acceleration in domestic policy change in countries that all underwent a rapid transition from being sending states to receiving ones.

The countries most clearly shaped by the EU context have been those that joined the EU in 2004 and 2007. They were signing up to a much more developed *acquis* and were joining the EU in an era when there was much more anxiety and unease about migration and asylum (and internal security generally). It is simply not possible to understand the eastwards enlargement of the EU without taking into account the centrality of migration and asylum. Similarly, for Croatia, Macedonia and Turkey, which currently have candidate country status, movement towards the EU will be affected crucially by the migration and asylum implications of membership, which are relatively slight in the former Yugoslavian countries' cases but are seen as potentially much more significant in Turkey's.

This focus on the effects of European integration does raise the issue of Europeanization. In the next section we analyse the extent to which member states have been Europeanized and relate this to a broader discussion of convergence.

Europeanization and convergence

In Chapter 3 we saw that the potential impacts of European integration are broad. Returning to the widely used definition provided by Radaelli (2000:4), Europeanization can refer to processes of construction, diffusion and institutionalization of formal and informal rules, procedures, policy paradigms, styles and 'ways of doing things'. It can also include the development of shared beliefs and norms which emerge at EU level and are then incorporated in domestic discourse, identities, political structures and public policies. Europeanization is thus broad, but can have far-reaching effects on domestic politics. Europeanization is not the same as convergence. Convergence could occur separately from European-ization, or Europeanization could be one factor among many that induces convergence.

We have already noted that the effects of European integration are more likely to be seen in some member states than others. We also saw that adaptation may occur with 'national colours', which can mean that established ways of doing things need not be abandoned if they are consistent with EU requirements, or can at least be made to appear so. The EU can thus provide pressure for convergence. We have seen, too, that the pressures for convergence differ by policy type, and have different implications for the constellations of actors and forms of politics and decision-making that are evident across different policy types. This does however still leave open the question of what we mean by convergence.

It is not the case that convergence must mean that an identical approach is pursued in all member states – that is, a one-size-fits-all policy for all 27 member states. Analyses of convergence typically focus on the development of policy similarity over time. As such it also relates to the idea of isomorphism, which means the way in which one unit in a population will begin to resemble other units that face a similar set of pressures from their environment (Di Maggio and Powell 1991:66). Following Knill (2005:5), policy convergence can be defined as:

> Any increase in the similarity between one or more characteristics of a certain policy (for example policy objectives, policy instruments, policy settings) across a given set of political jurisdictions (supranational institutions, states, regions, local authorities) over a given period of time. Policy convergence thus describes the end result of a process of policy change over time towards some common point, regardless of the causal processes.

If we look at it in these terms, then we can develop a more fine-grained account of policy convergence in the EU that is attuned to the different ways in which it might become evident.

In such terms, there is evidence of policy convergence in the EU, with shared objectives on key aspects of policy, common legal instruments, well-defined and quite highly developed decision-making processes. There has been a strong temporal dimension that has seen significant accretion of responsibility over time, particularly since the end of the 1990s. This does not mean that that we have a single, shared, common EU approach. We have already noted that it is partial and differential and does not impinge directly on the admissions policies of member states. Nor does it mean that the EU is the only driver of change. We have already seen the continued power of domestic factors that affect patterns of irregular migration and continued divergence within the EU in terms of attitudes towards regularizations. We identified this divergence as also being related to welfare state organization and interactions between social provision and labour markets.

It may also be the case that similar developments may occur in EU member states, but that underlying drivers of action may relate to broader processes. For example, there are some similarities between approaches to asylum and border management that are common to the USA, Australia and the EU. It is obviously not sensible to argue that all these changes are driven by the EU or are instances of Europeanization. Rather it may be the case that similar states with some important similarities in the constitution of politics do also experience similar dilemmas in the domain of immigration policy and develop similar responses. This is because they are liberal states and not just because they are members of the EU.

Our argument does not contest this observation. We do not claim that the EU is everywhere and at all times the driver of change. We have tried to show how the EU's role has developed, with its various gaps and inconsistencies. We have shown, too, that multilevel politics does not mean writing the member states out of the equation. Indeed, we showed their continued strong role in shaping policy. Moreover, we showed how these dynamics worked out in different ways across different policy types in order to specify the dynamics of the multilevel politics of migration and mobility in the EU. Our argument is not that the EU has somehow taken over and that all approaches other than an EU-centred approach are redundant; rather it is that migration and mobility must be explored alongside each other and that this cannot be done without accounting for the contemporary transformation of the European state system within which the EU has played a key role.

Bibliography

Adam, C. and A. Devillard (2008) *Comparative Study of the Laws in the 27 EU Member States for Legal Migration*. Brussels: European Parliament Directorate General Internal Policies of the Union, Policy Department C: Citizens' Rights and Constitutional Affairs.

Allen, R. (1999) 'Equal Treatment, Social Advantages and Obstacles: In Search of Coherence in Freedom and Dignity', in E. Guild (ed.) *The Legal Framework and Social Consequences of Free Movement of Persons in the European Union*. The Hague: Kluwer, 31–48.

Andall, J. (2000) *Gender, Migration and Domestic Service: The Politics of Black Women in Italy*. Aldershot: Ashgate.

Anderson, B. (1999) *The Devil is in the Detail: Lessons to be Drawn from the UK's Recent Exercise in Regularising Undocumented Workers*. University of Warwick Working Paper.

Ansell, C. (2004) 'Restructuring Authority and Territoriality', in C. Ansell and G. Di Palma (eds) *Restructuring Territoriality: Europe and the United States Compared*. Cambridge University Press, 3–18.

Arango, J. (2000) 'Becoming a Country of Immigration at the End of the Twentieth Century', in R. King, G. Lazaridis and C. Tsardanidis (eds) *Eldorado or Fortress: Immigration in Southern Europe*. London: Macmillan.

Arango, J. and C. Finotelli (2009) 'Spain', in M. Baldwin-Edwards and A. Kraler (eds) *REGINE: Regularisations in Europe*. Amsterdam University Press, 443–57.

Bache, I. (2008) *Europeanization and Multi-Level Governance*. Lanham, MD: Rowman & Littlefield.

Bade, K. (2003) *Migration in European History*. Oxford: Blackwell.

Baganha, M. (1997) *Immigration in Southern Europe*. Lisbon: Celta Editora.

Bailey, A. and P. Boyle (2004) 'Untying and Retying Family Migration in the New Europe', *Journal of Ethnic and Migration Studies*, 30(2), 229–41.

Balch, A. (2010) *Managing Labour Migration in Europe: Ideas, Knowledge and Policy Change*. Manchester University Press.

Baldwin-Edwards, M. (2009) 'Greece', in M. Baldwin-Edwards and A. Kraler (eds) *REGINE: Regularisations in Europe*. Amsterdam University Press, 297–330.

Baldwin-Edwards, M. and A. Kraler (eds) (2009) *REGINE: Regularisations in Europe*. Amsterdam University Press.

Bale, T. (2008) 'Turning Round the Telescope: Centre-Right Parties and Immigration and Integration in Europe', *Journal of European Public Policy*, 15(3), 315–30.

Balibar, E. (1998) 'The Borders of Europe', in P. Cheah and B. Robbins (eds) *Cosmopolitics: Thinking and Feeling Beyond the Nation*. Minneapolis: University of Minnesota Press, 216–33.

Barrot, J. (2008) *Intervention du M. Barrot, Vice-Président de la Commission Européenne au Sommet Européene sur le Peuple Rom*. Brussels: SPEECH/08/435.

Bauböck, R. (2005) *Citizenship Policies: International, State, Migrant and Democratic Perspectives*. Geneva: Global Commission on International Migration.

Bauer, T. and K. Zimmerman (1999) *Assessment of Possible Migration Pressure and Its Labour Market Impact Following EU Enlargement to Central and Eastern Europe*. Bonn: Institute for the study of Labour (IZA).

Bhabha, J. and S. Shutter (1994) *Women's Movement: Women Under Immigration and Nationality Law*. London: Joint Council for the Welfare of Immigrants.

Bhagwati, J. (1998) *A Stream of Windows: Unsettling Reflections on Trade, Immigration and Democracy*. Cambridge, MA: MIT Press.

Bigo, D. (2001) 'Migration and Security', in C. Joppke and V. Guiraudon (eds) *Controlling a New Migration World*. London: Routledge.

Bilous, A. (1999) 'Posted Workers and the Implementation of the Directive', *European Industrial Relations Observatory On-line*, September.

Boeri, T. and H. Bruecker (2000) *The Impact of EU Enlargement on Employment and Wages in the EU Member States*. Berlin: European Integration Consortium.

Bommes, M. and A. Geddes (2000) *Immigration and Welfare: Challenging the Borders of the Welfare State*. London: Routledge.

Borjas, G. (1995) 'The Economic Benefits from Immigration', *Journal of Economic Perspectives*, 9(2), 3–22.

Borjas, G. (2001) *Heaven's Door: Immigration Policy and the American Economy*. Princeton University Press.

Boswell, C. (2000) *EU Enlargement: What Are the Prospects for East-West Migration?* London: Royal Institute of International Affairs.

Boswell, C. (2003) *European Migration Policies in Flux*. Oxford: Blackwell/ Royal Institute of International Affairs.

Boswell, C. (2007) 'Migration Control in Europe After 9/11: Explaining the Absence of Securitization', *Journal of Common Market Studies*, 45(3), 589–610.

Boswell, C. (2008) 'The Political Functions of Expert Knowledge: Knowledge and Legitimation in European Union Immigration Policy', *Journal of European Public Policy*, 15(4), 471–88.

Boswell, C. (2009) *The Political Use of Expert Knowledge: Immigration Policy and Social Research*. Cambridge University Press.

Bourdieu, P. (1991) *Language and Symbolic Power*. Cambridge: Polity Press.

Bourdieu, P. and L. Wacquant (1992) *An Invitation to Reflexive Sociology*. Chicago University Press.

Bowker, G. and S. Leigh-Star (1999) *Sorting Things Out: Classification and Its Consequences*. Cambridge (Mass.) : MIT Press.

Brettell, C. and J. Hollifield (2000) *Migration Theory: Talking Across Disciplines*. London: Routledge.

Brubaker, R. (2001) 'The Return of Assimilation? Changing Perspectives on

Immigration and Its Sequels in France, Germany and the United States', *Ethnic and Racial Studies*, 24(4), 531–48.

Bruecker, H. (2000) *The Impact of Eastern Enlargement on Employment and Wages in EU Member States*. Brussels: European Commission DG Employment and Social Affairs.

Brunsson, N. (2003) *The Organization of Hypocrisy: Talk, Decision and Action in Organizations*. 2nd edn. Copenhagen Business School Press.

Byrne, R., G. Noll and J. Vedsted-Hansen (2002) *New Asylum Countries? Migration Control and Refugee Protection in an Enlarged European Union*. The Hague: Kluwer.

Caldwell, C. (2009) *Reflections on the Revolution in Europe: Can Europe be the Same with Different People in It?* London: Allen Lane.

Card, D. (1990) 'The Impact of the Mariel Boat Lift on the Miami Labour Market', *Industrial and Labor Relations Review*, 43(2), 245–57.

Card, D. (2005) 'Is the New Immigration Really So Bad?', *The Economic Journal*, 115(507), 300–23.

Carling, J. (2007) 'Unauthorized Migration from Africa to Spain', *International Migration*, 35(4), 3–37.

Carrera, S. and E. Guild (2007) *An EU Framework on Sanctions Against Employers of Irregular Immigrants: Some Reflections on the Scope, Features & Added Value*. Brussels: Centre for European Policy Studies Policy Brief no. 140.

Casado-Diaz, M., C. Kaiser and A. Warnes (2004) 'Northern European Retired Residents in Nine Southern European Areas: Characteristics, Motivations and Adjustment', *Ageing & Society*, 24(3), 353–81.

Castles, S. (1986) 'The Guestworker in Western Europe: An Obituary', *International Migration Review*, 20(4), 761–78.

Castles, S. (2004a) 'The Factors that Make and Unmake Migration Policies', *International Migration Review*, 38(3), 852–84.

Castles, S. (2004b) 'Why Migration Policies Fail', *Ethnic and Racial Studies*, 27(2), 205–27.

Castles, S. and M. Miller (1998) *The Age of Migration: International Population Movements in the Modern World*. Basingstoke: Palgrave.

Castles, S. and M. Miller (2009) *The Age of Migration: International Population Movements in the Modern World*, 4th edn. London: Palgrave.

Caviedes, A. (2004) 'The Open Method of Co-ordination in Immigration Policy: A Tool for Prying Open Fortress Europe?', *Journal of European Public Policy*, 11(2), 289–310.

CEC (Commission of the European Communities) (1997) *An Action Plan for Free Movement of Workers*. COM (97) 586. Brussels.

CEC (Commission of the European Communities) (2000) *Communication from the Commission to the Council and the European Parliament on a Community Immigration Policy*. COM/2000/0757 final. Brussels.

CEC (Commission of the European Communities) (2004) *Handbook on Integration for Policy Makers and Practitioners*. Brussels: Directorate General for Justice, Freedom and Security.

CEC (Commission of the European Communities) (2005) *Policy Plan on Legal Migration*. Brussels: Commission of the European Communities.

CEC (Commission of the European Communities) (2006a) *The Global Approach to Migration One Year On: Towards a Comprehensive European Migration Policy.* COM (2006) 735 final. Brussels.

CEC (Commission of the European Communities) (2006b) *Policy Priorities in the Fight Against Illegal Immigration.* COM (2006) 402 final. Brussels.

CEC (Commission of the European Communities) (2006c) *Screening report, Croatia, Chapter 24 – Justice, Freedom and Security.* Brussels: DG Enlargement, http://ec.europa.eu/enlargement/pdf/croatia/screening_reports/screening_report_24_hr_internet_en.pdf.

CEC (Commission of the European Communities) (2007a) *Applying the Global Approach to Migration to the Eastern and South-Eastern Regions Neighbouring the European Union.* COM (2007) 247 final. Brussels.

CEC (Commission of the European Communities) (2007b) *Communication from the Commission to the Council, the European Parliament, the European Economic and Social Committee and the Committee of the Regions. Mobility, an Instrument for More and Better Jobs: The European Job Mobility Action Plan (2007–2010).* COM (2007) 773 final. Brussels

CEC (Commission of the European Communities) (2008) *A Common Immigration Policy for Europe: Principles, Actions, Tools.* COM (2008) 359 Final. Brussels.

CEC (Commission of the European Communities) (2009) *Commission Staff Working Document: Former Yugoslav Republic of Macedonia – Progress Report.* Commission of the European Communities SEC (2009) 1335. Brussels.

Chaloff, J. and G. Lemaitre (2009) *Managing Highly Skilled Labour Migration: A Comparative Analysis of Migration Policies and Challenges in OECD Countries.* Paris: OECD.

Checkel, J. (2005) 'International Institutions and Socialization in Europe: Introduction and Framework', *International Organization,* 59(4), 801–26.

Cini, M. (1996) *The European Commission: Leadership, Organisation and Culture in the European Union Administration.* Manchester University Press.

Cohen, M., J. March and J. Olsen (1972) 'A Garbage Can Model of Organisational Choice', *Administrative Science Quarterly,* 17(1), 1–25.

Cornelius, W. (2001) 'Death at the Border: Efficacy and Unintended Consequences of US Immigration Control Policy ', *Population and Development Review,* 27(4), 661–85.

Cornelius, W., P. Martin and J. Hollifield (1994) 'Introduction: The Ambivalent Quest for Immigration Control', in W. Cornelius, P. Martin and J. Hollifield (eds) *Controlling Immigration: A Global Perspective.* Stanford University Press, 3–41.

Corriere della Sera (2009) 'Frattini: "Immigrati, problema europeo"', 23 August, http://www.corriere.it/politica/09_agosto_23/frattini_immigrati_problema_europeo_0ac51d2a-8fec-11de-ab60–00144f02aabc.shtml.

Corriere della Sera (2010a) 'Immigrati, il Pd attacca Berlusconi "Le sue parole istigano al razzismo"', 28 January, http://www.corriere.it/politica/10_gennaio_28/immigrati-berlusconi-reazioni_c75254fe-0c28–11df-8679–00144f02aabe.shtml.

Corriere della Sera (2010b) 'Immigrati, una giornata di guerriglia a Rosarno', 8 January, www.corriere.it/2010/genndio/08/immigrati_una_giornata–di_ guerriglia_rosarno_co_8_10010821, shtm1.

Council of the European Union (2004) *The Hague Programme: Strengthening Freedom, Security and Justice in the European Union*, Council Document 16054/04 JAI559. Brussels.

Dawson, R. and K. Prewitt (1969) *Political Socialization*. Boston, MA: Little, Brown.

de Haas, H. (2007) *The Myth Of Invasion: Irregular Migration from West Africa to the Maghreb and the European Union*, Research Report, International Migration Institute. Oxford, October.

DiMaggio, P. and W. Powell (1991) 'Introduction', in W. Powell and P. DiMaggio (eds) *The New Institutionalism in Organizational Analysis*. University of Chicago Press, 1–38.

Duncan, F. and S. Van Hecke (2008) 'Immigration and the Transnational European Centre-Right: A Common Programmatic Response?' *Journal of European Public Policy*, 15(3), 432–52.

Dustmann, C. *et al.* (2003) *The Impact of EU Enlargement on Migration Flows*. London: Home Office.

Düvell, F. and B. Jordan (2002) *Irregular Migration: The Dilemmas of Transnational Mobility*. Cheltenham: Elgar.

Eichenhofer, E. (1997) *The Social Security of Migrants in the European Union of Tomorrow*. Osnabrück: Universitätsverslag.

Einaudi, L. (2007) *Le Politiche dell'Immigrazione in Italia dall'Unità ad Oggi*. Rome: Laterza.

Ellermann, A. (2008) 'The Limits of Unilateral Migration Control: Deportation and Interstate Cooperation', *Government and Opposition*, 43(2), 168–89.

Elman, A. (2000) 'The Limits of Citizenship: Migration, Sex Discrimination and Same-Sex Partners in EU Law', *Journal of Common Market Studies*, 38(5), 729–49.

Elrick, T. and O. Ciobanu (2009) 'Evaluating the Impact of Migration Policy Changes on Migration Strategies: Insights from Romanian-Spanish Migrations', *Global Networks*, 9(1), 100–16.

Esping-Andersen, G. (1986) *The Three Worlds of Welfare Capitalism*. Cambridge: Polity.

European Commission (2008) *Justice, Freedom and Security: Securing Our Rights and Defending Our Interests*, europa.eu/pol/justice/index_en.htm.

European Council (1999) *Tampere European Council Presidency Conclusions*. Tampere, Finland: 15–16 October 1999.

European Council (2000) *Lisbon Special European Council: Towards a Europe of Innovation and Knowledge*. Brussels.

European Migration Network (2006) *Evaluating the Impact of Immigration on Europe's Societies*. Brussels: Commission of the European Communities.

Eurostat (2008) *Ageing Characterises the Demographic Perspectives of the European Societies*. Brussels. Statistics in Focus 72/2008.

Eurostat (2009) *The EU-27 Population Continues to Grow*. Brussels: Eurostat Data in Focus 31/2009.

Faist, T. (2000) *The Volume and Dynamics of International Migration and Transnational Social Spaces*. Oxford University Press.

Faist, T. and A. Ette (2007) *The Europeanization of National Policies and Politics of Immigration: Between Autonomy and the European Union*. Basingstoke: Palgrave.

Fassmann, H. and R. Muenz (1994) *European Migration in the Late Twentieth Century*. Laxenburg: International Institute for Applied Systems Analysis.

Favell, A. (2003) *Eurostars and Eurocities: Towards a Sociology of Free Moving Professionals in Western Europe*. San Diego: University of California Center for Comparative Immigration Studies.

Favell, A. (2007) *Eurostars and Eurocities: Free Movement and Mobility in an Integrating Europe*. Oxford: Blackwell.

Favell, A. and R. Hansen (2002) 'Markets Against Politics: Migration, Enlargement and the Idea of Europe', *Journal of Ethnic and Migration Studies*, 28 (4), 581–601.

Favell, Adrian (1998) *Philosophies of Integration: Immigration and the Idea of Citizenship in Britain and France*. London: Palgrave Macmillan.

Ferrera, M. (1996) 'The Southern Model of Welfare in Social Europe', *Journal of European Social Policy*, 6(1), 17–37.

Fleischmann, F. and J. Dronkers (2007) *The Effects of Social and Labour Market Policies of EU Countries on the Socio-Economic Integration of First and Second Generation Immigrants from Different Countries of Origin*. Working Paper EUI-RSCAS 2007/19 (European Forum Series). San Domenico di Fiesole: European University Institute.

Florida, R. (2002) *The Rise of the Creative Class*. New York: Basic Books.

Foucault, M. (1994) 'Governmentality', in M. Foucault (ed.) *Power: Essential Works of Foucault 1954–1984*. New York: New Press, 201–22.

Freeman, G. (1995) 'Modes of Immigration Politics in Liberal Democratic States', *International Migration Review*, 29(4), 881–902.

Freeman, G. (2006) 'National Models, Policy Types and the Politics of Immigration in Liberal Democracies', *West European Politics*, 29(2), 227–47.

FRONTEX (2007) *FRONTEX General Report*. Warsaw.

Geddes, A. (2003) *The Politics of Migration and Immigration in Europe*. London: Sage.

Geddes, A. (2005) 'Europe's Borders and International Migration Relations', *Journal of Common Market Studies*, 43(4), 787–806

Geddes, A. (2008a) 'Il rombo dei cannoni? Immigration and the Centre-Right in Italy', *Journal of European Public Policy*, 15 (3), 349–66.

Geddes, A. (2008b) *Immigration and European Integration: Beyond Fortress Europe?* Manchester University Press.

Geddes, A. and V. Guiraudon (2004) 'Britain and France and EU Anti-Discrimination Policy: The Emergence of an EU Policy Paradigm'. *West European Politics*, 27(2), 334–53.

Geddes, A., S. Scott, K. Nielsen and P. Brindley (2007) *Gangmasters Licensing Authority: Annual Review*. Nottingham: Gangmasters Licensing Authority.

Gibney, M. (2004) *The Ethics and Politics of Asylum: Liberal Democracy and the Response to Refugees*. Cambridge University Press.

Givens, T. and A. Luedtke (2005) 'European Immigration Policies in Comparative Perspective: Issue Salience, Partisanship and Immigrant Rights 'Comparative European Politics*, 3(1), 1–22.

Glover, S. *et al.* (2001) *Migration: A Social and Economic Analysis*. London: Home Office.

Green, S. (2004) *The Politics of Exclusion: Institutions and Immigration Policy in Germany*. Manchester University Press.

GLA Economics (2009) *Economic Impact on the London and UK Economy of an Earned Regularisation of Irregular Migrants to the UK*. London: Greater London Authority

Green-Cowles, M., J. Caporaso and T. Risse (eds) (2001) *Transforming Europe: Europeanization and Domestic Change*. Ithaca (NY): Cornell University Press.

Groenendijk, K. (2004) 'Legal Concepts of Integration in EU Migration Law', *European Journal of Migration and Law*, 6(2), 111–26.

Groenendijk, K., R. Fernhout, D. Dam and R. Oers (2007) *The Family Reunification Directive in EU Member States: the First Year of Implementation*. Nijmegen: Wolf Legal Publishers.

Guild, E. (1998) *The Legal Framework and Social Consequences of Free Movement of Persons in the European Union*. The Hague: Kluwer.

Guild, E. (1999) 'The Impetus to Harmonise: Asylum Policy in the European Union', in F. Nicholson and P. Twomey (eds) *Refugee Rights and Reality: Evolving International Concepts and Regimes*. Cambridge University Press, 313–35.

Guild, E. (2001) 'Moving the Borders of Europe', Inaugural Lecture, Catholic University of Nijmegen, 8 May.

Guild, E. (2005) 'Who Is Entitled to Work and Who Is in Charge? Understanding the Legal Framework of European Labour Mobility', in D. Bigo and E. Guild (eds) *Controlling Frontiers: Free Movement Into and Within Europe*. Aldershot: Ashgate, 100–39.

Guiraudon, V. (1998) *International Human Rights Norms and Their Interpretation: The Protection of Aliens in Europe*. San Domenico di Fiesole: European University Institute.

Guiraudon, V. (2000a) 'European Integration and Migration Policy: Vertical Policy-Making as Venue Shopping', *Journal of Common Market Studies*, 38(2), 251–71.

Guiraudon, V. (2000b) *Les Politiques d'immigration en Europe: Allemagne, France, Pays-Bas*. Paris: L'Harmattan.

Guiraudon, V. (2003) 'The Constitution of a European Immigration Policy Domain: A Political Sociology Approach', *Journal of European Public Policy*, 10(2), 263–82.

Hailbronner, K. (2004) 'Asylum Law in the Context of a European Migration Policy', in N. Walker (ed.) *Europe's Area of Freedom, Security and Justice*. Oxford University Press, 41–88.

Halfacree, K. (1995) 'Household Migration and the Structuration of

Patriarchy: Evidence from the USA', *Progress in Human Geography*, 19(2), 159–82.

Halfmann, J. (2000) 'Welfare State and Territory', in M. Bommes and A. Geddes (eds) *Immigration and Welfare: Challenging the Borders of the Welfare State*. London: Routledge, 34–50.

Hall, P. (1984) 'The Patterns of Economic Policy: An Organizational Approach', in S. Bornstein, D. Held and J. Krieger (eds) *The State in Capitalist Europe*, London: Allen and Unwin, 31–53.

Hammar, T. (1985) *European Immigration Policy: A Comparative Study*. Cambridge University Press.

Hampshire, J. (2008) 'Immigration Politics and Security in Britain Since 9/11', in T. Givens, G. Freeman and D. Leal (eds) *Immigration Policy and Security: U.S., European, and Commonwealth Perspectives*. London: Routledge.

Hansen, R. (2000) *Citizenship and Immigration in Post-War Britain*. Oxford University Press.

Hansen, R. (2002) 'Globalization, Embedded Realism and Path Dependence: The Other Immigrants to Europe', *Comparative Political Studies*, 35(3), 259–83.

Hansen, R. (2007) 'The Free Economy and the Jacobin State', in C. Swain (ed.) *Debating Immigration*. New York: Cambridge University Press, 223–36.

Hars, A. (1998) *Labour Migration and the Eastern Enlargement of the European Union: Lessons from the Hungarian Experiences*. Budapest: Kopint-Datorg Discussion Papers.

Heckmann, F. (2007) 'Illegal immigration: What Can We Know and What Can We Explain? The Case of Germany', in A. Portes and J. DeWind (eds) *Rethinking Migration: New Theoretical and Empirical Perspectives*. New York: Berghahn, 285–307.

Helton, A. (2002) *The Price of Indifference: Refugees and Humanitarian Action in the New Century*. Oxford University Press.

Herbert, U. (2001) *Geschichte der Ausländerpolitik in Deutschland: Saisonarbeiter, Zwangsarbeiter, Gastarbeiter, Flüchtlinge*. München: Beck.

Herman, E. (2006) 'Migration as a Family Business: The Role of Personal Networks in the Mobility Phase of Migration', *International Migration*, 44(4), 191–222.

Hoennekop, E. and H. Werner (2000) 'Is the EU's Labour Market Threatened by a Wave of Immigration?', *Intereconomics: Review of European Economic Policy*, 35 (1), 3–8.

Hoffmann, S. (1966) 'Obstinate or Obsolete? The Fate of the Nation State and the Case of Western Europe', *Daedalus*, 95(3), 862–915.

Hollifield, J. (1992) *Immigrants, States and Markets: The Political Economy of Migration in Europe*. Cambridge, MA: Harvard University Press.

Hollifield, J. (1999) 'Ideas, Institutions and Civil Society: On the Limits of Immigration Control in France', in G. Brochmann and T. Hammar (eds) *Mechanisms of Immigration Control: A Comparative Analysis of European Regulation Policies*. Oxford: Berg, 59–95.

Home Office and UK Border Agency (2009) *Accession Monitoring Report*,

May 2004–2009: A8 Countries. London: Home Office http://www.ukba.
homeoffice.gov.uk/sitecontent/documents/aboutus/reports/accession_moni-
toring_report/report-19/may04-mar09?view=Binary.

Honohan, I. (2008) 'Reconsidering the Claim to Family Reunification in
Migration', *Political Studies*, 57(4), 768–87.

House of Commons (2006) *House of Commons European Scrutiny
Committee, Thirty-First Report.* London.

House of Lords (2009) *The Stockholm Programme: Home Affairs.* London:
House of Lords EU Select Committee 25th Report.

Hughes, J. and O. Field (1998) 'Recent Trends in the Detention of Asylum
Seekers in Western Europe', in J. Hughes and F. Liebaut (eds) *Detention of
Asylum Seekers in Europe: Analysis and Perspectives.* The Hague: Kluwer,
5–48.

Hurwitz, A. (1999) 'The 1990 Dublin Convention: A Comprehensive
Assessment', *International Journal of Refugee Law*, 11(4), 646–77.

Huysmans, J. (2006) *The Politics of Insecurity: Fear, Migration and Asylum in
the European Union.* London: Routledge.

Hyndman, J. (2000) *Managing Displacement: Refugees and the Politics of
Humanitarianism.* Minneapolis: University of Minnesota Press.

International Organization for Migration (2008) *World Migration Report:
Managing Labour Mobility in the Evolving Global Economy.* Geneva.

Jandl, M. (2004) 'The Relationship Between Human Smuggling and the
Asylum System in Austria', *Journal of Ethnic and Migration Studies*, 30(4),
799–806.

Jileva, E. (2002) 'Visas and Free Movement of Labour: The Uneven
Imposition of the EU Acquis on the Accession States', *Journal of Ethnic
and Migration Studies*, 28(4), 683–700.

Joly, D. (1996) *Haven or Hell? Asylum Policies and Refugees in Europe.*
London: Macmillan.

Joppke, C. (1998) 'Why Liberal States Accept Unwanted Immigration', *World
Politics*, 50(2), 266–93.

Joppke, C. (2009) 'Limits of Integration: Britain and Her Muslims', *Journal of
Ethnic and Migration Studies*, 35(3), 453–72.

Joppke, C. and E. Morawska (2003) *Towards Assimilation and Citizenship:
Immigrants in Liberal Nation States.* Basingstoke: Palgrave Macmillan.

Kaufman, E. (2010) *Shall the Religious Inherit the Earth? Demography and
Politics in the Twenty-First Century.* London: Profile.

Kelly, L. (2005) 'You Can Find Anything You Want: A Critical Reflection on
Research on Trafficking in Persons', in F. Laczko and E. Gozdziak (eds)
Data and Research on Human Trafficking: A Global Survey. Geneva:
International Organization for Migration, 235–66.

King, R. and E. Zontini (2000) 'The Role of Gender in the South European
Immigration Model', *Papers*, 60, 35–52.

Kingdon, J. (1984) *Agendas, Alternatives and Public Policies.* Boston, MA:
Little Brown.

Knill, C. (2005) 'Cross-National Policy Convergence: Concepts, Approaches
and Explanatory Factors', *Journal of European Public Policy*, 12(5),
764–74.

Kofman, E. (1999) 'Female 'Birds of Passage' a Decade Later: Gender and Immigration in the European Union', *International Migration Review*, 33(2), 269–99.

Kofman, E. (2004) 'Family-Related Migration: A Critical Review of European Studies', *Journal of Ethnic and Migration Studies*, 30(2), 243–62.

Kofman, E. and V. Meetoo (2008) 'Family Migration', in International Organization for Migration (ed.) *World Migration 2008.* Geneva, 151–72.

Kofman, E., A. Phizacklea, P. Raghuram and R. Sales (2000) *Gender and International Migration in Europe: Employment, Welfare and Politics.* London: Routledge.

Kofman, E. and P. Raghurman (2006) 'Gender and Global Labour Migrations: Incorporating Skilled Workers', *Antipode*, 38(2), 282–303.

Kolb, H. (2005) 'Germany's "Green Card" in Comparative Perspective', in H. Lenke (ed.) *Crossing Over: Comparing Recent Migration in Europe and the United States.* Lanham, MD: Lexington.

Koser, K. (2002) 'Asylum Policies, Trafficking and Vulnerability', *International Migration*, 28(3), 91–111.

Koser, K. (2008) 'Why Migrant Smuggling Pays', *International Migration*, 46(2), 3–26.

Koser, K. and C. Pinkerton (2002) *The Social Networks of Asylum Seekers and the Dissemination of Information about Countries of Asylum.* Home Office Research, Development and Statistics, London.

Kostakopoulou, T. (2002) 'Long-Term Resident Third-Country Nationals in the European Union: Normative Expectations and Institutional Openings', *Journal of Ethnic and Migration Studies*, 28(3), 443–62.

Krasner, S. (1999) *Sovereignty: Organized Hypocrisy.* Princeton University Press.

Krissman, F. (2005) 'Sin Coyote Ni Patrón: Why the "Migrant Network" Fails to Explain International Migration', *International Migration Review*, 39(1), 4–44.

Kushner, T. and K. Knox (1999) *Refugees in an Age of Genocide.* London: Cass.

Laczko, F. (2005) 'Introduction', in in F. Laczko and E. Gozdziak (eds) *Data and Research on Human Trafficking: A Global Survey.* Geneva: International Organization for Migration, 1–14.

Lahav, G. (1997) 'International Versus National Constraints in Family-Reunification Migration Policy', *Global Governance*, 3(3), 349–72.

Lavenex, S. (1999) *Safe Third Countries: Extending the EU Asylum and Immigration Policies to Central and Eastern Europe.* Budapest: Central European University Press.

Lavenex, S. (2001) 'Migration and the EU's New Eastern Border: Between Realism and Liberalism', *Journal of European Public Policy*, 8(1), 24–42.

Lavenex, S. (2006) 'Shifting Up and Out: The Foreign Policy of European Immigration Control', *West European Politics*, 29(2), 329–50.

Leibig, T. (2004) 'Recruitment of Foreign Labour in Germany and Switzerland', in D. Bobeva and J.-P. Garson (eds) *Migration for Employment: Bilateral Agreements at a Crossroads.* OECD: Paris.

Levy, C. (2002) 'Harmonization or Power Politics? EU Asylum and Refugee Policy Five Years After Amsterdam', ECPR Joint Sessions of Workshops, March, Turin,

Majone, G. (1989) *Evidence, Argument and Persuasion in the Policy Process.* New Haven, CT: Yale University Press.

Majone, G. (1992) *Ideas, Interests and Policy Change.* Dan Domenico di Fiesole: European University Institute.

March, J. and J. Olsen (1983) 'The New Institutionalism: Organizational Factors in Political Life', *American Political Science Review*, 78, 734–49.

March, J. and J. Olsen (1989) *Rediscovering Institutions: The Organizational Basis of Politics.* New York: Free Press.

Marrus, M. (1985) *The Unwanted: European Refugees in the 20th Century.* New York: Oxford University Press.

Martin, P. (2003) *Managing Labor Migration: Temporary Worker Programs for the 21st Century.* International Institute for Labour Studies, Geneva.

Martin, P. and D. Papademetriou (1991) *The Unsettled Relationship: Migration and Economic Development.* Westport, CT: Greenwood.

Martineau, T., K. Decker and P. Bundred (2004) '"Brain Drain" of Health Professionals: From Rhetoric to Responsible Action', *Health Policy*, 1(70), 1–10.

Massey, D. (1990) 'Social Structure, Household Strategies and the Cumulative Causation of Migration', *Population Index*, 56(1), 3–26.

Massey, D. and C. Capoferri (2007) 'Measuring Unauthorized Immigration', in A. Portes and J. DeWind (eds) *Rethinking Migration: New Theoretical and Empirical Perspectives.* New York: Berghahn, 257–81.

Matland, R. (1995) 'Synthesizing the Implementation Literature: The Ambiguity–Conflict Model of Policy Implementation', *Journal of Public Administration Research and Theory*, 5(2), 147–74.

Mattli, W. (2000) 'Sovereignty Bargains in Regional Integration', *International Studies Review*, 22(2), 149–80.

Meo, N. (2008) 'Italians Welcome Army on Streets as Anti-Gypsy Sentiment Sweeps Country', *Daily Telegraph*, 8 May.

Meyer, J. and B. Rowan (1977) 'Institutional Organizations: Formal Structure As Myth and Ceremony', *American Journal of Sociology*, 83(2), 340–63.

Meyers, E. (2002) *Multilateral Co-operation in International Labor Migration.* San Diego: University of California Center for Comparative Immigration Studies.

Mincer, J. (1978) 'Family Migration Decisions', *Journal of Political Economy*, 86(5), 749–73.

Mitsilegas, V. (2007) 'Border Security in the European Union: Towards Centralised Controls and Maximum Surveillance', in H. Toner, E. Guild and A. Baldaccini (eds) *EU Immigration and Asylum Law and Policy: Whose Freedom, Security and Justice?* Oxford: Hart. 359–93.

Monar, J. (2001) 'The Dynamics of Justice and Home Affairs: Laboratories, Driving Factors and Costs', *Journal of Common Market Studies*, 39(4), 747–64.

Montanari, A. and A. Cortese (1993) 'South to North Migration in a

Mediterranean Perspective', in R. King (ed.) *Mass Migration in Europe: The Legacy and the Future*. London: Bellhaven, 212–33.

Morokvasic, M. (1984) 'Birds of Passage Are Also Women', *International Migration Review*, 28(4), 886–907.

Morrison, J. and B. Crosland (2000) *The Trafficking and Smuggling of Refugees: The End Game of European Asylum Policies*. Geneva: UNHCR.

Moyes, J. (1997) 'Asylum Seekers Win Right to Support', *The Independent*, 18 February.

Myrdal, G. (1957) *Rich Lands and Poor*. New York: Harper Row.

Neal, A. (2009) 'Securitization and Risk at the EU Border: The Origins of FRONTEX', *Journal of Common Market Studies*, 47(2), 333–56.

Nicholson, F. and P. Twomey (1999) *Refugee Rights and Realities*. Cambridge University Press.

Noll, G. (1997) 'Prisoners', Dilemma in Fortress Europe: On the Prospects of Burden Sharing in the European Union', *German Yearbook of International Law*, 40, 405–37.

Noll, G. (2000) *Negotiating Asylum: The EU Acquis, Extra-Territorial Protection and the Common Market of Deflection*. Leiden: Nijhoff.

Noll, G. (2003) 'Visions of the Exceptional: Legal and Theoretical Issues Raised by Transit Processing Centres and Protection Zones', *European Journal of Migration and Law*, 5(3), 303–41.

O'Reilly, K. (2007) 'Intra-European Migration and the Mobility-Enclosure Dialectic', *Sociology*, 41(2), 277–93.

OECD (2007) *Policy Coherence for Development 2007: Migration and Developing Countries*. Paris: Organisation for Economic Co-operation and Development.

OECD (2008) *International Migration Outlook: SOPEMI Report 2008*. Paris: Organisation for Economic Co-operation and Development.

OECD (2009) *International Migration Outlook 2009: SOPEMI Report 2009*. Paris: Organisation for Economic Co-operation and Development.

Parkes, R. (2009) *Mobility Partnerships: Valuable Addition to the ENP Repertoire? A Checklist for Revitalizing ENP*. Berlin: Stiftung Wissenschaft und Politik.

Pastore, F., P. Monzini and G. Sciortino (2006) 'Schengen's Soft Underbelly? Irregular Migration and Human Smuggling Across Land and Sea Borders to Italy', *International Migration*, 44(4), 95–119.

Pécoud, V. and P. de Guchteneire (2005) *Migration Without Borders: An Investigation into the Free Movement of People*. Geneva: Global Commission on International Migration.

Pierson, P. (1996) 'The Path to European Integration: An Historical Institutionalist Analysis', *Comparative Political Studies*, 29(2), 123–63.

Piore, M. (1979) *Birds of Passage: Migrant Labor and Industrial Societies*. Cambridge University Press.

Pisa, N. (2008) 'Italy Declares State of Emergency Over Roma Immigrants', *Daily Telegraph*, 25 July.

Post, D. and A. Niemann (2007) 'The Europeanisation of German Asylum Policy and the "Germanisation" of European Asylum Policy: The Case of the "Safe Third Country" Concept', in *European Union Studies Association (EUSA) Biennial Conference, May 17–19, 2007*, Montreal, QC.

Pressman, J. and A. Wildavsky (1982) *Implementation*, 2nd edn. Berkeley: University of California Press.

Purcell, M. and J. Nevins (2005) 'Pushing the Boundary: State Restructuring, State Theory, and the Case of U.S.–Mexico Border Enforcement in the 1990s', *Political Geography*, 24(2), 211–35.

Radaelli, C. (2000) 'Whither Europeanization: Concept Stretching and Substantive Change', *European Integration On-Line Papers*, 4(8), http://eiop.or.at/eiop/texte/2000–008a.htm

Reyneri, E. (1998) 'The Role of the Underground Economy in Irregular Migration to Italy: Cause or Effect?', *Journal of Ethnic and Migration Studies*, 24(2), 313–31.

Robinson, V. and J. Segrott (2002) *Understanding the Decision-Making of Asylum Seekers*. London: Home Office.

Ruggie, J. (1983) 'International Regimes, Transactions and Change: Embedded Liberalism in the Postwar Economic Order', in S. Krasner (ed.) *International Regimes*. Ithaca, NY: Cornell University Press.

Ruhs, M. (2002) *Temporary Foreign Workers Programmes: Policies, Adverse Consequences, and the Need to Make Them Work*. San Diego, CA: Centre for Comparative Immigration Studies.

Ruspini, P. (2009) 'Italy', in M. Baldwin-Edwards and A. Kraler (eds) *REGINE: Regularisations in Europe*. Amsterdam University Press, 351–70.

Sack, R. (1986) *Human Territoriality: Its Theory and History*. Cambridge University Press.

Salt, J. (1999) *Assessment of Possible Migration Pressure and its Labour Market Impact Following EU Enlargement to Central and Eastern Europe*. London: UCL Press.

Salt, J. and J. Stein (1997) 'Migration as a Business: The Case of Trafficking', *International Migration*, 35(4), 467–94.

Sandell, S. (1977) 'Women and the Economics of Family Migration', *Review of Economics and Statistics*, 59(4), 406–14.

Sandholtz, W. and A. Stone Sweet (1997) *European Integration and Supranational Governance*. Oxford University Press.

Sasse, G. and E. Thielemann (2005) 'A Research Agenda for the Study of Migrants and Minorities in Europe', *Journal of Common Market Studies*, 43(4), 655–71.

Schuster, L. (2000) 'Comparative Analysis of the Asylum Policy of Seven European Governments', *Journal of Refugee Studies*, 12(1), 118–32.

Schuster, L. (2004) *The Exclusion of Asylum Seekers in Europe*. University of Oxford Centre on Migration, Policy and Society (COMPAS).

Sciortino, G. (1999) 'Planning in the Dark: The Evolution of Italian Immigration Control', in G. Brochmann and T. Hammar (eds) *Mechanisms of Immigration Control: A Comparative Analysis of European Regulation Policies*. Oxford: Berg.

Scott, W. and J. Meyer (1991) 'The Organization of Societal Sectors', in W.

Powell and P. DiMaggio (eds) *The New Institutionalism in Organizational Analysis*. University of Chicago Press, 108–39.

Shaw, J. (2007) *The Transformation of Citizenship in the European Union: Electoral Rights and the Restructuring of Political Space*. Cambridge University Press.

Sinn, H.-W. (2002) 'EU Enlargement and the Future of the Welfare State', *Scottish Journal of Political Economics*, 49(1), 104–15.

Sitaropoulous, N. (2000) 'Modern Greek Asylum Policy and Practice in the Context of the Relevant European Developments', *Journal of Refugee Studies*, 13(1), 105–17.

Smith, D. (2004) 'An "Untied" Research Agenda for Family Migration: Loosening the "Shackles" of the Past', *Journal of Ethnic and Migration Studies*, 30(2), 263–82.

Soysal, Y. (1994) *Limits of Citizenship: Migrants and Post-National Membership in Europe*. University of Chicago Press.

Spiegel (2007) 'Reversing the Brain Drain: Poland Tries to Woo Its Young Back Home', *Spiegel Online International*, 21 September, http://www.spiegel.de/international/europe/0,1518,507079,00.html.

Stevens, A. with H. Stevens (2001) *Brussels Bureaucrats? The Administration of the European Union*. London: Palgrave.

Stone, D. (2002) *Policy Paradox: The Art of Political Decision-Making*. New York: Norton.

Straubhaar, T. (2000) 'Why Do We Need a General Agreement on Movements of People (GAMP)?', in B. Ghosh (ed.) *Managing Migration: Time for a New International Regime?* Oxford University Press, 110–35.

The Guardian (2009) 'Immigration: Act First, Think Later', 23 September 2009, http://www.guardian.co.uk/commentisfree/2009/sep/23/europe-immigration-asylum-and-refugees.

Tichenor, D. (2002) *Dividing Lines: The Politics of Immigration Control in America*. Princeton University Press.

Tirman, J. (2004) 'Introduction: The Movement of People and the Security of States', in J. Tirman (ed.) *The Maze of Fear: Security and Migration After 9/11*. New York: New Press, 1–16.

Tuitt, P. (1996) *False Images: The Law's Construction of the Refugee*. London: Pluto Press.

Tyson, A. (2001) 'The Negotiation of the European Community Directive on Anti-Discrimination', *European Journal of Migration and Law*, 3(2), 199–229.

UNHCR (United Nations High Commissioner for Refugees) (2010) *Asylum Trends in Industrialised Countries 2009*, produced by the Division of Programme Support and Management, http://www.unhcr.org/4ba7341a9.pdf.

van Selm, J. (2002) 'Immigration and Asylum or Foreign Policy: The EU's Approach to Migrants and Their Countries of Origin', in S. Lavenex and E. Uçarer (eds) *Migration and the Externalities of European Integration*. Lanham, MD: Lexington.

Waever, O., B. Buzan, M. Kelstrup and P. Lemaitre (1993) *Identity, Migration and the New Security Agenda in Europe*. London: Pinter.

Walker, N. (2004) *Europe's Area of Freeedom, Security and Justice*. Oxford University Press.

Walker, R. (2006) 'The Double Outside of the Modern International', *Ephemera: Theory and Politics in Organization*, 6(1), 56–69.

Wallace, C. (2002) 'Opening and Closing Borders: Migration and Mobility in East-Central Europe', *Journal of Ethnic and Migration Studies*, 28(4), 603–25.

Wallace, H. (2004) 'An Institutional Anatomy and Five Policy Models', in H. Wallace, W. Wallace and M. Pollack (eds) *Policy-Making in the EU*, 5th edn. Oxford University Press.

Weick, K. (1995) *Sensemaking in Organizations*. London: Sage.

Wiener, A. (1998) '"European"Citizenship Practice: Building Institutions of a Non-State*. Boulder, CO: Westview.

Willen, S. (2007) 'Exploring "Illegal" and "Irregular" Migrants' Lived Experiences of Law and State Power', *International Migration*, 45(3), 2–7.

Wimmer, A. and N. Glick Schiller (2002) 'Methodological Nationalism and Beyond: Nation-State Building, Migration and the Social Sciences', *Global Networks*, 2 (4), 301–34.

Winter-Ebner, R. and J. Zweimuller (1999) 'Do Immigrants Displace Young Native Workers? The Austrian Experience', *Journal of Population Economics*, 12(2), 327–40.

Wöger, A. (2009) 'Austria', in M. Baldwin-Edwards and A. Kraler (eds) *REGINE: Regularisations in Europe*. Amsterdam University Press, 175–86.

Woodbridge, J. (2001) *Sizing the Unauthorised (Illegal) Migrant Population in the UK*. London: Home Office On-Line Report 29/05.

Zincone, G. (1999) 'Illegality, Enlightenment and Ambiguity: A Hot Italian Recipe', *South European Society and Politics*, 3(3), 43–81

Zolberg, A. (1989) 'The Next Waves: Migration Theory for a Changing World', *International Migration Review*, 23(3), 403–30.

Zolberg, A., A. Suhrke and S. Aguayo (1983) 'International Factors in the Formation of Refugee Movements', *International Migration Review*, 20(2), 151–69.

Zürn, M. and J. Checkel (2005) 'Getting Socialized to Build Bridges: Constructivism and Rationalism, Europe and the Nation State', *International Organization*, 59(3), 1045–79.

Index

Key: **bold** = extended discussion or term highlighted in the text; b = box; f = figure; n = note; t = table.

Abdulaziz, Cabales and Balkandali case (ECHR, 1985)   114
accountability   61, 62, 65
acquis communautaire   165, 232
Action Plan for Free Movement of Workers (European Commission, 1997)   199
Action Plan for Skills and Mobility (European Commission, 2002)   199
Adam, C.   109, 235
adaptation   **71**
  migrant newcomers and host society   201
administrative practice and implementation   72, 73, **74–5**, 229
  asylum   156, **167–73**
  asylum (decoupling by changing categories)   **170–2**
  asylum (decoupling in welfare system)   **172–3**
  asylum (practical dilemmas)   **170**
  convergence (horizontal and vertical)   143, 145
  family migration   **118–20**
  immigrant integration   **217–21**, 222t, 223–9
  irregular migration   **143–8**
  labour migration policy   **97–102**
  mobility, citizenship, EU enlargement   **196–200**
admissions policies   7, 12, 76–7, 78, 92–6, 100, 102, 103, 109, 115, 130, 135, 144, 230, 234
  'dark side'   **123–4**
Adriatic   124
AENEAS Programme   140
Afghanistan/Afghans   3, 124, 126, 159, 160t
Africa   22t, 23,24f, 35, 144, 159, 237
age   37, 80b, 87b, 105, 107, 111, 116, 119, 196, 211, 217, 219, 221
ageing population   2, 5, 79, 81
  dependency ratio   80b
  versus labour migration   **80b**

agriculture   24, 27, 30, 85b, 86b, 92, 98, 139, 148, 193
  reliance on cheap labour   127
aid/development aid   133, 142
airlines   132
Al Qaeda   37
Albania   14t, 124, 166b
Albanian migrants   124, 147
Algeria   124, 166b
Alleanza Nazionale (AN)   136
Almería   145
America/s   23,24f, 35b
Amnesty International   161, 167
Amsterdam Treaty (1997; effective 1999)   9, 34, 51–2, 56, 57, 61, 63, 65, 66, 94, 150, 151, 161, 162b, 167, 197, 212, 216, 228, 245
  'Article 13'   211
  Articles 62–4 (border controls, TCNs)   9b
  citizenship   189
  incorporated Schengen provisions   58, 60t
  Title IV (free movement, migration, asylum)   9b
  UK opt-out   138
Andalucía   145
Andean Community   142
'annual quota' migration   192
Ansell, C.   12, 235
appeal rights   175
Arango, J.   148n, 235
'area of freedom, security, justice'   189
Argentinians   197
Asia   22t, 23,24f, 35, 159
Asian communities   111
asylum   19, **34–6, 150–75**; 6, 7, 9, 12, 16, 21, 35, 49, 50, 75, 140, 228, 229, 230, 231–2, 234, 241
  acquis imposed on new EU member-states   165
  administrative practice and implementation   **167–73**
  'area of [EU] common interest'   162b

asylum – *continued*
causes of flight 159
common policy (Lisbon Treaty)
10–11b
common procedure 52b
comparative studies (cross-national
legal) 168
concept 34
core dilemma **36**
cross-references ('chapter seven') 34,
46, 63, 88
EU cooperation 150–1, 174–5
EU cooperation (key developments)
162–3b
EU cooperation (themes) **151–7**
EU harmonization 155
EU policy aims **154–7**
EU 'raised level of protection' **155–6**
EU Resolutions, Decisions, Joint
Positions 162b
'extensively Europeanized' 34
harmonization 161
impact of restrictive entry policies
159, **161**
interactions between sending and
receiving countries 159, **160–1**
legislation 156
narratives **157–61**
policy-makers 'choose what sort of
knowledge to embrace' 161
political debate **161–6**
'post-Amsterdam framework' 151
systematic data 170
temporary 162b, 163b
trends in protection-seeking (academic
literature) 159
asylum applications/claims 11b, 63
common processing 53b
processing 174
asylum debate (polarization) 161
asylum legislation 160
asylum policy **19**, 88, 144
'complex interactions' 165
EU dimension **51–75**
'external dimension' 154
'first pillar' powers 162b, 163b
harmonization 164, 165, 168, 169,
245
implementation 156
potted history **8–9b**
asylum politics 46
asylum procedure 42, 53b, 151, 162b,
166b, 167
EU legislation (2005) 164
cooperation with third countries 152

lowest-common-denominator policymaking 152
minimum guarantees 162b
Asylum Procedures Directive (2005) 151
asylum statistics 156
asylum status
harmonization of procedures **63–4**
valid throughout EU (target) 167
asylum-seekers 30, 33, 35b, 35, 106,
109, 152, 153, 244
Afghan 1
countries of origin 49, 160t, 171
destruction of documentation 171
'disappearance' from the system
171–2
empirical evidence 158
failed 144
'non-genuine' applicants 154
reception 174
reception conditions (EU legislation,
2003) 151, 164
reception standards 162b, 163b, 164
rejected **171–2**
restrictive measures 154
schein (bogus) 157–8
selection of those qualifying for
protection (EU legislation, 2004)
164
'true sharing' of responsibility for
hosting 53b
Australia 25b, 26, 27f, 234
Austria 25t, 29, 39, 60t, 61, 77, 115,
117, 147, 150, 153t, 165, 171, 172,
179, 180, 184, 191, 192, 209, 212,
213, 216, 220t, 222t, 249
immigration legislation 109
number of migrants (2000–5) 4f
Azores 15t

Baganha, M. I. xiv, 235
Bailey, A. 108, 235
Baldwin-Edwards, M. 147, 148n, 235,
247
Bale, T. 209, 235
Balibar, E. 13, 235
Balkans 97, 139
Belarus 14t
Belgium 5, 25t, 61, 77, 87b, 100, 172,
180t, 220t, 222t
asylum-seekers 152, 153t
guest workers 29
intra-EU movement 177
Benelux 8b, 58, 231
Berlusconi, S. 27, 28, 92, 99, 136, 137,
193

Bersani, P. 28
bilateral agreements (migrant labour) 86b
birth rates 5
births (projected, 2008–60) 6t
'Blue Card' scheme (EU, 2009–) **95–6**, 102, 230
Boeri, T. 183, 236
Bolivia 24, 26f
Bommes, M. xiii, 173, 236
border controls 7, 19, 99, 123, 140, 142, 149, 152, 174, 191
border guards 146b
borders **12–15**, 132, 135, 227, 234
    air 60t, 124, 129
    'blue' (maritime) 15t, 15, 24, 91, 123, 124, 129, 133, 193, 230, 246
    external 10b, 14–15, 47, 52b
    'green' (land) 14t, 14–15, 33, 61, 60t, 123, 124, 129, 133, 230, 246
    internal 10b, 128
    organizational 14
    'social constructions' 15
    erritorial 14
Borjas, G. 85–6, 236
Bosnia-Herzegovina 166b
Bosnians 171
Bossi, U. 136
Bossi-Fini immigration law (Italy) (2002) 137
Boswell, C. xiii–xiv, 43, 45, 173, 185, 191, 229, **236**
'boundary build-up' (Purcell and Nevins) 134
Bourdieu, P. 125
Bowker, G. 13, 236
Boyle, P. 108, 235
brain drain 47–8, 196
Brazil 124, 141
Brazilians 197
Brindley, P. 241
'British jobs for British workers' (Brown) 186b, 209
British National Party (BNP) 67, 209, 210
British Nationality Act (1948) 29
Brown, J. G. 186b, 209
Brubaker, R. 202, 236
Bruecker, H. 183, 236
Brunsson, N. 45–7, 237
Brussels 55, 56, 66, 189, 190
'brute logic' (economic) 108–9
budget line B7–667 97
Bulgaria 5, 14t, 25t, 60t, 147, 153t, 195
Bulgarians (in Spain) 192–3

Bundestag 89
burden-sharing 150, 162b, 164, 165, 174
bureaucracies
    division of competence 99
    and labour migration **98–102**
    'officials'/'civil servants' 55, 61, 64, 68–9, 70, 74, 81, 189
    see also decision-making
bureaucratic practice 72, **73–4**
'bus stop' principle 135, 138
Bush, G. W. 134
business interests 81, 82, 84, 90, 98, 190

Caldwell, C. 37, 237
Canada 22t, 126
Canary Islands 15t, 145
'capacity bargains' 54, 228
Cape Verde 97
capitalism 35
Capoferri, C. 134, 245
Card, D. 86, 237
CARDS 139
care/care sectors 26, 27, 137
Carling, J. 144, 145, 237
Carrera, S. 142, 237
carriers' liability 132
Casa delle Libertà 136
Catalonia 92
Caucasus countries 97
centre–periphery differences 100
CEPOL 146b
'certain margin of appreciation' 117
Ceuta 24
'chain migration' 101
Chaloff, J. 77, 78, 238
Chavez, H. 141
cheap labour 33, 127, 231
Chechnya 159
Checkel, J. 69, 238
Chen, Mrs 176, 198
child support 196
children 32, 78, 105, 106, 107, 110, 116–17, 119, 130, 141b, 198
China 124, 138, 166b, 176
Christian Democrats 89, 90, 210
Church of England 111
churches (organizations) 90, 137, 158
circular migration **96–7**
citizens (non-EU) 25t
citizenship 35, 37, 38, 73, 170, 176–7, 178, 180, **187–90**, 201, 203, 215, 230, 248
    European project 'dismal failure' 190
    political rights 188

citizenship provisions, used to secure free-movement rights 197
civic integration 207, 208, 219, 221, 223
Civic Integration Examination Abroad 202
civil liberties 61, 163
civil rights 101
civil war 171
climate 192, 193, 194b
co-decision 9b, 10b, 55, 58, 65, 66, 140b, 141, 228, 229
coalition governments 27, 46, 88, 92, 99, **136–7**, 212
cohabitation 107
colf and *badanti* (domestic work and care) 137
Colombia 24, 26f
colonies/colonization 21, 29
Comité Interministériel de Contrôle de l'Immigration (France) 109
Common Agricultural Policy 183b
Common European Asylum System (prospective, 2012) 52b, 163b, 167–8, 169
Common Fisheries Policy 183b
Common Foreign and Security Policy 183b
Common Trade Policy 183b
Commonwealth 26, 27f, 29
Communication on a Community Immigration Policy (CEC, 2000) 94, 237
'Communications' (European Commission) 64, 167
communism 21, 33, 35
see also political spectrum
Community Immigration Policy 94
'competence creep' 96
competitiveness 180
compromise 44
Confindustria (Italy) 137
Conservative Party 67, 89, 138, 186–7
constitutions (national) 32, 34, 41, 42, 104
construction sector 26, 27, 30, 86b, 86, 92, 123, 192, 193, 204
cheap labour 127
convergence 70–1, **232–4**, 244
definition (Knill) 233
not same as 'Europeanization' 232–3
Copenhagen School 162–3
Correa, R. 141–2
Council Directions (2004, 2005), 95

Council of Europe 161, 194
Council (of Ministers) 55, 56, 66, 141b, 156, 167
'Council' 57, 58, 65, 116, 140b, 142, 168
not same as 'European Council' (1974–) 55
QMV 51
courts 57, 101, 112, 113, 114, 120, 172–3
guarantors of rights 18
crime 61, 144, 193–4
crimes against humanity 35b
Croatia 4, 23, 25t, 142, 232
cultural adaptation 206, 207
cultural biases 120
cultural capital 84
cultural diversity 90
'source of innovation' 84
culture 38
norms 'deeply contested' 206
customs checks 190
Customs Union 183b
Cyprus, 5, 15t, 25t, 30, 129t, 147, 153t, 220t, 222t
Czech Republic 3, 5, 25t, 30, 60t, 90, 147, 153t, 165, 220t, 222t

Dam, D. 241
Danish People's Party 110
data deficiencies 25t, 77, 148t, 172, 204, 219, 220t, 222t
databases 42, 58, 61
'dawn raids' 172
Dawson, R. 69, 239
de Haas, H. 133, 239
deaths (projected, 2008–60) 6t
decision-making 118, 162, 223, 233, 248
behind 'gilded doors' (Guiraudon) 113
bureaucratic 75, 113
public-administrative 73–4
venues 104
decision-making processes 233
tensions, ambiguities, contradictions 149
decision-making venues 114, 155, 164, 210, 229
'decisions' 56
declaratory politics 65
'decoupling' **46–7**, 74, 76–7, 81, 92–3, **98–9**, 101, 151, 156, 174–5
by changing categories **170–2**
in welfare system **172–3**
see also rhetoric

'deliberate malintegration' (Hall) **47–8**, 50, 72, 76–7, **99**, 102, 137, 156, 169, 225, 230
demography **5–6**, 94, 195
'demography as destiny' 37
denizens/denizenship 203, 215, 216
Denmark 25t, 60t, 77, 95, 104, 114, 115, 119, 153t, 180t, 209, 216, 220t, 222t
  family reunion laws 110
  marriage tests 111
deportation **139–43**, 172
  see also Returns Directive
detention centres 170, 172
developing countries 48
'less-developed countries' 120, 127
Devillard, A. 109, 235
Directive on Family Reunion (2003) 32, 103, 105–6, 107–8, 110, 114, **115–17**, 217, 231, 241
  Articles 4(1), 4(6), and 8 116
  Article 7(2) 119
  negotiating process 115
  problems **116**
Directive on Long-Term Residents (2003) 182, 197, 204, 213–14, **214–17**, 221, 231
  Articles 5(2) and 15(3) 216
Directive on rights of legally resident TCNs (2003) 202–3
Directives 16, 53b, 56–7, 70, 95
  asylum 231
  asylum (2001–4) **163b**
  equal treatment (1976) 178
  presented and rejected 94
  Directive 2004/38/EC (mobility consolidation directive) **177–8**
disability 211
'discarded solutions' (fished out) 49
discourse *see* rhetoric
discrimination/anti-discrimination 38, 52b, 111, 119–20, 157, 178, 194, 196, 202, 203, 211–12, 213, 223, 224
  Directives 57, 201, 216
displacement effects 86, 90
divorce 107
DNA testing 61, 110
domestic employment 24, 26, 27, 86b, 86, 92, 137, 147
  see also employment
drivers of change **70–1**
Dronkers, J. 221, 240
Dublin Convention 162b
Dublin II 'Regulation' (2003) 151, 162b, 163b

Düvell, F. 127, 239
Duncan, F. 210, 239

economic activity 178, 188, 197
economic crises
  (1973) 30
  (2007–) 5, 24, 68, 76, 91, 186b, 200
economic development 142
  global 82
  versus migration 82
economic growth 83, 101, 182, 204
economic integration 54, 205, 209, 212, 215, 228
economic participation 107
economic performance 208
economic prosperity 30
Economic and Social Research Council xiii
economics
  labour migration 82
  supply-side 83–4
economists 182, 190
Ecuador 141
Edinburgh University xiii
education 33–4, 38, 78, 95, 107, 115–16, 173, 196, 197, 201, 217, 218
educational attainment 77, 120, 206
Egypt 124
election times 136
electoral campaigns (Italy) 149
electorates 46, 47, 62, 73, 88, 92, 155, 172, 173, 188
Eleventh of September (2001) 42, 163, 214, 236
elites 164, 190
emigration countries 42, 91, 183–4, 232
  conversion into host nations 30
empiricism 17, 50
employers 40, 86, 87b, 92, 137, 199, 231
  agents of immigration control authorities (resentment) 143
  of irregular migrants (proposed sanctions) 142
  recruitment of people they need 181
employment 38, 76, 83–4, 128, 137, 157–8, 176, 191, 196–202, 206, 208, 213, 217, 218, 219
  high-skilled 95
  illegal 132
  irregular 127
  unlawful practices 86–7
  see also full employment
employment benefits 86

employment contracts 31
employment rates 219, 220t, 222t
employment status
  regular versus irregular 129, 130
employment-based programmes,
  recruitment of migrant labour 86–7b
empowerment 12
engineering 31, 86b
entire family migration 106
environment 194b
Equal Treatment Directives
  (1976) 212
  (2000) 202, 213
equal treatment principle 178
equality 41
Eritrea 124, 160t
Esping-Andersen, G. 219, 239
Estonia 5, 14t, 25t, 60t, 90, 153t, 220t,
  222t
ethics 13, 48
ethnic minorities 38, 82, 211, 212
  see also Roma
ethnicity 20, 21, 157, 173, 203, 204,
  208, 211, 213
Euro (currency) 190
Eurocities 190
Europe 21–2, 35b, 160t
  borders (paradox) 12–15
  geopolitical shake-up (1989) 7
  loss of self-confidence 37
  migrant population (2010) 22t
  migration 'puzzle' 112
  migration and refugee flows (1945–)
  23–8
Europe: A8 countries 90–1, 159, 180,
  180t, 185, 193, 195–6
Europe: central 3–4, 7, 19, 30, 68, 98,
  110, 159, 166b, 179, 182–3, 184,
  192, 195, 247
Europe: eastern 7, 30, 33, 68, 98, 110,
  144, 159, 166b, 179, 182–3, 184,
  192, 195, 247
  labour mobility 89
Europe: non-EU 23,24f
Europe: north-west 83
Europe: northern 143, 184
Europe: southern 19, 33, 50, 54, 68,
  110, 122–3, 152, 153t, 230
  welfare-state type (Ferrera) 219, 240
Europe: western 3–4, 32, 34, 35
European Asylum Support Office 151
European asylum system (target date
  2012) 151
European border surveillance system
  (EUROSUR) 123

European Commission/Commission of
  European Communities (CEC)
  8–9b, 54, 55, 57, 58, 66, 76, 79,
  115, 123, 139, 142, 151, 156, 163b,
  167, 169, 181, 189, 190, 194, 195,
  198, 211, 212–13, 215, 216, 230,
  237–8
  attempt to expand involvement in
    labour migration policy 102
  'constantly pushing pace of reform'
    168
  forays (labour migration policy)
    94–6
  'greater role' foreseen 229
  harmonization of national labour-
    migration policies 94
  institutional status 62
  involvement in labour migration
    'paradoxical' 93–4
  legitimation 64
  'multi-organization' 229
  new thinking on migration and mobility
    96–7
  power and responsibility 228
  responsibility for management and
    implementation of policy 56
  rights of initiative 65
  role 61–4
  'sole right of initiative' 63
  treaty-guardian role 63
  worker mobility 199
European Commission: Directorates-
  General (DGs) 61–2, 63, 229
  Employment (DG EMP) 62
  Foreign Affairs (DG RELEX) 62
  Justice and Home Affairs (DG JHA,
    1999–) 61–4,
  Justice, Liberty and Security (DG JLS)
    61–2, 63, 64
European Commissioners 62, 73
European Community (EC) 63
European Conservatives and Reformists
  Group 67
European Convention on Human Rights
  (ECHR) (1953) 105, 111, 113–14,
  172
  'Articles 8 and 14' 116
European Council [heads of
  state/government, 1974–] 10b, 55,
  56, 65–6, 167, 168, 181
  follow-ups 'can be disappointing' 66
  meetings (2003, 2004) 94
  presidencies 65, 73, 156, 168, 169
European Council Conclusions 66, 168,
  190

European Council for Refugees and Exiles (ECRE)　161, 167
European Court of Justice　8–9b, 55–6, 57, 63–4, 106, 116–17, 156, 163b, 176, 196, 198, 228, 229
European Economic Area (EEA)　3–4, 86b, 88, 92, 94, 182, 183b, 190, 191
European Employment Strategy　132
European Free Trade Area (EFTA)　x, 183b
European integration　17, 62, 63, 66, 68–9, 71, 75, 162, 168, 169, 228, 231, 233, 241
　definition (Radaelli)　70, 232
　economic impetus　227
　effects　70
　'ontological' dimension　69
　see also　harmonization
European Integration Fund　140
European migration politics: framework for analysis　45–50
　deliberate mal-integration　47–8, 50
　policy stream　48–50
　'talk', 'decision', 'action' (Brunsson)　45–7, 50, 237
European Parliament (EP)　8–9b, 10b, 51, 55, 56, 57, 58, 65, 66–7, 116, 140b, 141, 141b, 142, 163b, 167, 188, 194, 209, 210, 211, 228, 229–30
　centre-left and centre-right federations　210
　elections (June 2009)　67
　MEPs　66, 73
　'multi-site' problem　66
European Parliament: Civil Liberties Committee　66
European People's Party　67
European politics of migration　17
European Refugee Fund　140
European Single Market　183b, 205, 211, 216, 218
　see also　Single European Act
European treaties　190
European Union　21–2, 44, 160t
　accession process　133
　'added value' to citizens　189
　area of freedom, justice, security　140b
　aspirations (economic versus political-cultural)　188–9
　budget　56
　candidate countries　142, 144, 174, 232; see also　Croatia, Macedonia, Turkey

common migration and asylum policy　7, 52b, 227–8; see also　European Union asylum policy
'convenient scapegoat'　155–6
cooperation on asylum (key developments)　162–3b
cooperation outside treaty framework　61
core economic objectives　36, 223
creation of area of freedom, security, justice (budget, 1998–2013)　140
differential impact　34, 231
governance structures　12, 227–9
hybridity　56
issue of return　139–43
'key role'　234
legal outputs　69, 70
limited role in labour migration policy　93–4
meaning contested　229
migration and mobility (new thinking)　96–7
migration policy (temporal shifts)　68
ministerial meetings　51
mobility, migration, asylum policy (potted history)　8–9b
multilevel policy setting　54–67, 75
multilevel system　82
'pendulum-like' policy-oscillation　66
politics　212
population　5–6, 6t, 24f
raised level of protection' for asylum-seekers　155–6
role in irregular migration　122–3
social relocation　68–9
spatial relocations of competence and capacity to act　67, 68
treaties　57
'treaty-based organization'　55
Turkish membership (prospective)　179
voluntary system for sharing responsibility for refugees　163b
European Union: EU-15　159, 212
European Union: EU-25　220t, 222t
European Union: EU-27　25t, 75, 129t, 152, 153t, 178, 205, 225, 233
European Union: member-states　12–13, 16, 17, 23, 24f, 31, 54, 57, 62, 64, 67, 68, 69, 95, 102, 115, 116–17, 120, 122–3, 127, 141b, 142, 164, 168, 169, 174, 175, 201, 203, 205, 217, 218, 219, 224, 229, 230, 241
'collective suicide pact' notion　227–8

Europen Union: member-states – *continued*
  constraints (family migration policy)
    114
  discretion in regulation of family
    migration **118–19**
  'shape policy' versus 'shaped by policy'
    231
  shaped by EU context 232
European Union asylum policy
  castigated 161–2
  divergent perspectives 167
  good-cop, bad-cop labels 156
  institutional conflict 156
  institutional interests and constraints
    169
European Union citizens 203
  'EU nationals' (relocation to another
    EU country) 196
European Union citizenship 19
European Union competencies 7, 40, 52,
    57–8, 67, 68, 69, 76, 96, 117, 204,
    211, 215, 227
  asylum 9b, 34
  immigration 9b
European Union enlargement 54, 62,
    68, 75, 93, 138, 177, 191, 236, 247,
    248
  (1980s, southern Europe) 179
  (2004) 89, 90, 195
  (2004, 2007) 19, 33, 58, 159, 179,
    180, 182–3, 183b, 193, 197, 232
European Union framework 17
  differences across policy types **230–1**
  partial 12
European Union institutions 54–5, **55–8**
European Union migration and asylum
  policy 17, 18, 50, **51–75**, 182,
    229
  'external' dimension 52b
  five-year work plans 52
  key role 53
European Union migration and asylum
  policy: analysis of effects **71–5**
  implementation **74–5**
  narratives and ideas **72–3**
  politics and political mobilization 73
  public-administrative decision-making
    73–4
European Union series i-ii
European Union system
  'new actors' **229–30**
  'rebundling' of authority 228
Europeanization 51, **69–71**, 247
  and convergence 226, **232–4**
  definition (Radaelli) 70

driver (differential and partial) of
    domestic change **70–1**
  five key questions **70–1**
EUROPOL 146b
Euroscepticism 67, 164, 191–2
Eurostat 24–7n, 170, 219, 220t, 222t,
    240
everyday life 201
executive branch 57, 101, 103, 112,
    113, 118, 120
experience 73
expert knowledge 73, 229, 236
exploitation 27
external security 133

failed states 159
family 1, 2, 8b, 13, 16, 87b, 95, 101,
    141b, 176, 178, 179, 196, 219
  'decision-making unit' 114
  definition **107–9**
  'different' norms 104
  extended 109, 119
  'gender-based inequalities' 108
  power of definition 119
  restrictive definition 105
  see also nuclear family
family care services 123–4
family life 105, 112, 116, 117
family migration 18, **32–3, 103–21**;
    19, 30, 31, 34, 53b, 75, 229, 235,
    247
  administrative practice and
    implementation **118–20**
  age profile 107
  centrality **103–5**
  cross-references 78, 102, 217
  core dilemma **33**
  demand **109–12**
  EU's role **114–15**
  forbidden 30
  narratives **106–12**
  'no positive right' **105–6**
  political debate **112–17**
  types **106**
  'unproductive' 110
  see also illegal immigration
family reunification 106, 109, 118, 188,
    203, 231, 243
  conditions 116
  rights 115–16
  waiting periods 105
  see also Directive on Family
    Reunion
fascism 21
Favell, A. xii, 200, 208, **240**

Federal Agency for Migration and
    Refugees (Germany)   99
federalism   190
Fernhout, R.   241
Ferrera, M.   219, 240
fertility rates   37, 80b
'fight against illegal immigration'   131,
    132–5, 139, 152, 230, 238
fingerprints   61
Fini, G.   136, 137
Finland   5, 14t, 25t, 60t, 153t, 180t,
    220t, 222t
Finotelli, C.   148n, 235
'fire-fighting'   44
Fleischmann, F.   221, 240
Follini, M.   136
forestry   139
'fortress Europe'   40, 66, 161, 162, 237,
    241
    idea contested   151
Foucault, M.   42, 164, 240
France   1, 5, 8b, 25t, 58, 61, 87b, 104,
    113, 116, 118, 119, 124, 129t, 146,
    150, 179, 180t, 186, 192, 202, 204,
    210, 212, 220t, 221, 222t, 231, 240,
    241, 242, 243
    ageing population   80b
    asylum-seekers   152, 153t
    ethnic origin data   213
    family migration   32, 109–10
    guest workers   29
    immigration legislation (2006, 2007)
        110
    labour migration strategy   **78**
    maritime borders   15t
    migrant population (2010)   22t
    Muslim integration   38
    nationality laws   208
    number of migrants (2000–5)   4, 4f
    'republican approach' (migrant
        integration)   208
    Roma people   **194–5**
Frattini, F.   5, 238
free market   180, 181
free movement   3, 57, 58, 78, 84, 90, 93,
    105, 134, 177, **181–5**, 227
    costs   85
    'expansionist dynamic'   198
    general right (2004–)   7, 8b
    long-term/short-term   197
    low proportion of EU population
        exercising the right   179
    restrictions   180
    use of citizenship provisions   197
    see also mobility

free trade   181
Freedom Party (Austria)   212, 213
Freeman, G.   xiii, 70, 240
French Republicanism   38
friends   2, 101
Front National (France)   67, 209, 210
FRONTEX (2005–)   124, 129n, 145,
    149, 246
    full title   xi, 122
    roles   **146b**
FRONTEX: Common Core Curriculum
    146b
full employment   84b
    see also labour

gangmasters   **138–9**
Gangmasters Licensing Authority (GLA)
    139, 241
GDP   184
Geddes, A.   xiii–xiv, 45, 63, 140, 173,
    188, 213, 236, **240–1**
Geddes, A., *et al.* (2007)   139, 241
    Brindley, P.   241
    Nielsen, K.   241
    Scott, S.   241
gender   103, 110, 111, 119, 165, 203,
    212, 217, 219
General Agreement on Trade and Services
    (GATS)   230
general public   18
Geneva Convention on Status of Refugees
    (1951)   34, **35b**, 106, 167, 170
    'Article 31'   166b
Georgia   97, 160t
Germany/West Germany   5, 8b, 25t,
    31, 36, 39, 50, 58, 61, 68, 77, 100,
    104, 113, 115, 116, 118, 119, 147,
    150, 157, 164, 171, 172, 179, 180,
    184, 186, 192, 194b, 202, 204, 210,
    214, 216, 220t, 221, 222t, 231,
    242
    ageing population   80b
    asylum policy   154
    asylum-seekers   152, 153t
    bureaucracies (division of competence)
        99
    case for labour migration   **88–91**
    constitutional court rulings (1970s,
        1980s)   101
    constitutional reform (1993)   165
    family migration   32
    guest workers   29
    immigration commission   88–9
    intra-EU movement   177
    labour migration strategy   **78–9**

Germany/West Germany – *continued*
  mechanisms for recruiting labour
    migrants 86b
  migrant integration 208
  migrant population (2010) 22t
  number of migrants (2000–5) 4, 4f
  recruitment ban (1973) **98–9**
  'two-level game' 165
  upper house 90
  welfare state type (Esping-Andersen)
    219
Gibney, M. 109, 241
Givens, T. 210, 241
global inequality 131
globalization 2, 21, 180
'good practice' 155
government agencies 47, 62, 99
'governmentality' 42, 240
governments 18–19, 30, 31–2, 43–4, 49,
  54, 57, 64, 66, 67, 72, 73, 76, 79, 80,
  83, 89, 91, 92, 110, 112, 114, 115,
  120, 122, 155, 156–7, 158, 161,
  168–9, 170, 172, 173, 175, 179,
  187b, 191–2, 196
  active in shaping debates and ideas 81
  business-friendly 100
  conflicting interests (mollification)
    101
  diversity of interests 98
  judicial constraints 118
  policy failure **39–41**
  responsiveness to business interests 81
  see also coalition governments
Gozo 15t
Granada 145
Greece 7, 25t, 29, 77, 87b, 122, 124,
  129t, 143, 145, 147, 158–9, 180t,
  192, 220t, 222t, 232, 235
  accession to EC (1981) 183–4
  asylum-seekers 152, 153t
  borders 14t, 15t
  regularizations 136, **147–8**, 148t,
    235
'Green Card'
  Germany **86b**, 88, 100, 112
  Greece 147
  SA 88
Green Papers (European Commission)
  64, 95
Green Party (Germany) 88
Groenendijk, K., *et al.* (2007) 120, 241
  Dam, D. 241
  Fernhout, R. 241
  Oers, R. 241
Guardian 1

guest workers **29**, 39, 98, 107, 113
  'becoming permanent residents'
    29–30
Guild, E. 142, 199, 237, 241
Guiraudon, V. xiii, 45, 47, 113, 115,
  210, 213, **241–2**

Hague Programme (2005–9) 52, 52–3b,
  55, 140b, 151, 163b, 239
Hall, P. **47–8**, 242
Hamburg 85b
Hammar, T. 203, 242
Hansen, R. xii, 38, 242
harmonization 63–4, 94, 102, 118, 155,
  161, 164, 165, 168, 169, 245
  see also European integration
heads of state/government 55
  see also European Council
health 38, 78, 80b, 173, 201
health insurance 178, 188
health professionals 48
health and safety 87
health services 33–4, 194b
healthcare 14, 107, 204, 217
Heckmann, F. 131–2, 145, 242
Herman, E. 131, 242
High Court (UK) 111
High-Level Panel on Free Movement of
  Persons 199
Highly-Skilled Migrants Programme
  (HSMP/UK) 89
Hollifield, J. xii, 64, 112–13, 116, 243
Holocaust 21
Hong Kong 166b
Honohan, I. 109, 243
'host third country' (concept) 166b
hotels (and catering) sector 30, 31, 86b,
  98
housing 14, 38, 78, 106, 107, 188,
  194b, 198, 201, 217, 218
  'accommodation' 33, 185
human capital 84
human rights 18, 37, 41, 42, 63–4, 103,
  115, 142, 158, 159, 160, 167, 169,
  171, 175, 194, 241
human-trafficking 11b, 39–40, 52b,
  123, 125–6, **131–2**, 135, 144, 243,
  244, 247
  UN definition 130
  versus people-smuggling 130
humanitarian assistance 167
Hungary 5, 14t, 25t, 30, 60t, 90, 153t,
  165, 220t, 222t

Iceland 4, 60t, 183b

identity   179, 201, 208, 219
  collective   42
  national   2, 37, 70, 90, 103
identity cards   145, 178
illegal immigration   6, 9b, 9, 11b, 28,
    52b, 61, 86–7, 242
  terminology   128
  see also   immigration
immigrant integration   *see*   migrant
    integration
immigration   179
  'back route'   18
  'displacement effect'   83
  economic benefits   236
  entry and settlement programmes
    30–1
  'goes to heart of self-definition of states'
    13
  host countries (old versus new)   91
  irregular   16
  'liberalization by stealth'   32
  'limited analytical usefulness'   17
  'new focus for insecurity'   163
  'not a panacea' for ageing population
    80b
  positive impact   83
  'public resistance'   31–2
  timing   144
  'wanted' versus 'unwanted' forms
    113, 134, 230
  see also   irregular migration
Immigration Act (Spain, 2000)   92
Immigration Act (Spain, 2005)   93
  amendment (2009)   100
immigration controls
  enforcement costs   126
immigration countries
  'newer'   50, 69, 110, 152, 153t, 159,
    221, 232
  'older'   50, 221, 225
immigration hotspots   24
Immigration Law (Germany, 2004)   99
Immigration and Nationality Directorate
    (IND/UK)   161
immigration policy
  potted history (EU)   **8–9b**
Immigration Reform and Control Act
    (USA, 1986)   134
immigration status   **30–1**
'immigration stop' (early 1970s)   103,
    111, 112, 120
income tax   182
India   22t, 26, 27f
Indian sub-continent   29
inflationary pressures   83

informal economy   91, 130, 132, 136,
    144, 230–1
information deficits (labour mismatch)
    85b
information exchange   132
information technology   31, 86b
  ICT specialists   88
information-sharing   58, 61
innovation   84
'institutional sectors'   46, 124, 143
institutionalization
  EU legal and political framework   69
institutions   38, 80
  liberal-democratic   40–1
  social and political   37, 38–9
Integrated System of External Vigilance
    (SIVE, Spain)   145
integration   33, 201, 214
  basic questions   206
  core dilemma   **37–9**
  national approaches   37
  term 'widely used, deeply contested'
    206
  see also   migrant integration
integration handbook   201
'integration measures'   216
  versus 'integration conditions'   110,
    115, 119
'integration outcomes'   20
'integration policy'   20
'intensive transgovernmentalism'
    (Wallace)   **54–5**
inter-ethnic relations   43
inter-state negotiation   69
interest groups   47, 62, **72**
intergovernmentalism   54–5, 56, 61,
    168, 169
interior ministries   44, 99, 133, 156,
    171
  'cautious about publicizing
      compromising data'   172
  officials   64, 68–9
  see also   ministries
internal security   35b, 36, 48, 83, 97,
    128, 133, 135, 227, 231, 232
  'global approach'   133
International Centre for Migration Policy
    Development (ICMPD)   154
international criminal organizations
    144
International Labour Organization (ILO)
    85
international law   32, 55, 57, 104, 105,
    141b
  refugees   63–4

international migration, could not exist
    without state borders   13
International Organization for Migration
    (IOM)   4n, 21, 22t, 146b, 154, 243,
    244
international organizations   65, 79
intra-company transfers (migrant labour)
    87b
Iran   160t
Iraq   159, 160t
Iraqi migrants   124
Ireland   25t, 30, 60t, 77, 89, 95, 101,
    114, 115, 153t, 180, 184, 196, 216,
    220t, 222t
  citizenship   176–7, 198
  intra-EU movement   177
IREM   186–7b
irregular migrants   152, 173, 193
  deaths   122, 124
  exploitation   135
  expulsion   58
  interception costs   145
  sanctions on employers (proposed)
      142
irregular migration   18–19, 33–4,
    122–49; 6, 7, 40, 46–7, 52b, 75, 82,
    99, 101, 158, 174, 229, 234, 237,
    239, 245, 246
  'absence of clear definition'   125
  administrative practice and
      implementation   143–8
  convergence between law and practice
      (five factors)   144–5
  core dilemma   34
  cross-references   27, 32, 58, 86
  deaths (USA-Mexico border)   134
  detections of illegal entry (2007)
      129t
  economic drivers   131
  empirical evidence   144
  enforcement-evasion spiral   134
  epiphenomenal   127
  'epistemological uncertainty'   143
  EU role   145, 149
  expulsion (policy option)   135
  forms   130
  internal checks   19
  issue-definition contest   126–7
  narratives   125–8
  'notoriously difficult to measure'   34
  policy options   135–6
  political debate   135–43
  'pull' factors   134, 144, 146
  'push' and 'pull' factors   123
  push factors   127

regularization (policy option)   135,
    136
  terminology   129, 131
  terms and their consequences
      128–35
  toleration (policy option)   135
  UK   138–9
  see also labour migration
Islamophobia   202
isomorphism   233
issue linkages   142
issue-definition   125–6
  contest   126–7
Italians (in UK)   186b
Italy   7, 19, 25t, 29, 30, 36, 60t, 87b,
    97, 104, 122, 123, 124, 129t, 133,
    143, 145, 147, 150, 158, 180t, 191,
    192, 197, 204, 209, 220t, 232, 240,
    248
  asylum-seekers   152, 153t
  deliberate malintegration   99
  electoral campaigns   136, 149
  family migration   32
  immigration hotspot   27–8, 28f
  irregular migration (ambiguities of
      policy responses)   136–7
  irregular migration (court files)   144,
      246
  key issues   27
  maritime borders   15t
  new immigration country   91–3
  number of migrants (2000–5)   4, 4f
  regularizations   136, 137, 148t, 247
  Roma (people)   193–4

Jacobin state   38, 242
Jenkins, R.   207
Job Mobility Action Plan (2007–10)
    199
Johnson, B.   138
Joppke, C.   37–8, 41, 113, 114, 243
Jordan, B.   127, 239
judicial branch/judiciary   41, 57, 103,
    104, 112, 113, 118
judicial cooperation   60t
judicial decisions   138
Justice and Home Affairs (JHA)   63,
    183b, 189–90
  cooperation   152, 154, 162b
  'external dimension'   154
  inter-governmental pillar   8–9b
  'structural fatalists' versus 'naive
      separatists' (Walker)   169
  'third pillar' of Maastricht Treaty
      162b, 228

Justice and Home Affairs (JHA) Council (EU)   56, **64–5**, 163b, 168

K-4 Committee   64–5
Kaliningrad   14t
Kelly, L.   125, 243
Kingdon, J.   48, 244
Knill, C.   233, 244
knowledge-based economy   81, 83–4, 181–2, 216
Kofman, E.   111, **244**
Koser, K.   126, 244
Kosovo   150

labour/workers   16, 44, 188
    casual   87
    illegal   40
    indigenous/'native'   18   86–7, 126
    low-skilled 76, 77, 86, 91, 126, 193
    mobility rights   7, 8b
    preferences mismatch   85b
    seasonal   85b, 86b, 92, 96, 148, 192, 230
    semi-skilled   91
    skilled   1, 6, 46, 48, 68, 75, 76, 77;
        see also   professionals
    supply and demand   84–5b, 182
    temporary   86b, 87
    unskilled   85b
    see also   labour migrants
Labour Government (UK)   89, 93, 138
labour laws   36
labour market
    efficiency   180
    inspection   142–3
    needs   93, 94–5, 99
    policies   99
    segmentation   85, 107
    shortages   36
    structures   144
    test   **86b**
    trends   75
labour markets   14, 19, 20, 33–4, 38, 47, 53b, 173, 181, 188, 195, 200, 204, 206, 208, 218, 219, 220t, 221, 222t, 223, 234, 240
    flexible   87
    gendered   107
    migration-driver   134
    pull factors   135, 137, 138
    skill range   77
labour migrants/migrant labour   76, 98, 107
    recruitment mechanisms   84, **86–7b**
    see also   self-employment

labour migration   **18, 28–31, 76–102;** 34, 47–8, 68, 75, 107, 118, 127, 158, 170, 186, 192, 245
    academic studies   82–3
    versus ageing population   80b
    beneficial forms   43
    bureaucracies   **98–102**
    common admission procedure (proposed, 2005)   94–5, 237–8
    core dilemma   **31–2**
    costs and benefits 'unevenly distributed'   82
    duration   77
    economic arguments   82–3, **83–7**, 89–90
    global approach   97
    information and advice centres   97
    liberal approaches   98
    liberal economic interests   40–1
    narratives   **82–7**
    negative consequences (for immigrants and ethnic minority groups)   **85**
    negative consequences (for indigenous population)   **85–7**
    negative social impacts   91
    new thinking (EU)   **96–7**
    notion of 'skill'   120
    political debate   **88–97**
    productive'   110
    public debate based on academic research   90
    seasonal   97
    sector specificity   77
    selective   89
    spatial specificity   78
    see also   migration
labour migration policy   **77–82**
    administrative practice and implementation   **97–102**
    determinants   80–1
    dilemmas   77–8
    EU's 'limited role'   **93–4**
    forays by European Commission   **94–6**
    harmonization   102
    rhetoric decoupled from practice   79, 81
    strategies   **78–9**
labour mobility
    new thinking (EU)   **96–7**
labour recruitment   86–7b, 181
    bilateral agreements   193
    see also   recruitment programmes
labour shortages   30, 31, 79, 80b, 84, **84–5b**, 86b, 89, 94, 98, 185
    coexistence with unemployment   85b

labour shortages – *continued*
  complex causes   100
Laczko, F.   125, 244
land borders   *see* borders
language   78, 87b, 106, 110, 111, 119,
  148, 161, 193, 196, 198, 202, 206,
  214
Latin America   22t, 35–6, 159
Latvia   5, 14t, 25t, 60t, 90, 147, 153t,
  220t
Lavenex, S.   97, 244–5
law   33, 57, 104, 105, 115, 116, 118, 120,
  132, 195, 203, 212, 225, 227, 235
  see also   international law
Lega Nord (LN)   136
legal aid   141b
legal expertise   211
legal status   173
legislation   32, 34, 47, 49, 66, 75, 156,
  164, 174
legislative branch   57
legislative proposals   66
legitimacy/legitimation   44, 45–6, 64
Leigh Star, S.   13, 236
Lellouche, P.   194–5
Lemaitre, G.   77, 78, 238
level-playing field   164, 165
Levy, C.   168, 245
'liberal constraint'   41
liberal democracy   37, 113, 114, 234,
  240, 241
liberal economic goals   48
Libya   122, 123, 133, 145, 152
Liechtenstein   4, 183b
life expectancy   80b
'Life in UK' website   202
Lin Liang Ren   138–9
Lindsey Oil Refinery   186–7b
linguistic adaptation   20
  see also   language
Lisbon Strategy/Agenda (2000–)   95,
  181–2, 216, 239
Lisbon Treaty (signed 2007, ratified 2009)
  7, 51, 56, 57, 58, 65, 66, 150, 156,
  228
  Article 77(1) (absence of internal border
    controls)   10b
  Article 77(2) (external borders)   10b
  Article 77(3) (mobility rights)   10b
  Article 78 (common policy on asylum)
    10–11b
  Article 79 (common immigration
    policy)   11b
  Article 79(3) (re-admission agreements)
    11b

Article 79(4) (TCN-integration
  measures)   11b
Article 79(5) (TCN-admission)   11b
  76
Article 80 (responsibility-sharing)
  11b
'encountered strong opposition'   8
provisions   9, **10–11b**
rejected in referenda   8
Lithuania   5, 14t, 25t, 90, 153t, 220t
lobby groups   211, 213
local authorities   78, 83, 172–3, 185
local government   100
London   138, 163, 190
longevity   194b
long-term care   80b
long-term residents   197, 204, 223,
  231
  see also   Directive on Long-Term
    Residents
long-termism   62
losses in translation   75
Luedtke, A.   210, 241
Lula da Silva, L. I.   141
Luxembourg   5, 25t, 61, 66, 77, 153t,
  180t, 220t, 222t
Luxembourg [City]   55

Maastricht Treaty (Treaty on European
  Union, 1992)   7, 8b, 19, 63, 64,
  152, 227
  Article 17(1)   187
  'Articles 18–21'   188
  effective (1993–)   3
  JHA pillar   162b, 228
Macao   166b
Macedonia (FYR)   14t, 23, 25t, 142,
  166b, 232
MacFadden, P.   187b
Madeira   15t
Madrid   92, 163
Maghreb   239
Malta   5, 15t, 25t, 60t, 122, 123, 129t,
  147, 153t, 220t
'managed migration'   68, 135
Maroni, R.   28
marriage   32, 113
  'arranged', 'forced'   111
marriage migration/family formation
  106
Martelli Law (Italy, 1990)   158
Martin, P.   219, 245
Massey, D.   134, 245
'maximalism'   231
MEDA   139

media/mass media   32, 40, 44, 47, 62, 73, 83, 89, 90, 98, 102, 161, 164, 171, 184, 185, 193, 194b, 226
  'press coverage'   65
median age   5
medical sector   191
Mediterranean   122–4, 132, 139
Meetoo, V.   111, 244
Melilla   24
men   26, 78, 107, 110, 130, 221
Meyer, J.   46, 248
Middle East   35b, 36, 159
migrant integration/immigrant integration   19–20, 201–24; 16, 53b, 73, 82, 106, 110, 111–12, 115, 117, 230, 240
  administrative practice and implementation   217–21, 222t, 223
  'component of broader debate'   219
  context (social and institutional)   201
  cross-references   182, 197
  EU action (multi-causal bundle of concerns)   205
  EU level debate   208–9
  EU measures (member-state priorities)   201
  EU rights-based framework   218
  family members   104
  versus 'immigration-control'   **119–20**
  'intervening variables'   206, 217
  levels and dimensions   204–9
  lowest-common-denominator policy (averted)   212
  meaning 'not clear'   217
  'means different things in different places at different times'   207
  narratives   203–9
  organizational context   217
  philosophies   208, 240
  policy outputs and outcomes (gap)   217
  political debate   **209–17**
  political debate (EU dimension)   **210–14**
  'reframing of debate'   222–3
  socio-economic   202
  terminological disputes   206
  two-way process   201
  see also   integration
migrant integration sites   218
migrant labour   *see* labour migrants
migrants
  categories   13

cheap labour   33
  economic   157
  entry (regular versus irregular)   129, 130
  'expatriate communities'   194b
  favoured destinations (2010)   22t
  by geographic region (2010)   22t
  high-skilled   78–9, 83, 89, 106, 107, 112, 181, 203, 229, 230
  'individuals' versus 'family units'   104, 108
  integration capacity   214
  lower-skilled   78, 79, 85, 107, 203, 229
  networks   101
  numbers   3–4
  pre-entry tests   202
  productiveness (differential approach)   112
  quota systems   117
  returning to country of origin   25t
  seasonal   2, 30, 98
  selected   18
  skilled   31, 32, 77, 81, 99, 192, 196
  temporary   2, 30, 98, 113, 245
  temporary (transition to permanent settlement)   40, 82
  tests   208
  treatment variations   1
  young   196
  see also   regularizations
migration   232, 234
  analytical approaches   39
  'cumulative causation'   108
  decision-making venues   112, 117, 118
  differentiated from 'mobility'   3
  dilemmas   **31–9**
  driver of population growth   5–6, 6t
  versus 'economic development'   82
  economic rationale   42
  internal   2
  intra-European   24
  intra-EU versus extra-EU   57
  literature   39
  misunderstanding of phenomenon by policy-makers   40
  versus 'mobility'   **23**, 36, 54
  narrative constructions   118
  paradigms   181
  permanent-type   103–4
  policy responses 1
  post-cold-war context   3
  'primary' versus 'secondary'   107, 110, 113

migration – *continued*
  productive' versus 'supposedly
    unproductive' 104
  'productive' versus 'unproductive'
    110
  return of people to country of origin
    23
  'rhetorical construction' 39
  'threatening' (versus 'beneficial'
    intra-European mobility)
    180–1
  'twelve-month' definition 2
  types 6–7, **28–37**, 50
  'unwanted' 134, 230
  see also sunset migration
migration categories **16–17**
  fluidity 16
  re-definition 17
'migration industry' 123, **131–2**,
    135, 247
'migration business' 134, 144
migration management
  global approach 149
*Migration and Mobility in European
  Union*
  analytical framework 1–20,
    225–6
  approach 54
  conclusions 20, 225–34
  focus 2
  key questions 6–7
  'mobility' aspect 2–3
  objectives 17
  organization 18–20
migration policy 21–50
  complexities 15–17
  cross-references 17, 18, 71–2, 81,
    88, 143, 205, 223, 228
  economic logic 164
  EU dimension 51–75
  external dimension 132–3
  making and operation (temporal shifts)
    68
  shaping and reshaping 231–2
'Migration Policy and Narratives of
  Societal Steering' (seminar series,
  2007–9) xiii
migration policy-making 43–4
  face value 43
migration politics
  complexities 15–17
  illiberal tendencies 121
migration type 225
minimum wage 86, 109
ministers 55, 62

ministries of
  development 48
  economic affairs 44, 99, 100
  foreign affairs 44, 48, 99, 133
  health 148
  justice 44, 148
  labour 44, 99, 100
  public order 148
  see also interior ministries
mobility 2–3, 51, 75, 76, 79, 204, 214,
    224, 228, 229, 234
  'beneficial' (versus 'threatening'
    migration by TCNs) 180–1
  costs 85
  differentiated from 'international
    migration' 3
  EU framework **177–8**
  higher-skilled 190
  low-skilled, semi-skilled 181
  narratives **178–90**
  obstacles 198
  problems **186–7**
  rhetoric versus practice 177
  see also free movement
mobility, citizenship, and EU enlargement
    19, **176–200**
  administrative practice and
    implementation **196–200**
  core dilemma **36–7**
  cross-references 20, 36, 93, 204
  free movement of workers **181–5**
  political debate **190–6**
mobility partnerships **96–7**, 246
mobility rights 230
  potted history **8b**
  transition arrangements 179, 180,
    184, 192, 195
mobility versus migration **23, 36**
'Mode 4' liberalization 230
modernising agenda 89
Moldova 14t, 97, 166b
Montenegro 166b
Monzini, P. 246
Morecambe Bay (2004) **138–9**
'Moroccan mafias' 144
Moroccans 124, 193
Morocco 24, 26f, 29, 97, 124, 133,
    145, 166b, 215
multiculturalism 20, 37, 38, 202,
    205–6, **207–8**, 210, 214, 222, 223,
    226
multilevel governance 131, 177
multilevel migration politics **226–32**
  'differences across policy types'
    230–1

multilevel policy setting   54–67
multilevel politics   10–12, 234
   definition   226–7
multilevel system   16
multinational companies   96
   intra-company transfers   98
'multiple adjustments'   38, 201
Muslims   37–9, 202, 203, 223, 243
'mutual recognition' principle (asylum-
   seekers)   53, 53b
Myrdal, G.   108, 246
'myth of invasion'   34, 122, 239

narratives   xiii
   asylum   157–61
   family migration   106–12
   and ideas   72–3
   immigrant integration   203–9
   irregular migration   125–8, 135
   labour migration   82–7
   mobility, citizenship, EU enlargement
      178–90
   'technocratic'   73
nation-state   54–5, 180
   core functions   41
   'power-maximizing agents'   41–2
'national colours'   233
National Institute of Employment (Spain)
   100
national insurance   129
national interests   190
national sovereignty   12, 41, 94, 117,
   168, 176
   ceded to EU   179, 200
nationality   35b, 173, 178, 201, 203,
   211, 212
   transfer to subsequent generations
      197
nationality laws   215
Neal, A.   145, 246
necessary malintegration   120–1
neo-liberalism (challenged)   85
Netherlands   19, 25t, 29, 39, 50, 61,
   104, 106, 113, 115, 118, 119, 153t,
   180t, 191, 194b, 204, 208, 210–14,
   216, 220t, 221, 222t, 242
   asylum policy   154
   immigrant integration   201–2
   labour migration strategy   78
   'minorities policy'   207
   number of migrants (2000–5)   4f
networks   67, 101, 131, 135, 161
Nevins, J.   134, 247
'New Commonwealth'   29
new institutionalism   248

New World   21
New York Protocol (1967)   35b
NGOs   65, 156, 157, 158, 159, 161,
   194, 212
Nice Treaty (2001)   9b, 58, 65, 66, 116,
   150, 163b, 228
Nielsen, K.   241
Nigeria   160t
non-refoulement principle   35b, 141b,
   166b, 174
non-state actors   165
Nordic free movement area   60t
North Africa   29
North America   22t, 23
North American Free Trade Agreement
   145
North Lincolnshire   186–7b, 187
Northern Ireland   176
Norway   4, 60t, 183b, 220t, 222t
nuclear family   105, 106–7, 119

Oceania   22t, 23,24f
OECD   19, 32, 62, 80b, 85, 103–4, 246
Oers, R.   241
oil price crisis (1973)   30
Ombudsman   188
'open method of coordination' (OMC)
   94, 237
'opinions'   56
opt-outs   95, 114, 115, 216
organizational memory   73
organizations   74
organized crime   28
overstay   40, 122, 128, 130, 193

Pakistan   124, 126, 160t, 166b
Pakistani people   147
Palestine   124
Paris   190
Parkes, R.   97, 246
Partito Democratico   28
party politics   40, 73, 74, 102, 185, 209,
   229
   declaratory types   72
   dynamics   72
   see also   political parties
passports   178, 190
Pastore, F., *et al.* (2006)   144, 246
   Monzini, P.   246
   Sciortino, G.   246
patera (wooden boats)   124
pensioners   179
   see also   sunset migration
pensions   80b, 95, 137, 196, 198, 199,
   204

people-smuggling 11b, 19, 40, 52b, 123,
124, 126, 128, **131–2**, 135, 138–9,
144, 244, 246
versus 'human-trafficking' 130
permanent residence 35, 79, 170–1, 178
permanent settlement 31, 32, 40, 82,
97, 113
persecution 21, 34, 35b, 35, 157, 159
'well-grounded fear' 165
Pew world values survey (2004) 38
Pinar E (cargo ship) 122
Plan Greco (Spain, 2000) 104
points systems 31, 78, **87b**
Poland 5, 14t, 25t, 26, 27f, 60t, 77, 90,
153t, 159, 165, 180t, 185t, 195–6,
220t
intra-EU movement 177
loss of labour skills 196
migration to UK and Ireland (2004–)
101
police 60t, 61, 189
policy convergence *see* convergence
policy cycle 43, 49
policy dilemmas **31–9**, 50, 77–8,
147–8, 170
policy failure 2, 27, **39–41**, 48, **81–2**,
99, 101, 112, 120, 137, 169, 207,
218, 219, 221, 225, 231
reasons **40–1**
'simplistic' thesis 43
policy outputs **74–5**
policy pragmatism 144, 145
*Policy Priorities in Fight against Illegal
Immigration* (CEC, 2006) 132,
238
policy process 17, 71–2
outcomes 45, 46, **74–5**, 231
'policy failure' versus 'securitization'
39–44
policy stream 48–50, 72
policy types **230–1**
policy-making
ambiguity 50
credit-seeking 49
discourse versus practice **72**
'evidence-based' 125
multi-level and multi-dimensional 71
'opaque process' 45
problems versus solutions 72
relocation (spatial, temporal, social)
69
simplistic 40
political debate
asylum **161–6**
family migration **112–17**

immigrant integration **209–17**
irregular migration **135–43**
labour migration **88–97**
mobility, citizenship, EU enlargement
190–6
political mobilization 72, **73**, 75
political opinion 34, 35b
political participation 218
political parties 84, 87
business-friendly 88, 89
incumbent versus opposition 72, 73,
88, 89, 90, 164, 172, 191
mainstream 209–10
protectionist, welfare-oriented 88
see also party politics
political process 1, 6–7, 70
political sociology 44, 242
political spectrum 39
left-wing 87, 88, 158, 209
centre-left 28, 89, 92–3, 100, 136,
209–10
centre-right 27, 90, 92, 93, 99,
136–7, 158, 191, 209–10, 235,
239, 240
right-wing 87, 88, 90, 191–2, 193,
209, 210
extreme right 67, 209–10, 212
see also communism
politicians 49, 69
anti-immigration, anti-EU 230
liberal 190
politics 6–7, 9, 21, 70, 71, 73, 78, 233
constitutional and judicial 113
'high' versus 'low' 227
national 69
rights-based 64
territorial basis 227
politics of migration in Europe **17**
Popolo delle Libertà coalition (Italy)
92
Popular Party (Spain) 92
population control 12–13
population registration 145
populism 40, 62, 73, 83, 90, 136, 184,
209
'populist gap' 191
Portugal 15t, 25t, 29, 30, 60t, 87b, 104,
153t, 180t, 192, 220t, 222t, 232
accession to EC (1986) 183–4
family migration 32
Portuguese 186b, 204
post-Cold War era 7, 34, 68, 227–8
post-imperial era 39
post-war era (1945–) 18, 21, 29, 34, 39,
83, 84b, 247

post-war era – *continued*
  migration and refugee flows in Europe
    23–8
posted workers   **186–7b**
Posted Workers Directive (1996)   186,
  187b, 192
poverty ('push factor')   123
power (legal, social, political)   209
preferences mismatch (labour)   85b
Prewitt, K.   69, 239
productivity   83–4, 101, 182, 188
professional footballers
professionals/professions   77, 87b, 197
  skills shortages   86b
  see also 'labour/skilled'
proportional representation   210
'proposals'   64
protectionism (EU-level)   190
Prüm Treaty (2005)   61
public administration   73–4
public debate   39, 62, 113
public health   178
public opinion   44, 48, 62, 81, 89, 90,
  161, 193
public policy   18, 39, 44, 71–2
public services   156, 182
Puglia (Italy)   124
pupil exchange   95
Purcell, M.   134, 247

qualifications, recognition   95, 198
Qualifications Directive (2004)   152
qualifications mismatch (labour)   84b
qualified majority voting (QMV)   9b,
  10b, 16, 51, 58, 63, 65, 163b
quality of life   192

race   20, 34, 35b, 203, 208
Race Equality Directive (2000)   202,
  213
race relations   38
racial harassment   193
racism/xenophobia   27, 28, 141, 205,
  206, 209, 211, 213
Radaelli, C.   70, 232, 247
rape   193
rapid border intervention teams (RABITs)
  146
readmission agreements   **166b**, 171, 174
'rebundling' of authority (Ansell)   12,
  228, 235
'reception capacity'   116
reception centres   49
'recommendations'   56
recruitment programmes   101

recruitment quotas   100
  see also labour recruitment
Reding, V.   195
referenda   8, 183b
reforms
  'easy to initiate, hard to achieve'
    48–9
refugee
  concept   34, 165
  definition   35b
  joint EU position (1996)   162b
refugee camps   49
refugee flows   **34–6**
  causes   **159**
  core dilemma   **36**
refugee groups   175
refugee recognition   162b
refugee resettlement   99
refugee status   9b, 34–5, **170–1**, 174,
  175
refugees   **19**, 32, 163b
  protection in 'regions of origin'   49
  see also asylum
regional development   227
regional mismatch (labour)   85b
regional protection programmes   53b
regionalism   100
regularizations (of migrants)   27, 87b,
  92, 93, 99, 130, 134, **135**, 137, 138,
  143, **145–7**, 158, 193, 235, 247,
  249
  implementation (and dilemmas in
    practice)   **147–8**
  member-state policy-spectrum   **146–7**
  number of people involved
    (1996–2008)   136
  'pull' factor   146
  see also third-country nationals
Regulations   16, 51, 56–7, 70, 177
  asylum   231
religion   34, 35b, 111, 211
relocation: types   **67–71**
remittances   231
repatriation   171
research projects (EU-funded)   70
residence permits   11b, 119, 199
residence rights, for more than six months
  (conditions)   178
residence status, regular versus irregular
  129, 130
residents
  long-term   198
  long-term (non-EU citizens)   20
retirement   5, 24, 80b
return (deportation) issue   **139–43**

'return to assimilation' (Brubaker) 202, 236

Returns Directive (EU, 2008) 58, 66, 132, **140–1b**, 141, 143, 145
'Article 15' 141b
'Article 36' 127
issue linkages 142
see also safe countries
rhetoric 44, 45, 46, 72, 74, 76, 79, 106, 143, 189–90, 213, 217
'securitarian' 42
rhetoric versus practice 72, 81, 151, 155–6, 170, 174–5, 191–2
EU mobility provisions 177
Spain and Italy 92–3
West Germany **98–9**
rhetoric versus reality 104, 123–4, **136–7**, 200
see also 'talk, decision, action'
rights framework 208–9, 224
rights-based politics 103, 112, 229
Rodríguez Zapatero, J. L. 93
Roma (people) **193–5**
Romania 5, 14t, 24, 25t, 26f, 60t, 101, 147, 153t, 194–5
Romanians (in Spain) 192–3
rombo dei cannoni **136–7**
Rome 193
Rosarno (Reggio Calabria) 27–8
Ruggie, J. 112–13, 247
rural areas 78
Ruspini, P. 148n, 247
Russian Federation 14t, 22t, 160t, 166b
'Ryanair effect' 5, 190

safe areas 49
'safe (third) countries' 162b, 165, **166b**, 174
EU Resolution (1992) 166b
see also deportation
Salt, J. 132, 247
same-sex partnerships 107
Sanctions Directive (proposed, 2007–) 142–3, 237
'sanctity of law' 144
Sangatte 1, 3, 165
SAP 139
Sarkozy, N. 109
Saudi Arabia 22t
Schengen Agreement (1985) 8b, 58, 60t, 63, 197, 231
Schengen area xiv, 58, 59(map), 59, 190, 193, 246
history (1990–2008) 60t

Schengen Borders Code (2006)
'Article 5' 127–8
Schengen Convention (1990) **58–61**
effective (1995–) 58, 60t
signed (1990) to implement 'Schengen Agreement' 60t
single external border 58, 60t
Schengen Information System (SIS) 59, 60t, 128
central system (C.SIS) versus national system (N.SIS) 61
SIS second-generation (SIS II) 61
Schengen system 123, 133, 138
Schroeder, G. 90
science and technology 99
scientific research 73, 95
Sciortino, G. 142–3, 246, 248
scoreboards 66
Scotland 85b
Scott, S. xiii, 241
Scott, W. 46, 248
sea borders *see* borders
sector specificity 78
sector-based programmes (recruitment of migrant labour) **86b**
sectors (of economy) 87b, 95, 96, 138–9
skills shortages 86b
secularism 119
securitization **41–3**, 162–4, 174, 236
'simplistic' thesis 43
security officials 61
self-employment 76, 178, 179, 188, 197
see also unemployment
Senegal 97
Serbia 14t, 124, 160t, 166b
service sector 92, 107
sex discrimination 114
sex workers 130
sexual orientation 211
Shaw, J. 188–9, 248
Sheffield University xiii
Single European Act (1986) 63, 68
see also European Single Market
Sinn, H.-W. 184, 248
skill shortages 2, 79, 84, **84–5b**, 86b, 89, 93, 94
skills (vocational) 77
skills-based programmes (recruitment of migrant labour) 87b
Slovak Republic/Slovakia 5, 25t, 30, 60t, 90, 153t, 220t
Slovakians (in UK) 185
Slovenia 5, 15t, 25t, 30, 60t, 90, 147, 153t, 220t
social citizenship 208

social cohesion   42, 90, 109, 182, 227
Social Democrat Party (Germany)   88
'social dumping'   186, 191, 192, 200
social group   34, 35b
social inclusion   211, 215
social relocation
   effects on migration and mobility in EU
      68–9
social security   14, 33, 95, 185, 188,
   199, 202
social services   82–3
Socialist Party (France)   213
Socialist Workers' Party (PSOE)   93
socialization   69, 70, 74, 238
societal sectors   46, 248
'Solidarity and Management of External
   Migration Flows'   140
Somalia   124, 159, 160t
South Africa   26, 27f
'sovereignty bargains'   54, 106, 228
Soviet Union   139
Spain   7, 19, 29, 30, 31, 36, 60t, 61, 77,
   87b, 97, 100, 119, 122, 123, 124,
   129t, 143, 144, 145, 147, 153t, 180t,
   192, 220t, 222t, 232, 237
   accession (1986)   183–4
   immigrants (country of origin)   26f
   immigration hotspot   24–6
   maritime borders   15t
   migrant population (2010)   22t
   new immigration country   91–3
   number of migrants (2000–10)   4f,
      4–5
   property market collapse (2008–)   24
   regularizations   136, 148t, 235
   Romanian migration   101
   sunset migration   194b
spatial relocations (of competence)   67,
   68, 96, 223–4, 228
spatial specificity   78
'special agricultural workers' (USA)   134
spouses   105, 106, 110, 112, 113, 119,
   198
Sri Lanka   166b
standard of living   157
state controls (ineffectiveness)   40–1
state cooperation   54
state interests (complexity)   45
state power   127, 249
state role   37
state sovereignty   227
state-building   13
state-centricity   64
Stein, J.   132, 247
stigma   160

Stockholm Programme (2010–14)   52,
   53b, 55, 76, 150–1, 163b
Stone, D.   125, 248
Strasbourg   55, 66
Strategic Committee on Immigration,
   Frontiers, and Asylum (SCIFA)   51,
   56
Straubhaar, T.   182–3, 248
'street-level bureaucrats'   148
strikes   186b
students   179
   foreign/international   78, 87b
sub-Saharan Africa   132, 133
subsidiarity principle   204
sunset migration   192, 193, 194b
   see also   family migration
supermarket power   139
supranationalism   54–5, 56, 67
surveillance   42, 44
Sweden   5, 25t, 60t, 77, 89, 153t,
   164, 180, 184, 196, 207, 220t, 221,
   222t
   asylum-seekers   152, 153t
   number of migrants (2000–5)   4f
   welfare state type (Esping-Andersen)
      219
Switzerland   4, 4f, 29, 39, 60t, 220t,
   222t
   bilateral agreements with EU   183b
symbolical accords   47

TACIS   139
'talk', 'decision', 'action' (Brunsson)
   45–7, 50, 71, 72, 73, 105, 118,
   149, 173, 221, 223, 225, 230–1,
   237
   irregular migration   126
   see also   'decoupling'
Tampere action plan (1999–2004)   52,
   52b, 55, 151, 163b
Tampere European Council (1999)
   163b, 167, 216, 239
Tampere 'Scoreboard'   167
taxation   80b, 129, 188
technocratic debate   89–90, 91
'temporary leave to remain'   171
'temporary protection'   171
terminology
   and consequences (irregular migration)
      128–35
   irregular migration   125
territoriality   227
terrorism   42, 61, 214
'theory effect' (Bourdieu)   125
think tanks   211, 212, 213

third-country nationals (TCNs) 3, 7, 8,
9b, 10–11b, 23, 24, 37, 76, 94, 102,
113, 118, 120, 127, 142, 177, 179,
200, 202, 204, 211, 223, 224, 227
Council Directions (2004, 2005) 95
employment rates 219, 220t, 222t
EU parlance 203
EU's role 'relatively weak' 32–3
fair treatment 52b
free-movement provisions 196–7
'incomplete membership' status 205
long-term residents 215–16
mobility 182
mobility rights (policy options)
214–15
'not subject of EU legislation' 31
rights acquired by residence rather than
nationality 216
rights framework 205
'stronger labour-market exclusion'
221
unemployment rates 221, 222t
see also migrants
Tichenor, D. 134, 248
Tier 1 migrants (UK) 112
time 68
top-down projects 189
torture 166b
Total (oil company) **186–7b**
tourism 2, 24, 91, 190, 193
trade 142
trade talks 141–2
trade unions 90, 186, 187b, 199
training 95, 115–16, 146b, 178, 188,
196, 197, 217, 218
transgovernmentalism 67
transit 130, 164–5, 166b
transit countries 159
terminology 'value-laden' 133
transit migration 133
transparency/openness 97, 101
travel documents 128, 132, 164–5, 175
treaties (international) 41
Treaty of Rome (1957) 3, 8b, 19, 178,
183b, 203, 212, 227
'Article 3' 181
Title III 181
see also Maastricht Treaty
Treaty on European Union *see*
Maastricht Treaty
trust 38
Truszczynski, J. 195
Tunisia 29, 97
Turkey 4, 4f, 14t, 29, 124, 157, 166b,
179, 184, 192, 215, 232

Turks (in Germany) 113

Ukraine 14t, 22t, 166b
underclass 85
'undocumented migration', terminology
128
unemployment 5, 30, 90, 107, 182,
186–7b, 196, 221
coexistence with labour shortages
85b
sectors 181
see also domestic employment
*Unione dei Democratici Cristiani e di
Centro* (UDC) 136, 137
United Kingdom 1, 5, 26f, 36, 39, 49,
50, 68, 95, 99, 104, 113–14, 115,
119, 126, 150, 164, 165, 168–9, 180,
184, 191, 194b, 196, 198, 202, 204,
207, 208, 210, 211, 212–13, 216,
220t, 222t, 231, 240, 241
ageing population 80b
asylum policy 154
asylum-seekers 152, 153t, 172–3
case for labour migration **88–91**
emigrants to Spain 24
family migration 32
full market access for A8 nationals
(2004–) 185
gangmasters and irregular migrants
138–9
government citizenship survey (2008)
38
immigrants 29
immigration hotspot 25t, **26**, 27f
immigration legislation (1962–71) 26,
29, 147
intra-EU migration 78, 79
labour migration strategy 78
'limits of integration' 37–8, 243
migrant population (2010) 22t
migrants (professional status) 77
number of migrants (2000–5) 4, 4f
open door to East European labour
90–1
points system 31
Polish immigration (2004–) 101
regularizations 146–7
secures partial participation in
Schengen system (2000) 60t
welfare state type (Esping-Andersen)
219
United Kingdom: Department for Trade
and Industry 100
United Kingdom: Department for Work
and Pensions 100

United Kingdom: Home Office   99, 111, 138, 176, 185, 185n, 249
United Kingdom: PMO (Performance and Innovation Unit)   100
United Nations   80b
UN Commissioner for Human Rights 194
UN High Commissioner for Refugees (UNHCR)   122, 146b, 154, 160n, 161, 167, 170, 249
United States   85–6, 126, 219, 234, 236, 237, 248
    migrant population (2010)   22t, 23
    US–Mexico border   134, 145, 245
Universal Declaration of Human Rights (UDHR) (1948)   105
unsafe countries   141b
urban areas   78
urbanizaciones (Spain)   194b
'us and them'   15

Van Hecke, S.   210, 239
vehicle registration   61
Veil, S.   199
Venezuela   141
Vietnam   171
violence   **159**, 202
visa policy   52b
visas   9b, 11b, 37, 57, 59, 123, 128, 157–8, 175, 190, 193
vocational training   178, 197
voluntary service   95

wage rates   196, 200
    under-cutting   186b, 186, 204
wages   83, 85b, 86–7, 191
waiting periods   110, 113, 116–17, 119
Walker, N. 169, 249
Walker, R.   13, 249

Wallace, H.   54–5, 249
'ways of doing things'   232, 233
welfare   44, 81, 93, 149, 159, 160, 175, 200, 217
welfare agencies   99
welfare burden   190
welfare rules   36–7
welfare services   82–3, 176, 194b
'welfare shopping'   184
welfare states   14, 20, 34, 38, 107, 184, 208, 218, 223, 234, 236, 248
    types   219, 221, 239, 240
welfare systems   157–8, 204
    decoupling (rhetoric versus practice) **172–3**
West Africa   29, 239
West Indies   29
White Card (provisional residence, Greece)   147
Willen, S.   127, 249
Wöger, A, 134, 249
women   26, 78, 108–9, 110, 130, 137, 193, 221, 247
    guest-worker era   107
    work (paid and unpaid)   111
work permits   92, 199
Worker Registration Scheme (WRS/UK) applications (2004–8)   185, 185t
workers   *see*   labour
working population   5
World Bank   62, 85
World Trade Organization (WTO)   84–5
World War II   21

Year of Workers' Mobility (2006)   199
youth   196, 221, 223
Yugoslavia   29, 139, 150, 171
Yugoslavs (in Germany)   113

'zero-immigration' policies   30, 79